I0795018

IMAGES
of America

NORTH BRANFORD AND NORTHFORD 1950–1981

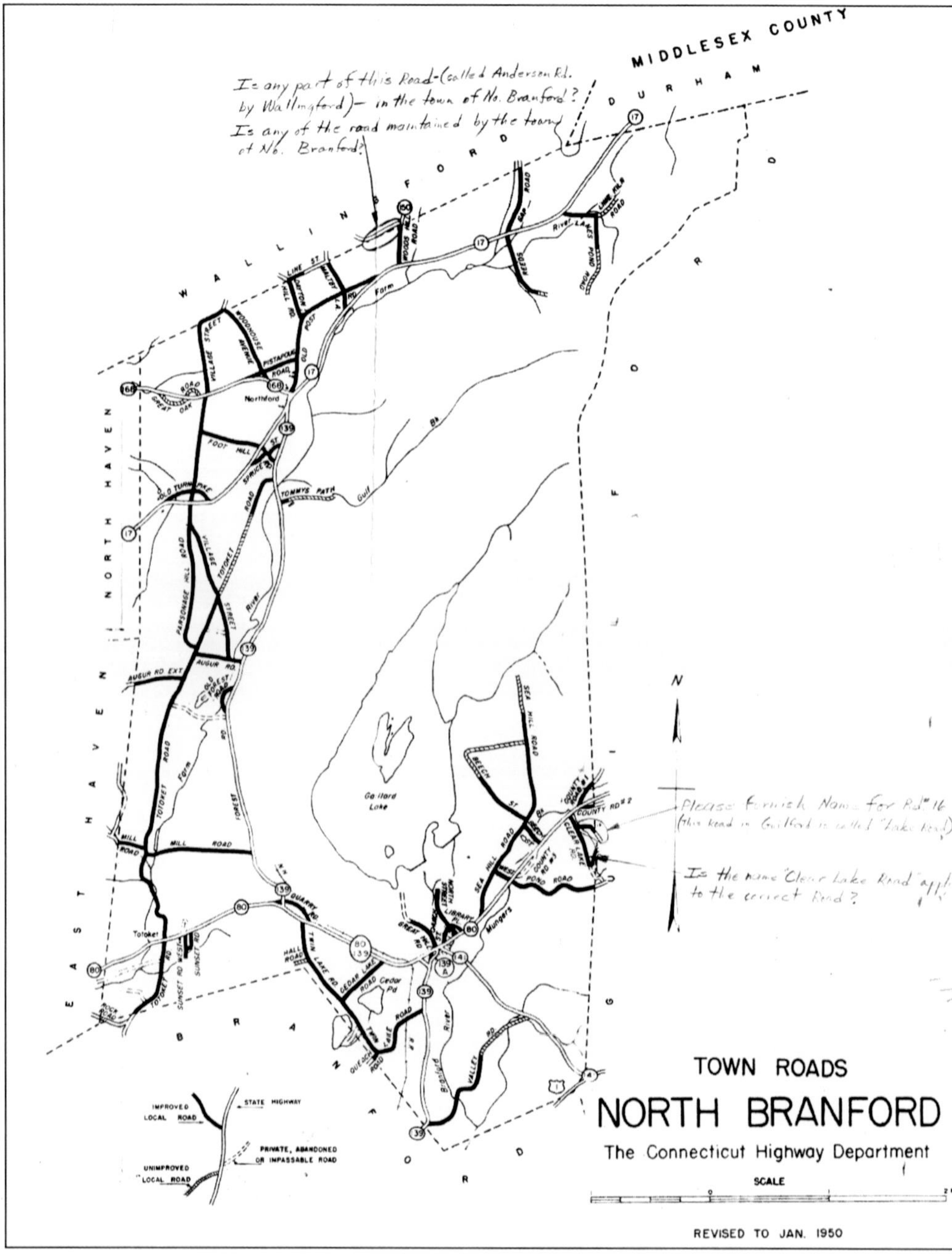

This highway map shows the North Branford roads in 1950. The state highways are white and the town roads are black. Note the unimproved and private roads. Sunset Road and Sunset Road West, the roads in the town's first housing development, are shown off Route 80 near Totoket Road. (Totoket Historical Society.)

IMAGES
of America

NORTH BRANFORD AND NORTHFORD 1950–1981

Janet S. Gregan and Grace Rapone Marx
for the Totoket Historical Society

ARCADIA
PUBLISHING

ISBN 978-0-7385-1343-0

Published by Arcadia Publishing
Charleston, South Carolina

Printed in the United States of America

Library of Congress Catalog Card Number: 2003110505

For all general information, contact Arcadia Publishing:
Telephone 843-853-2070
Fax 843-853-0044
E-mail sales@arcadiapublishing.com
For customer service and orders:
Toll-free 1-888-313-2665

Visit us on the Internet at www.arcadiapublishing.com.

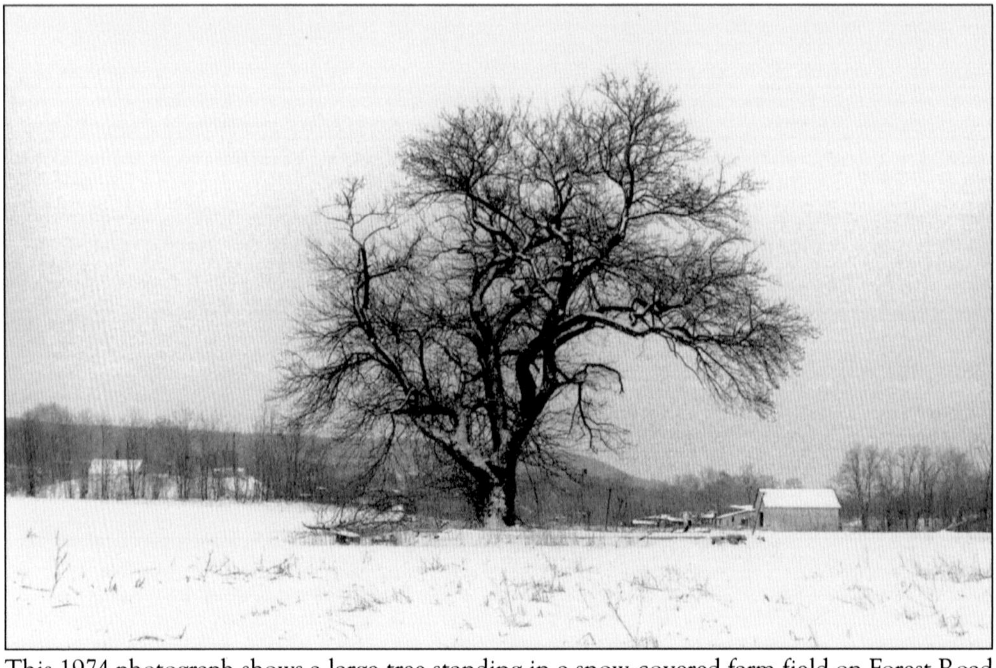

This 1974 photograph shows a large tree standing in a snow-covered farm field on Forest Road (Route 22). The fields are across from Arbor Lane, a 2003 subdivision that was built on the property of the old Malachi Cook house. The fields originally were part of the farm. There are now several homes located there. (Jane Leschuk.)

Contents

ACKNOWLEDGMENTS

Most of the photographs in this publication are from the collection of the Totoket Historical Society (THS). There is not enough space to individually recognize all of the photographers, residents, and other people who have donated photographs to the society, however the authors wish to express our appreciation for their contributions, both in the past and present, to the society photograph collection.

The authors especially wish to thank the following individuals and organizations who responded to the appeal for photographs to illustrate the theme of this book: Jane Leschuk, Tom Smith, Phyllis Peterson, Wally Anderson, Donald Guyer, Shirley Cole, Grace Marinuzzi, Grace Marx, Barbara Amatrudo, Joyce Hintz, Carl Battista, Linda Bunnell, Louise Mason, E. Robert Gregan, Marion Doody Bradley, the North Branford Volunteer Fire Department Companies No. 2 and No. 3, the North Branford Parks and Recreation Department, the North Branford Women's Club, the Northford Women's Club, the North Branford Congregational Church, the Northford Congregational Church, and the Zion Episcopal Church. We also wish to thank the members of the board of directors of the Totoket Historical Society for their help and support.

The authors regret that many of the events, activities, and organizations that were part and parcel of this particular time period could not be covered in this book due to a lack of photographs, timely information, and restrictions of format. There are many stories to be told, and we urge all who lived in North Branford during the 20th century to take the time to record memories on paper, tape, videotape, or computer disk and to compile albums of photographs and clippings. For those with special information, booklets, reports, photographs, and other memorabilia pertaining to the history of the town, we urge you to donate them to the Totoket Historical Society so those memories will not be lost.

—Janet S. Gregan and Grace Rapone Marx

INTRODUCTION

In the mid-20th century, North Branford was a small rural town with a population of 1,207. The town consisted of two villages: North Branford Center to the south and Northford to the north, situated on two main roads, Route 80 (the Foxon-Essex Turnpike) and Route 17 (the Middletown Turnpike), both of which were crossed by state Route 22, which served as a north-south corridor. Farmlands and secondary roads surrounded the two villages. The town boasted of five churches, three schools, three stores, a lumberyard, a couple of gas stations, a tavern, two package stores, and a small volunteer fire department.

Settled as the North Farms of Branford in 1695, the town's early economy was based on farm and wood products. During the 19th century, several small manufactories were established along the Farm and Branford Rivers, but lack of sufficient waterpower and rail transportation prevented expansion. By the 20th century, most of the industry had moved out of town. With the construction of the Lake Gaillard reservoir in 1926, approximately one-third of the town's lands came under the ownership of the New Haven Water Company. The New Haven Trap Rock Quarry was established in 1914 on the top of the Great Hill and soon became the town's largest employer, attracting immigrants from Italy and other countries. Many of those immigrants purchased farm properties. After World War II, the town changed rapidly. The combination of low-cost land, better roads, inexpensive automobiles, and veterans eager to own their own home in the country started a population boom that continues today. Farms were sold to developers, subdivisions sprang up all over town, and people moved in until, in 1981, the population had soared to 11,700.

The burgeoning student population sent the town on a school building spree that lasted for 20 years. Additions were built onto two of the three existing schools. Five new schools were built, and each of them required more additions as time went on. Center School, with a large vault added to the rear, became the town's first administration building, housing in its three rooms the offices of the town clerk, the selectmen, the finance department, the assessor, and the tax collector. Later, the police, building, and planning departments were located in the basement.

The town government struggled to keep pace with the rapid population growth by adding new services, such as recreation, planning and zoning, and police departments. Another fire company was established to serve many new homes. And in 1971, spearheaded by the League of Women Voters, a new charter was voted in that changed the government from a three-man selectmen form to a nine-member town council form overseeing a professional town manager. North Branford was recognized as an All-America City that same year. In 1979, a new town hall was built.

Churches also needed more space for religious education and meetings. The North Branford Congregational and St. Andrew's Episcopal Churches built new parish halls; a brand-new church was built for St. Augustine's Catholic Church; the Zion Episcopal Church moved from its original site and added a parish hall; and a new Roman Catholic parish, St. Monica's, was established in Northford.

Newcomers, who sought opportunities for themselves and their children to integrate, serve, and socialize, founded many new organizations, including the historical society, two women's clubs, two garden clubs, three men's organizations, the Conservation Land Trust, Little League, Midget Football, Girl and Boy Scout troops, and a fife-and-drum corps.

One of the most notable changes during the last 50 years was in social mores. As the authors researched annual town reports, histories, scrapbooks, newspaper articles, and other items in the historical society's collection, they noticed the difference in the wording of publicity articles and the way people dressed. Men and women both dressed much more formally for church services and organizational meetings than they do today. Married women were always identified by their husbands' names. The period between 1950 and 1981 saw great changes in the town but also created a paradox.

Despite the great growth in population and housing subdivisions, North Branford continued to retain the atmosphere and reputation of a rural town. Several farms remained productive, and farm stands were very evident on the town's main arteries. Today, in 2003, the town is endeavoring to preserve its open spaces despite a continued growth in housing and population.

One

From Farms to Suburbs

During the second half of the 20th century, many of the family farms in North Branford and Northford were sold to developers, who subdivided the land and built new houses. Most of the early subdivisions featured entry-level homes. The first housing development, Sunset Homes I and II, was built in 1949 and 1950 on new loop roads Sunset, Sunset West, Arthur, and Edward, off the western end of Foxon Road (Route 80). The second large subdivision was North Branford Estates, built on the farmlands sold by the Forte family on Mill Road. Soon, there were subdivisions all over town.

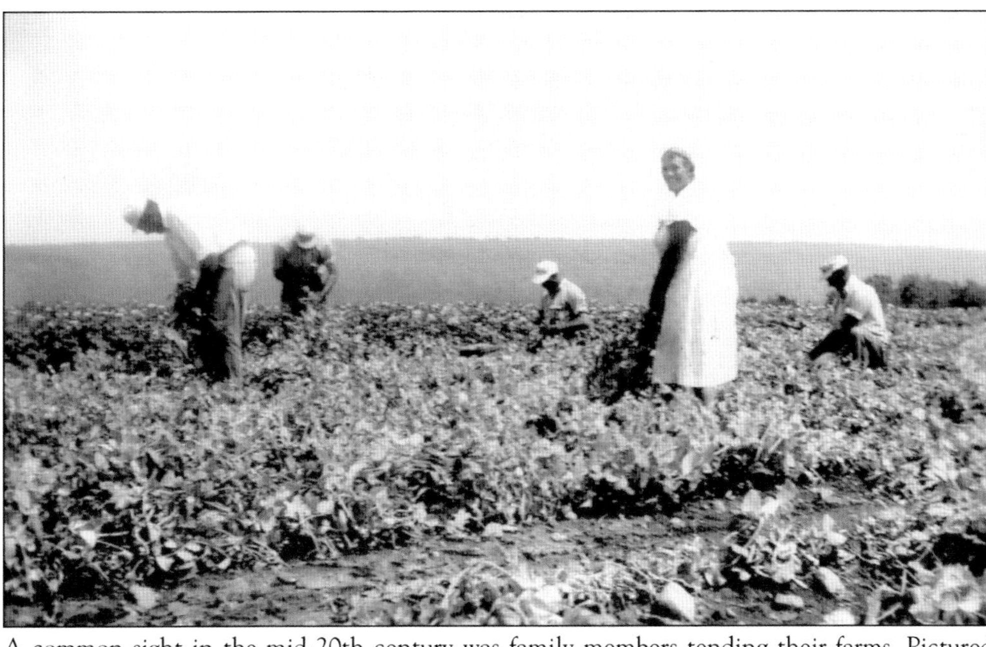

A common sight in the mid-20th century was family members tending their farms. Pictured here are Angelina Cecarelli and four of her eight sons working in the fields of their market farm on Old Post Road in Northford. (Tom Smith.)

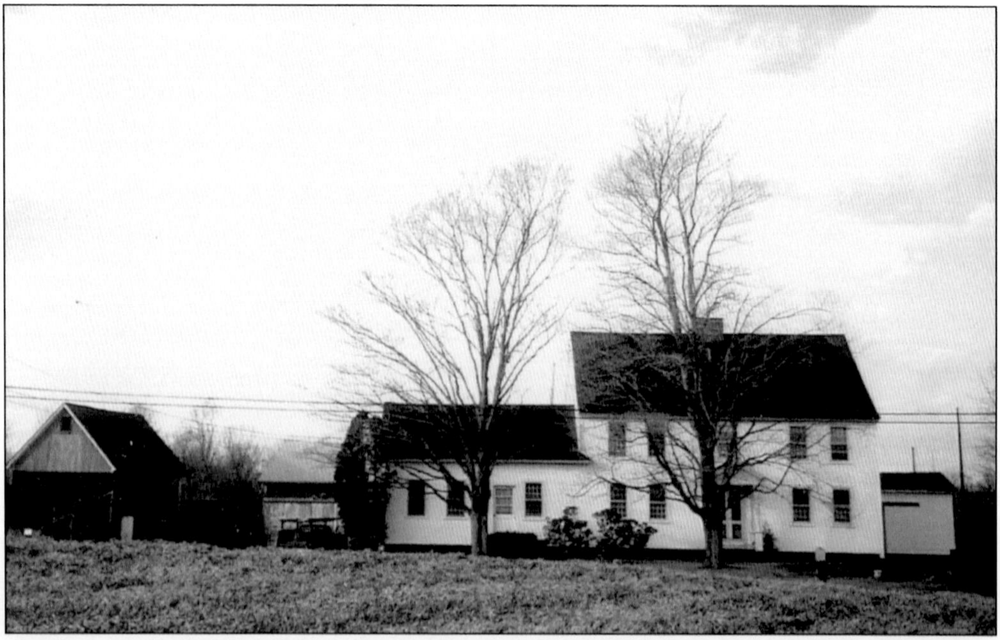

Frank Cecarelli purchased the 38-acre Lorenzo Harrison property on Old Post Road on September 5, 1911, to start a vegetable farm. Over the years, Frank continued to purchase additional acreage, and by 1979, his eight sons were growing fresh vegetables for roadside and wholesale markets on 275 acres. It is interesting to note that the first store in Northford was originally located in this house. (Phyllis Peterson.)

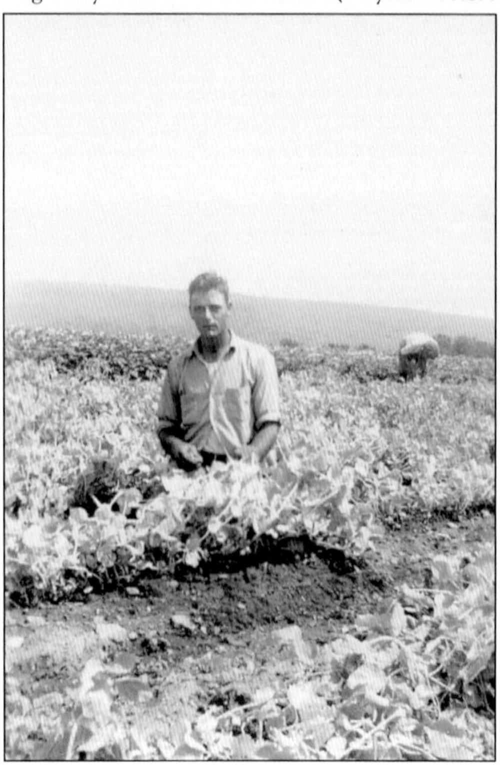

One of Frank and Angelina's sons, Louis Cecarelli picks vegetables on the family farm. In 1996, the Cecarelli family sold their development rights to the state under the Connecticut Department of Agriculture's Farmland Preservation Program, insuring that the remaining 150 acres of this family farm would remain forever as farmland. (Tom Smith.)

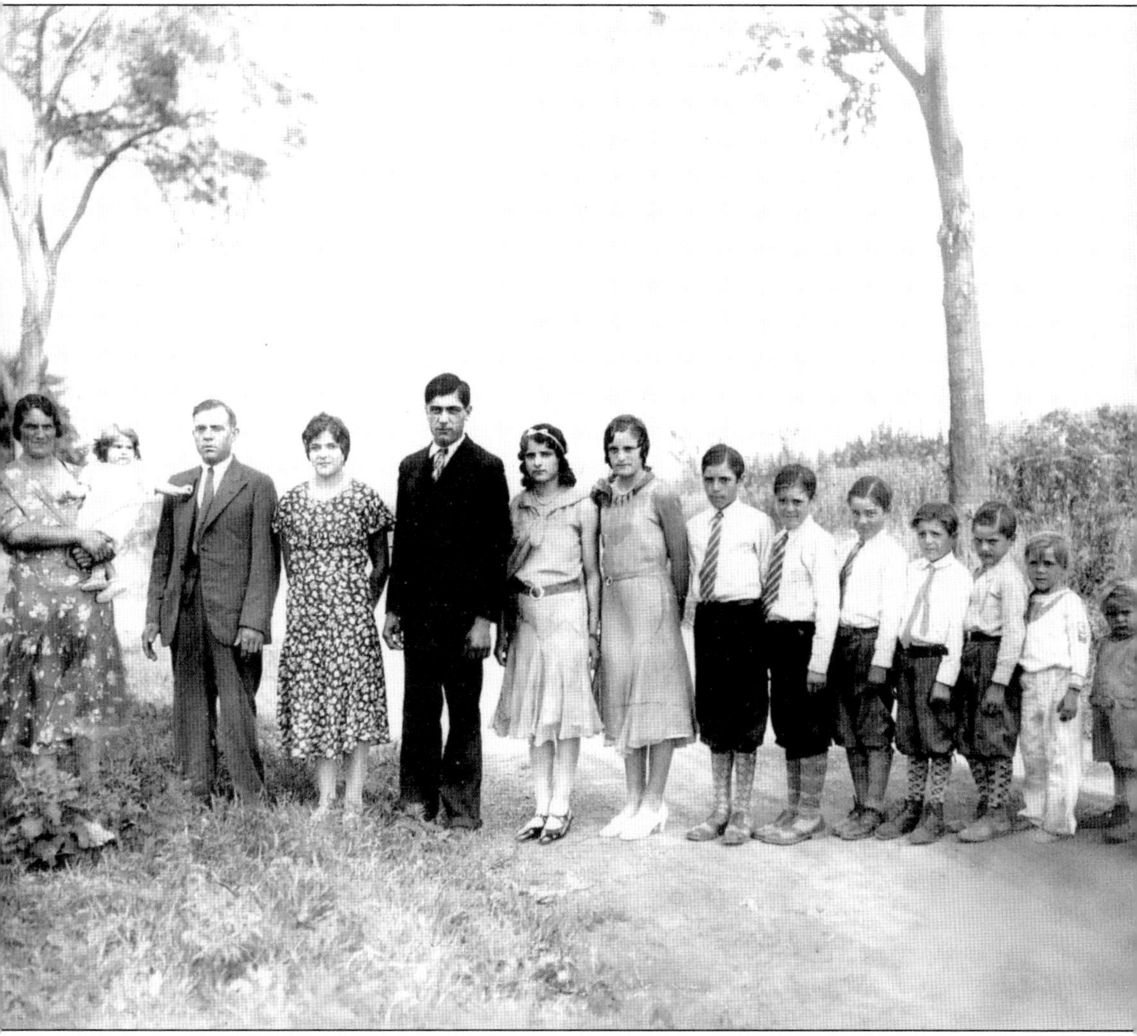

The Cecarelli family lines up for a photograph in the fields across from their farmhouse on Old Post Road in 1931. Pictured from left to right are Angelina (41) holding Clara (8 1/2 months), Frank Sr. (45), Mary (18), Tony (17), Alice (15), Helen (14), Frank Jr. (12), Thomas (11), Andrew (9), Nelson (8), Joseph (7), John (5), and Louis (2 1/2). (Tom Smith.)

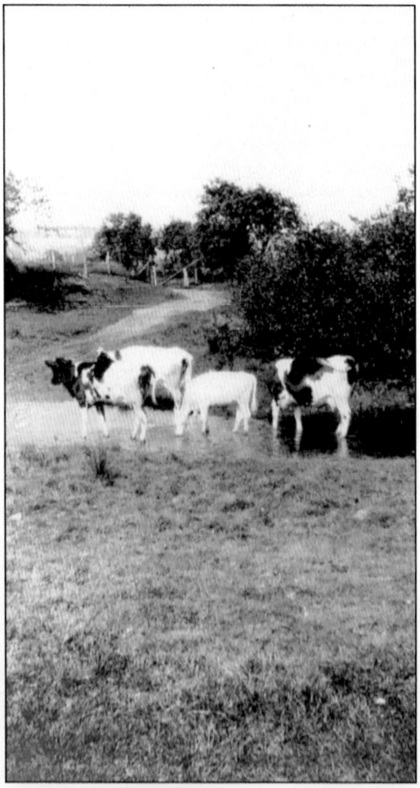

Cows cross Burr Brook in the fields next to the Doody farm on Foxon Road in this photograph taken by Dan Doody. Arthur Road now crosses the brook at this spot. The land was originally granted to John Linsley in the late 1600s and was passed down through the family until it was sold by Carrie G. Doody. (Totoket Historical Society.)

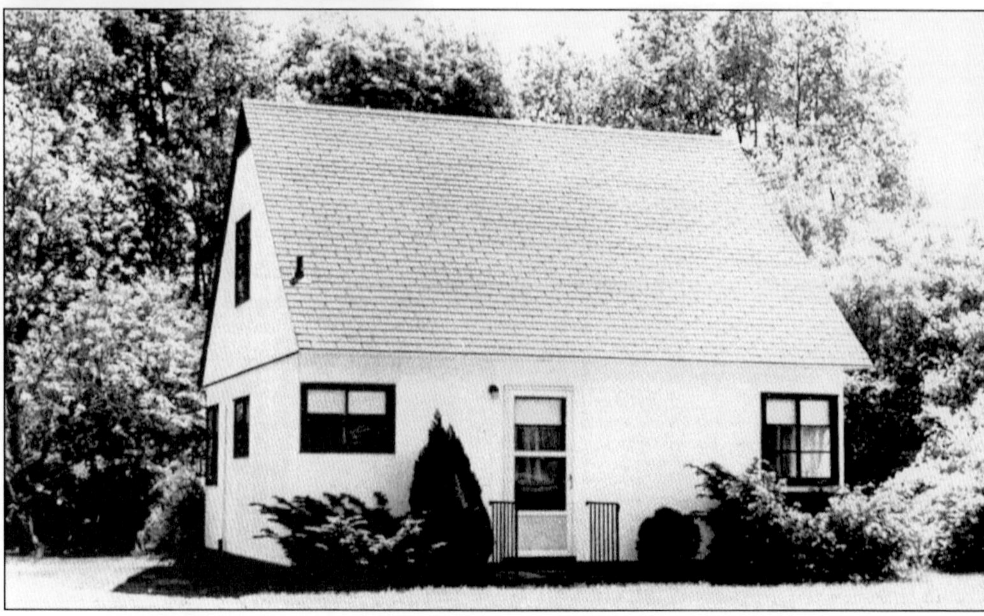

This house at 18 Sunset Road was built in the first housing development in town in 1949. The development was one of the first GI loan and Federal Housing Administration subdivisions in the area. Ten of the 30 lots in Sunset I were sold to the Casade Company, a development branch of the DeForest and Hotchkiss Lumber Company of New Haven. The houses built on these lots, including the one above, were prefabricated Homola units. (Totoket Historical Society.)

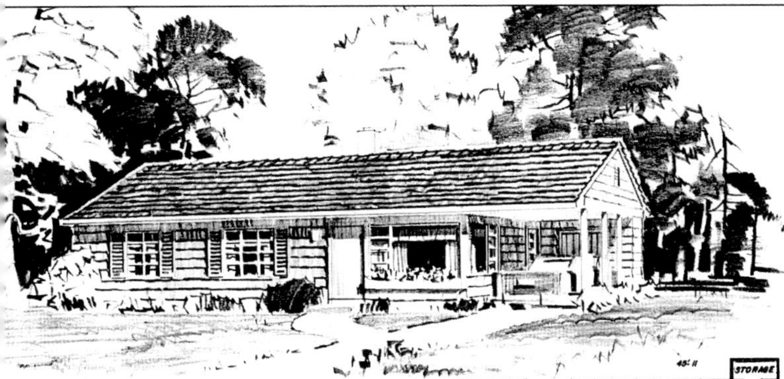

GROTON

$13,500

VETERANS down payment — $300.00
monthly — 82.00

NON-VETERANS down payment — $1,900.00
monthly — 76.00

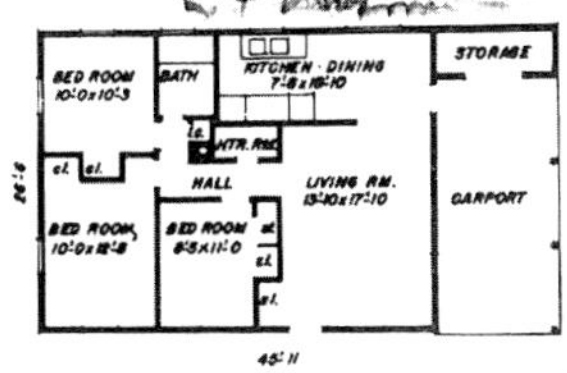

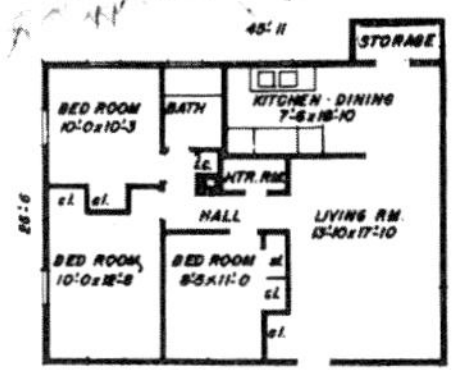

HARVARD
w/o CARPORT

$12,900

VETERANS down payment — $300.00
monthly — 79.00

NON-VETERANS down payment — $1,700.00
monthly — 75.00

KNOLLWOOD

$14,500

VETERANS down payment — $300.00
monthly — 89.00

NON-VETERANS down payment — $2,150.00
monthly — 83.00

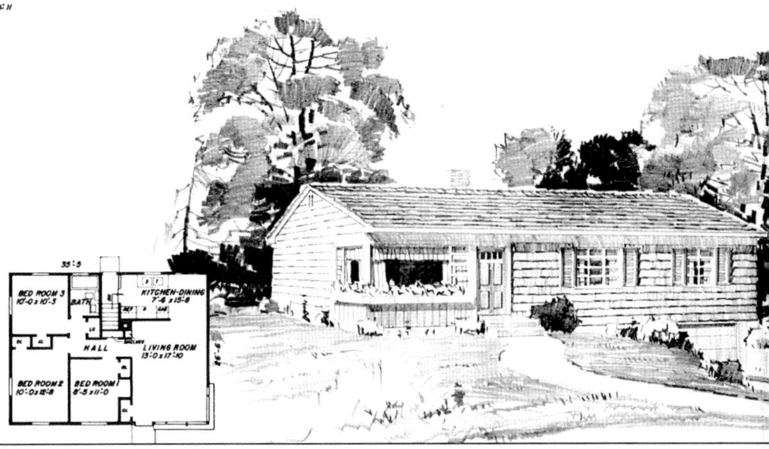

A page from the brochure for the homes at North Branford Estates is depicted here. This housing subdivision was built on the farmlands belonging to the Forte family. It consisted of 100 houses built on five new roads and along the existing Mill Road. (Donald Guyer.)

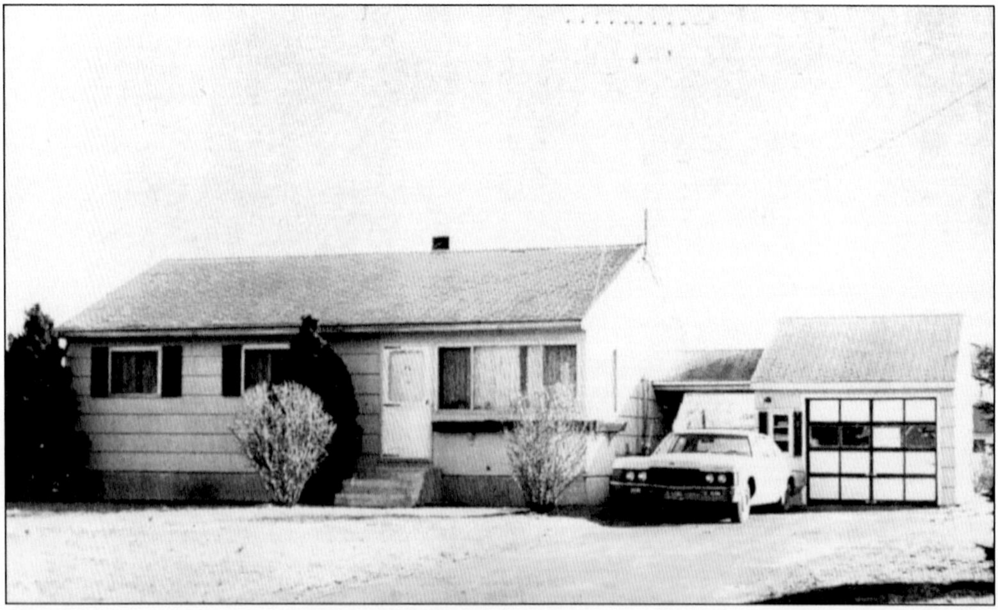

This house at 26 Marjorie Drive in North Branford Estates is an example of the Groton model (see the brochure on the preceding page) that originally sold for $13,500. The one-car garage was added later. In 1972, this house sold for $23,100. (Totoket Historical Society.)

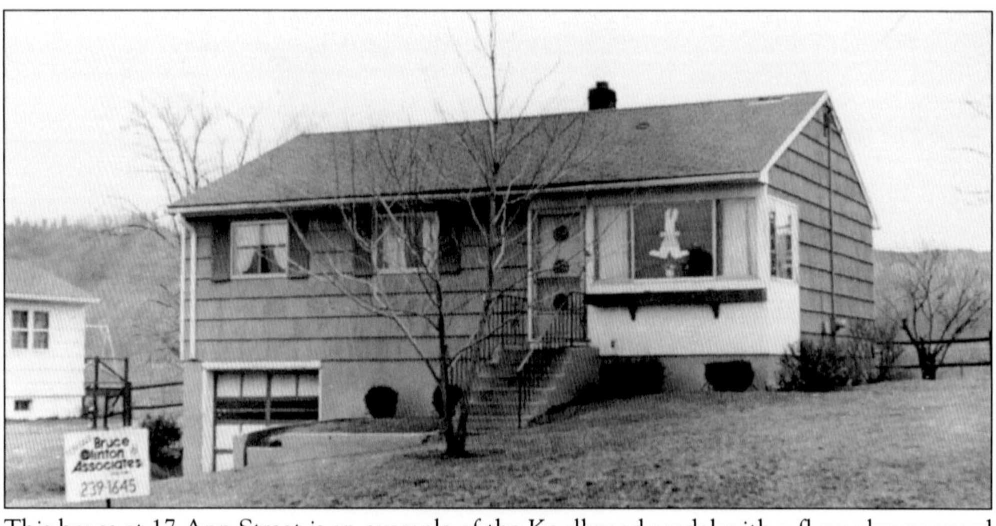

This house at 17 Ann Street is an example of the Knollwood model with a floor plan reversed from the one shown on the brochure on the preceding page. It originally sold for $14,500 and in 1975, sold for $30,520. (Totoket Historical Society.)

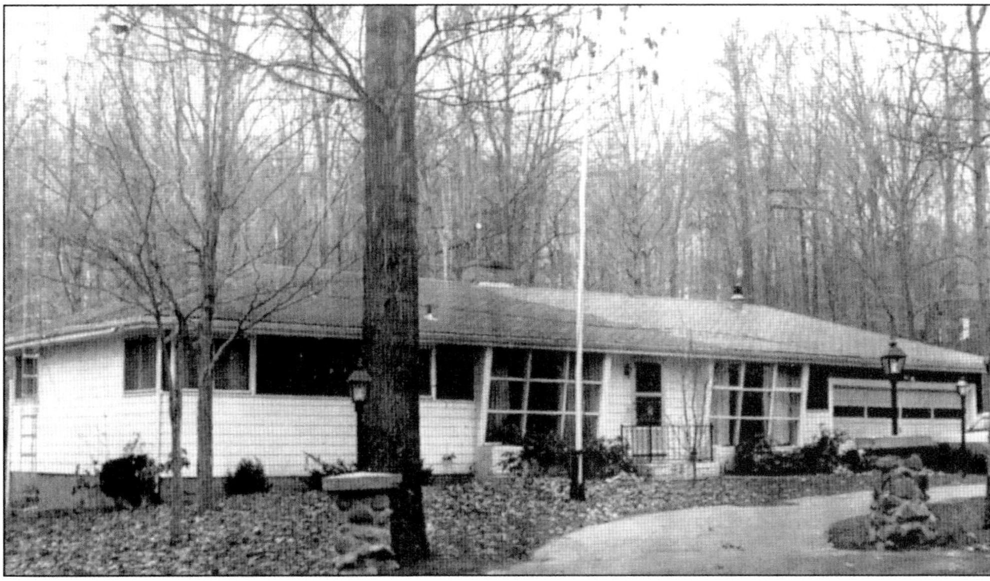

This six-room ranch house was built *c.* 1954 on Lakeview Drive in Northford as more housing developments were built in both ends of town. It depicts the popularity of the ranch house style at this time. (Totoket Historical Society.)

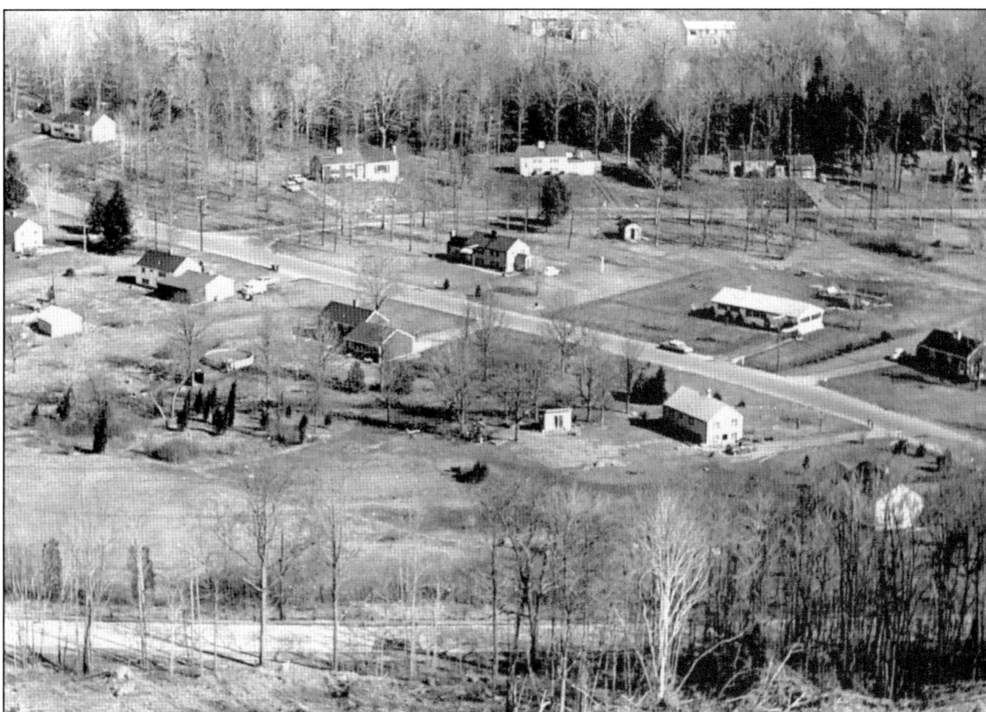

This is a view of the new housing developments in Northford taken from the top of the mountain at Pistapaug Pond near the Durham line. (Company No. 3.)

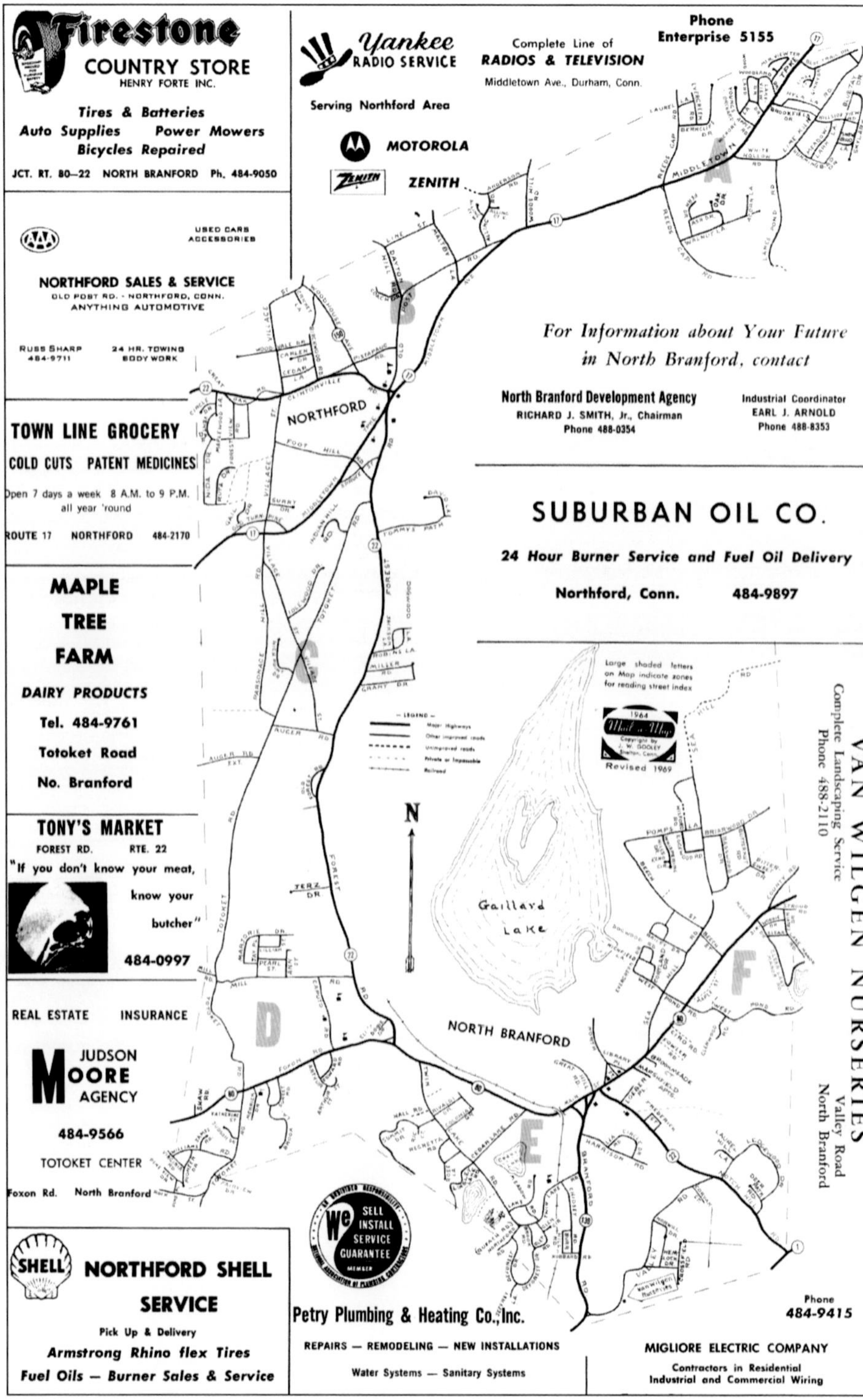

Compare this 1969 road map of North Branford to the map on page two. Note all of the new roads located off the town and state roads of 1950 in subdivisions all over the town. (Totoket Historical Society.)

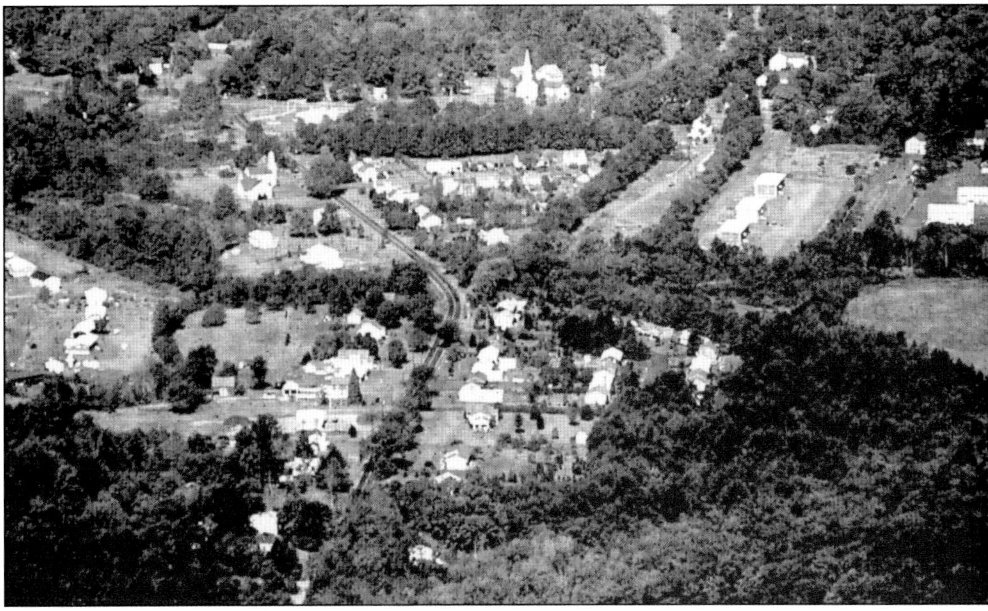

This 1965 aerial photograph shows the proliferation of housing in North Branford Center. Notch Hill Road can be clearly seen with Zion Episcopal Church located near the upper left and the houses on Loeber Place and Frederick Street in the middle of the photograph. The North Branford Congregational Church is in the middle of the upper portion. The Marshfield and Brookmeade Court apartment houses are on the right. (Totoket Historical Society.)

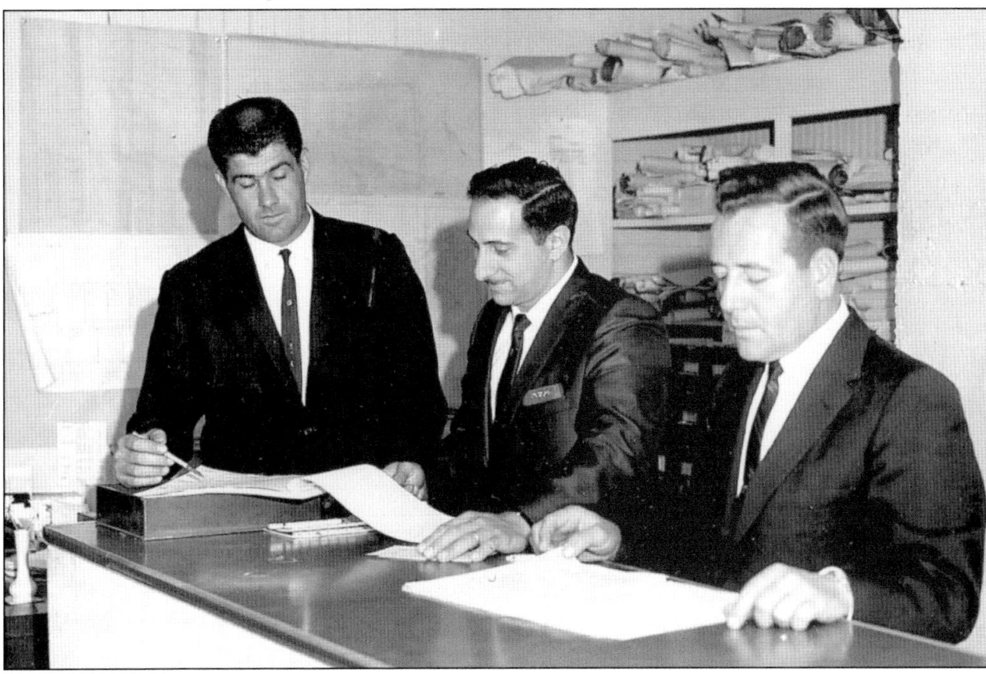

The town building inspectors are reviewing some plans in this 1966 photograph. They are, from left to right, John Gaiolini, plumbing inspector; Lawrence Migliore, electrical inspector; and Andrew Criscuolo, building inspector. The inspectors were part-time employees. (Totoket Historical Society.)

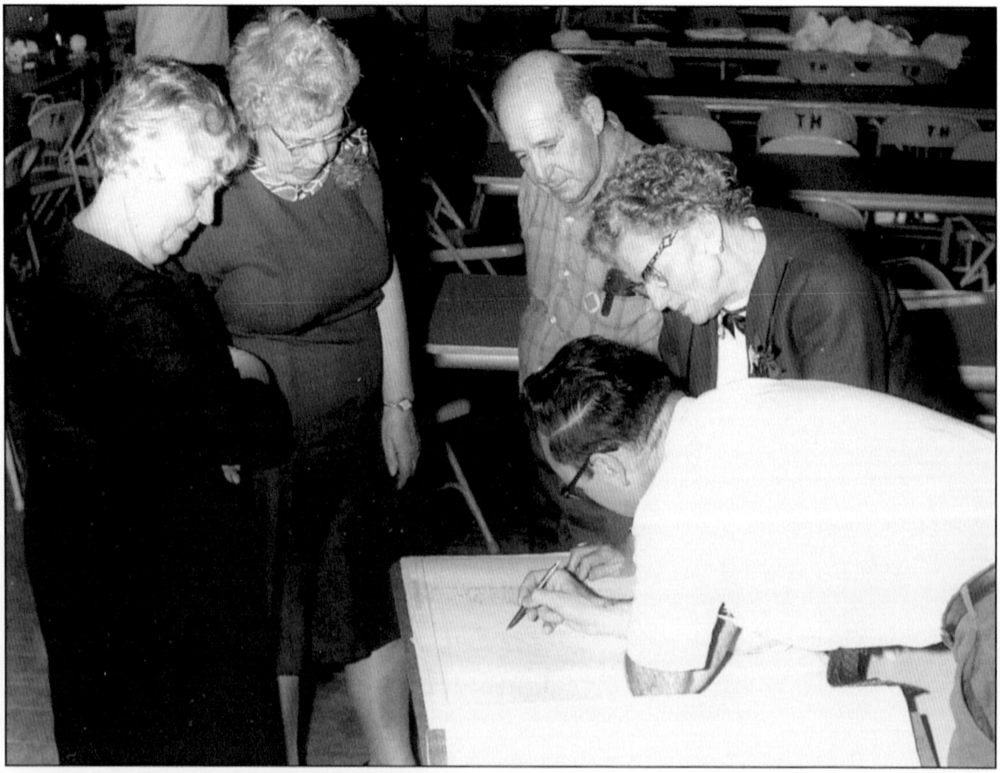

In 1970, senior citizens were recruited to help check and correct the house numbers in town. This photograph, taken by John Welch, shows, from left to right, Mary Camorata, Emma Pombino, William Coutois, Irene Vahldick, and an unidentified man checking the numbering system. (North Branford Parks and Recreation Department.)

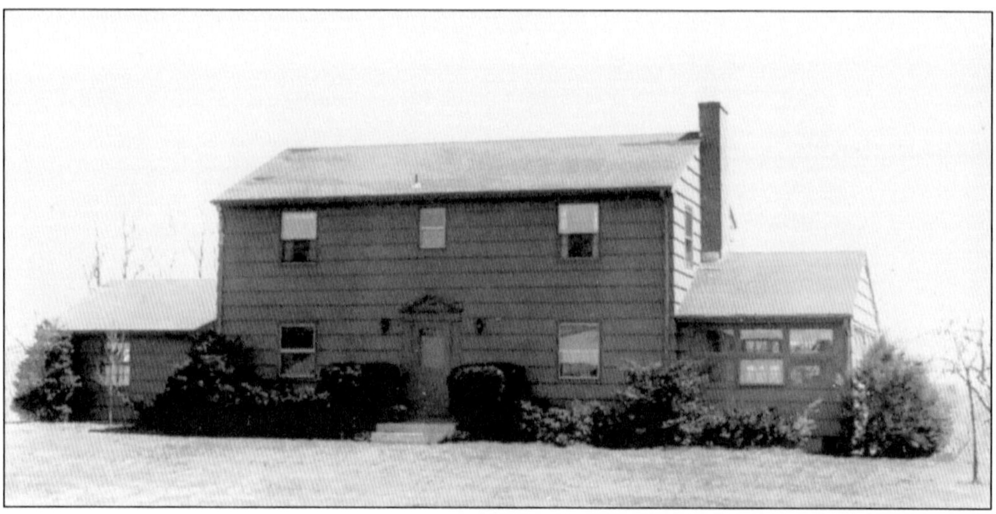

In 1961, North Branford was reported as the fastest-growing town in Connecticut. The houses built at the Deerfield Hills subdivision in the 1960s were more elaborate than houses in the earlier developments. This house at 3 Dogwood Road was built in the popular Colonial style and featured nine rooms, four bedrooms, and two and a half bathrooms. (Totoket Historical Society.)

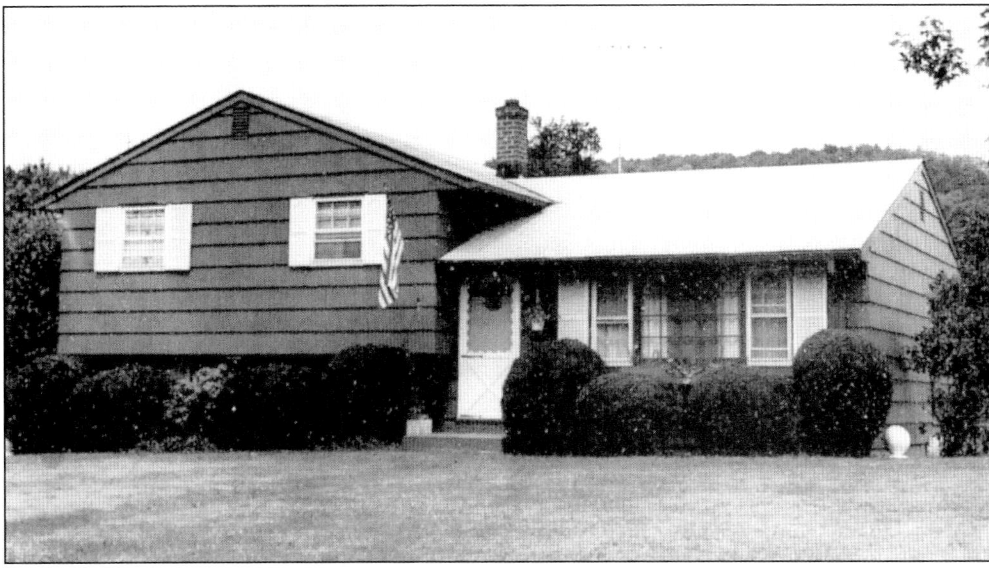

This home at 46 Brookfield Drive was built in 1965 as part of a Northford housing development and depicts a popular style of the era, the split-level house with seven rooms and three bedrooms. (Totoket Historical Society.)

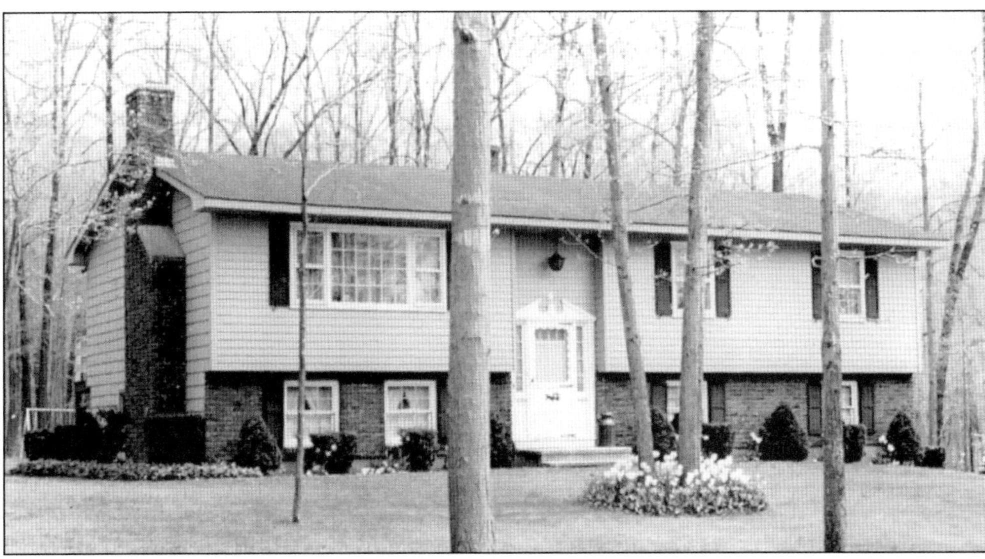

The raised ranch was another very popular style. This house, built in 1968, was part of the Whispering Hills subdivision in the North Branford end of town. (Totoket Historical Society.)

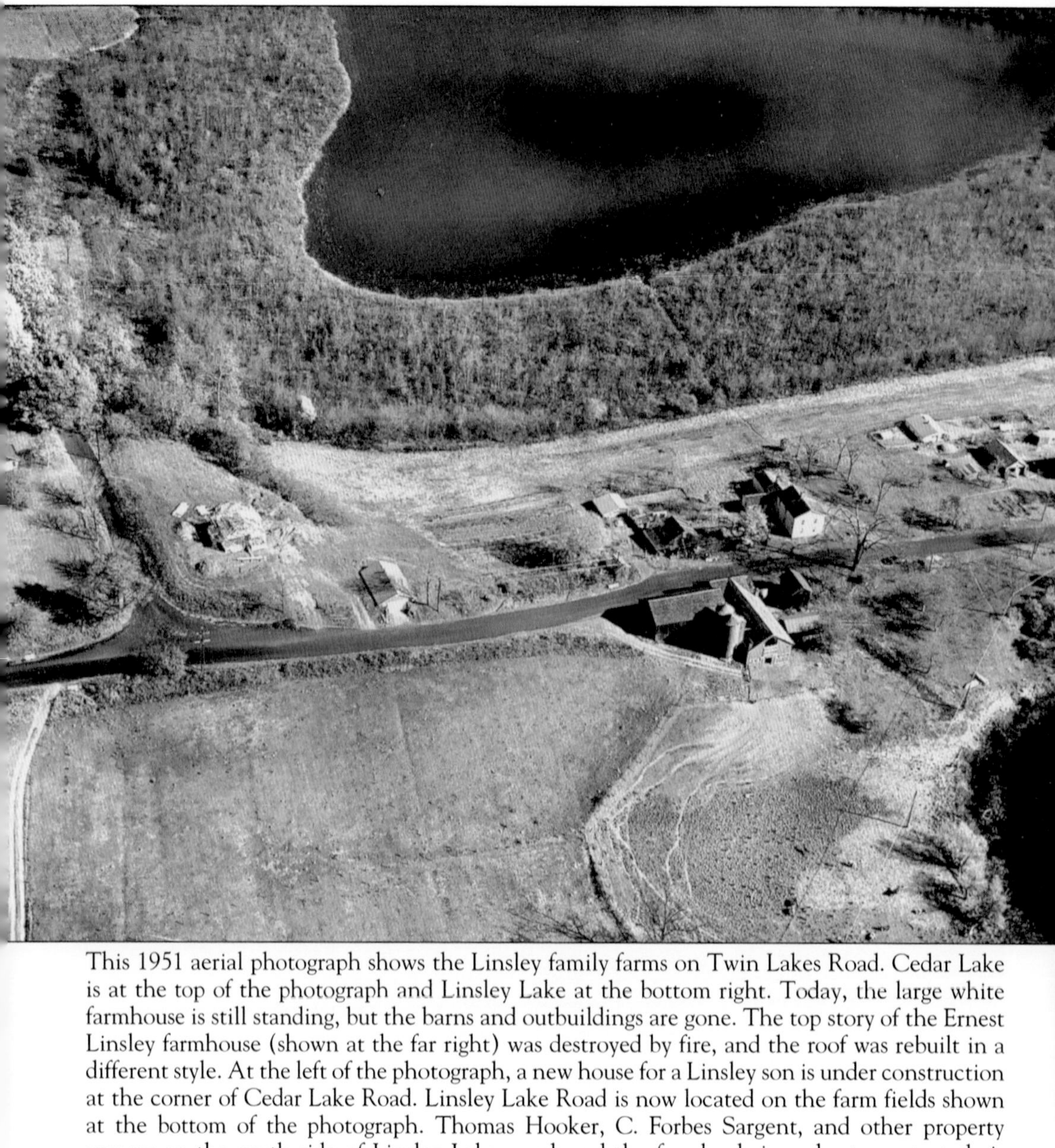

This 1951 aerial photograph shows the Linsley family farms on Twin Lakes Road. Cedar Lake is at the top of the photograph and Linsley Lake at the bottom right. Today, the large white farmhouse is still standing, but the barns and outbuildings are gone. The top story of the Ernest Linsley farmhouse (shown at the far right) was destroyed by fire, and the roof was rebuilt in a different style. At the left of the photograph, a new house for a Linsley son is under construction at the corner of Cedar Lake Road. Linsley Lake Road is now located on the farm fields shown at the bottom of the photograph. Thomas Hooker, C. Forbes Sargent, and other property owners on the south side of Linsley Lake purchased the farmlands in order to protect their view. In 1966, the sale of a building lot to architect David Wight precipitated the formation of the Linsley Lake Development Corporation and a unique housing development. (Totoket Historical Society.)

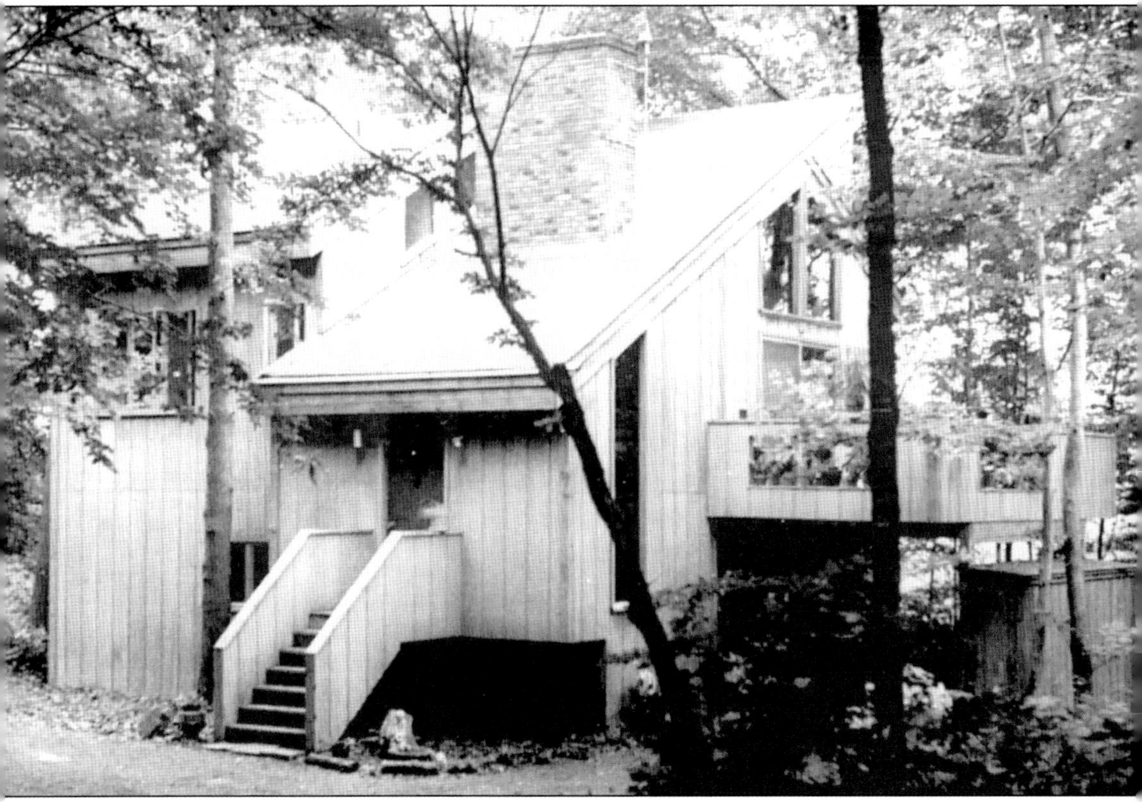

The houses built during the late 1960s on Linsley Lake Road were originally subject to a design review by the Linsley Lake Development Corporation, which included architect Bradford Tilney. This created a unique cluster of custom contemporary homes in town. Later, the design review was turned over to the Linsley Lake Association. This 1976 photograph shows an architect-designed house at 99 Linsley Lake Road. (Totoket Historical Society.)

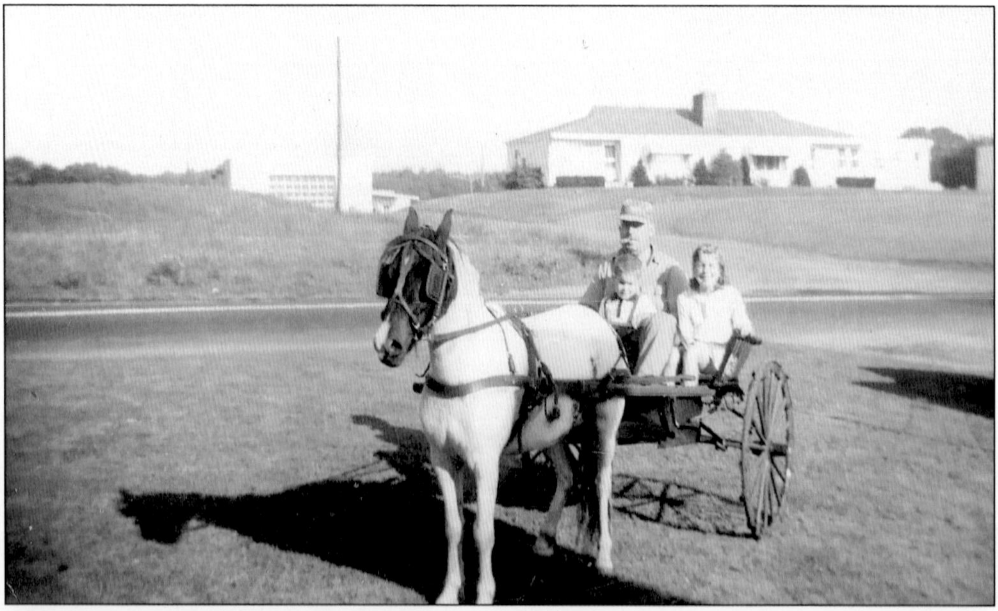

Owen Cole, his daughter Cynthia, and nephew Richard Venna pose in Cole's pony cart for this photograph taken in front of his house on Branford Road (Route 139) near Twin Lakes Road. Across the street is a house that was newly built for Alden and Paul Hill. Their construction business was located in the building on the left. This 1960 photograph shows the rural appearance of what is now a busy state highway. (Shirley Cole.)

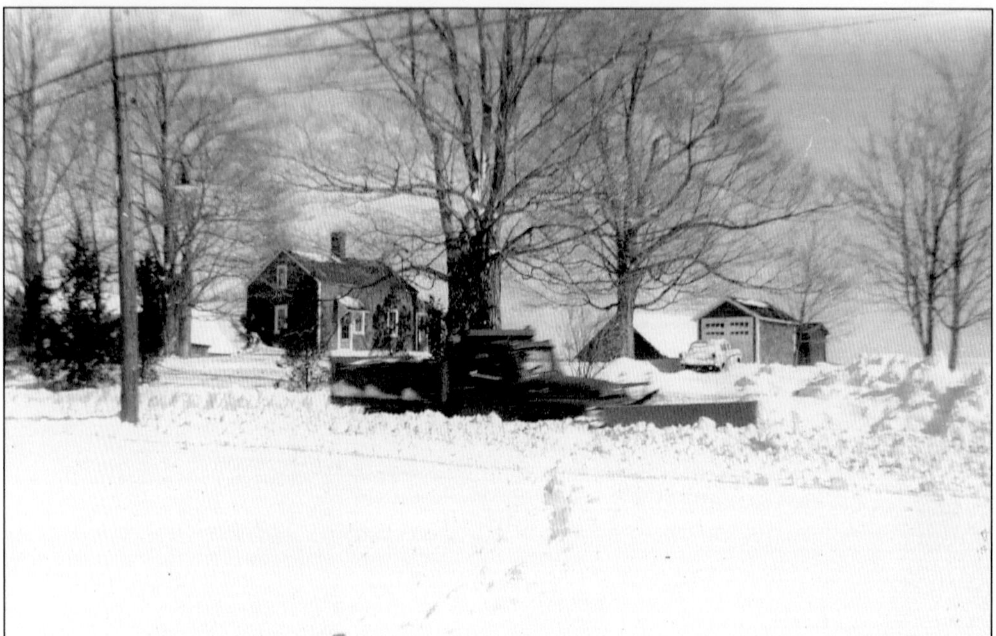

This photograph was taken from the yard of Owen Cole's house in 1961 after a big snowstorm. It shows the old Noah Foote house across the street, with a snow-covered roof at the far left. The barn was used for a lumber business on the Day property. The condominiums at North Farms were built on that property in the late 1970s. (Shirley Cole.)

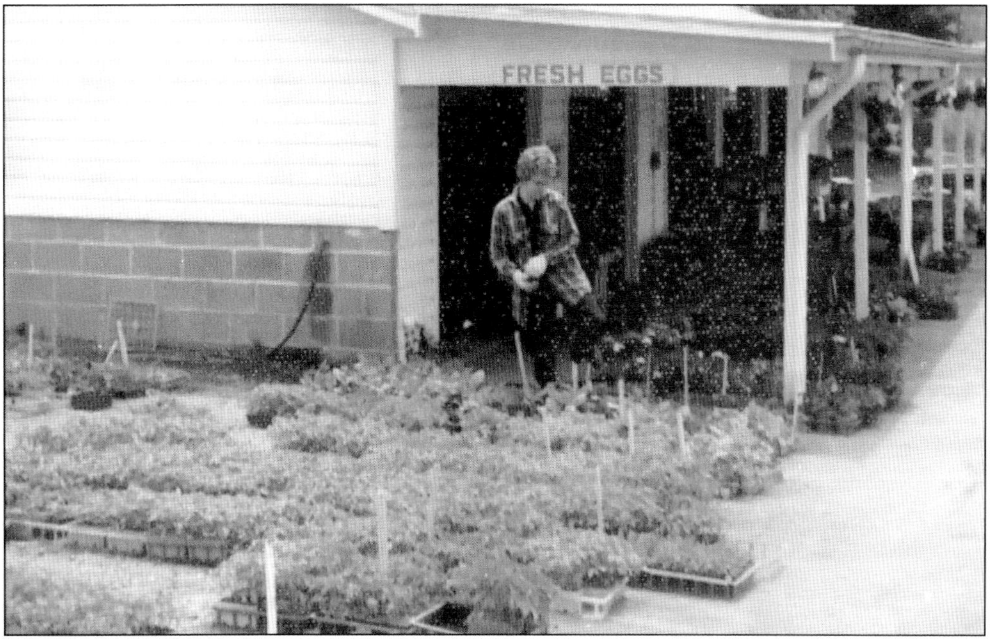

During this period of town growth, farm stands could be found along the town's main roads, featuring the produce and products of family farms. The Marinuzzi Farm Market located on Forest Road sold bedding plants, fresh eggs, and vegetables. In this photograph, Grace Marinuzzi looks over the vegetable plants for sale. (Grace Marinuzzi.)

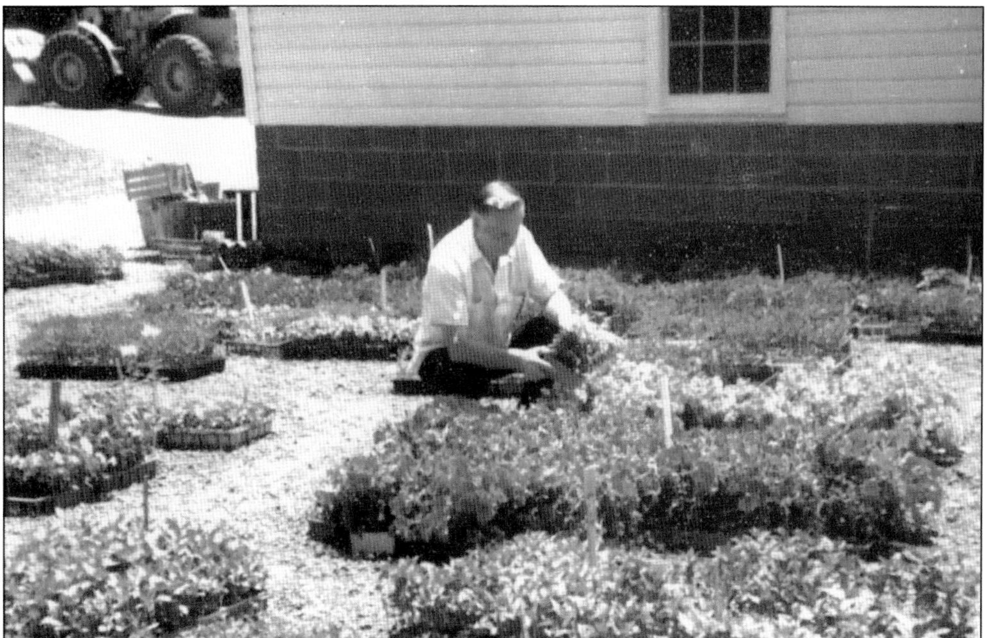

In this 1978 photograph, Michael Chatary readies a flat of flowers for sale at the Marinuzzi Farm Market on Forest Road. The building is still standing but is no longer open for retail sales. However, the Cristoforos, who took over the business, still raise bedding plants for the wholesale market. (Grace Marinuzzi.)

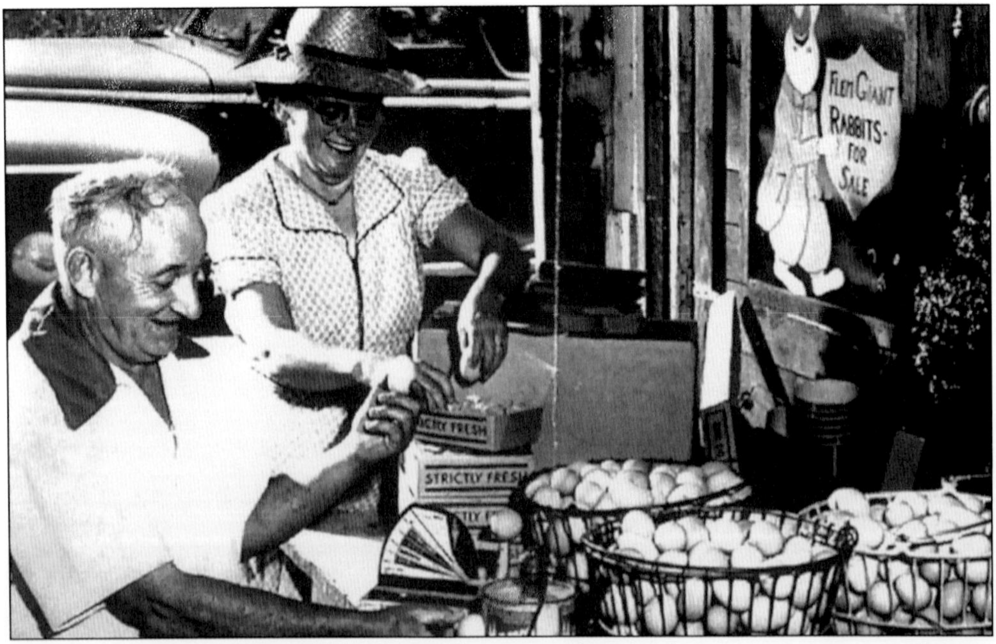

Upon his retirement, Gus Vahldieck started an egg and poultry business at his property located on the eastern end of Route 80. His poultry houses contained more than 2,000 chickens to produce eggs and chickens for his farm stand. His orchards and gardens supplied the fruits and vegetables sold there. In this photograph, Gus and Irene Vahldieck candle, weigh, and pack the eggs for sale. (Wally Anderson.)

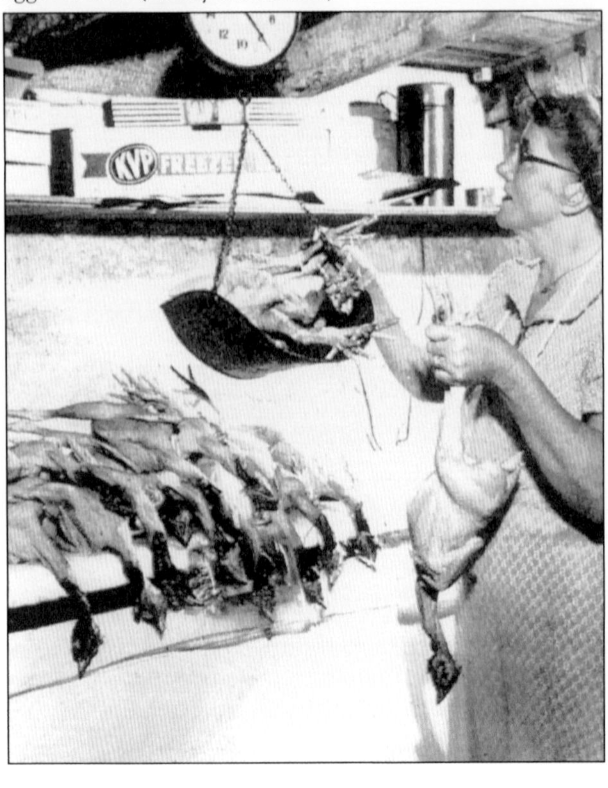

Irene Vahldieck weighs chickens before preparing them for the freezer. Along with the retail sales at the farm stand, chickens and eggs were taken to the Hamden co-op market to be auctioned off to food stores in Hamden, North Haven, and New Haven. (Wally Anderson.)

Two

A 20-Year School Building Spree

In 1950, there were three schools in town—Center School in the North Branford end of town, William Douglas School on Old Post Road in Northford, and Jerome Harrison School near Totoket Road—housing 290 students in kindergarten through eighth grade. With the increase in student population, additions were built onto William Douglas and Jerome Harrison in the early 1950s. Five years later, a new junior high school was constructed on Foxon Road, and within the next five years, two new elementary schools, Cedar Lake School on Twin Lakes Road and Stanley T. Williams on Middletown Avenue, were built. In 1964, the high school was built; it was the first one in town. Previously, students had to attend schools in other towns and cities to receive a high school education. In 1971, a new school was constructed, the Northford Intermediate School.

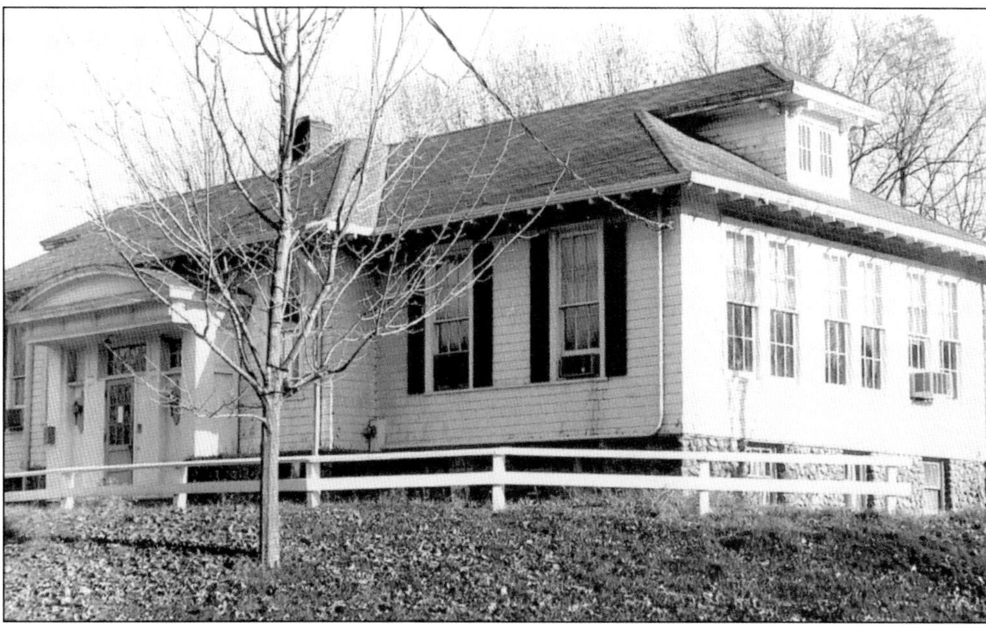

Center School, shown here, was built in 1920 as the first multi-room school building in town. Its three rooms housed eight grades of students. Later, when Jerome Harrison School became a junior high, there were six grades at Center School. When Cedar Lake Elementary School was built in 1960, the old school became the town's first administrative building. (Totoket Historical Society.)

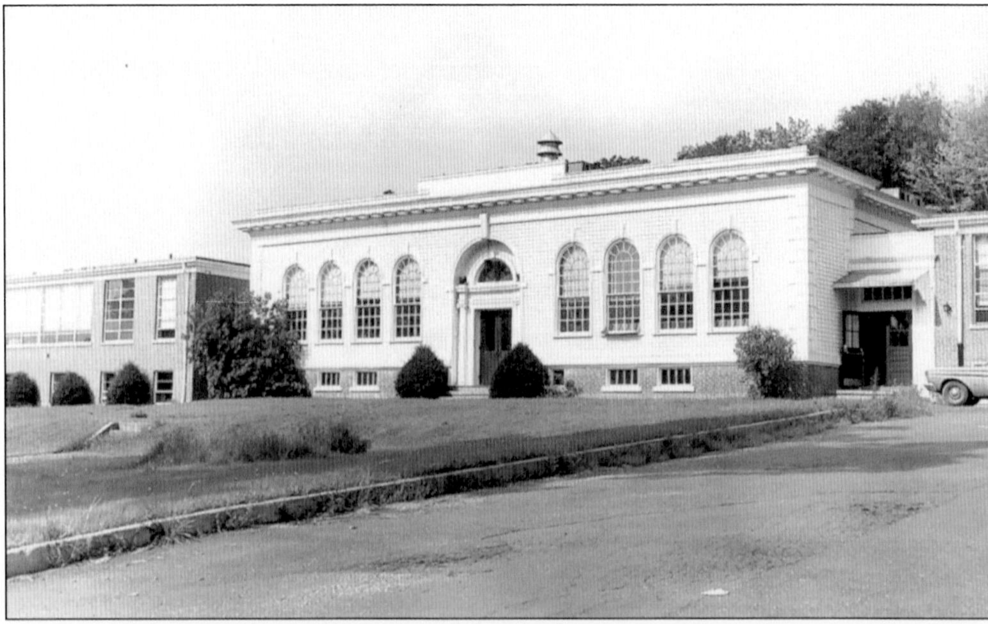

The four-room William Douglas School, built in 1925 to serve the students in the Northford area, received two additions during this era. Classrooms were created in the basement, and the brick ell on the right was built for offices and an assembly hall (that also served as a cafeteria) in 1952. The brick classroom addition on the left was built in 1960. (Totoket Historical Society.)

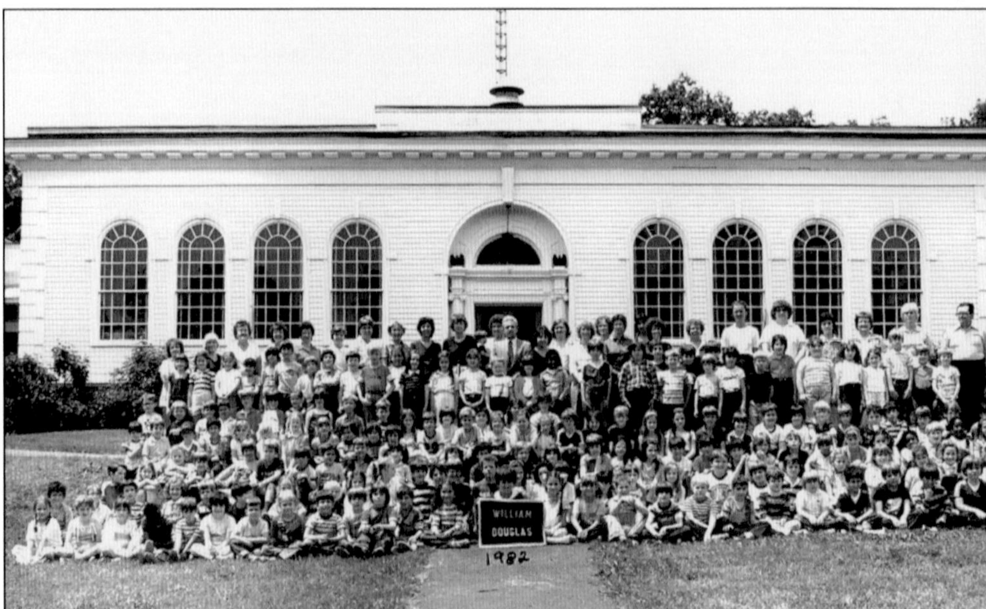

William Douglas School was vacated in 1982, when the student population began to decrease. This photograph of the students and faculty was taken on the last day. An attempt to utilize it as a community center failed; the building was sold and renovated as an office complex. Later, it was sold to Area Community Education Services (ACES), and the central and oldest portion was demolished and rebuilt to use as a regional school. (Totoket Historical Society.)

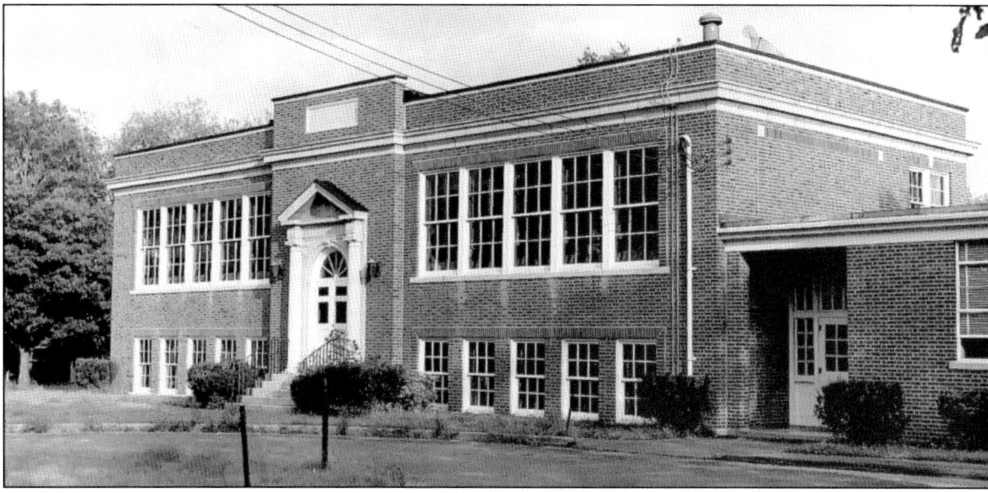

Jerome Harrison School acquired two additions, one in 1953 and another in 1955. The new part is the low-roofed portion on the right of the photograph. It served as an elementary school until 1999, when the entire building was demolished and a new school was built at the rear of the property. (Totoket Historical Society.)

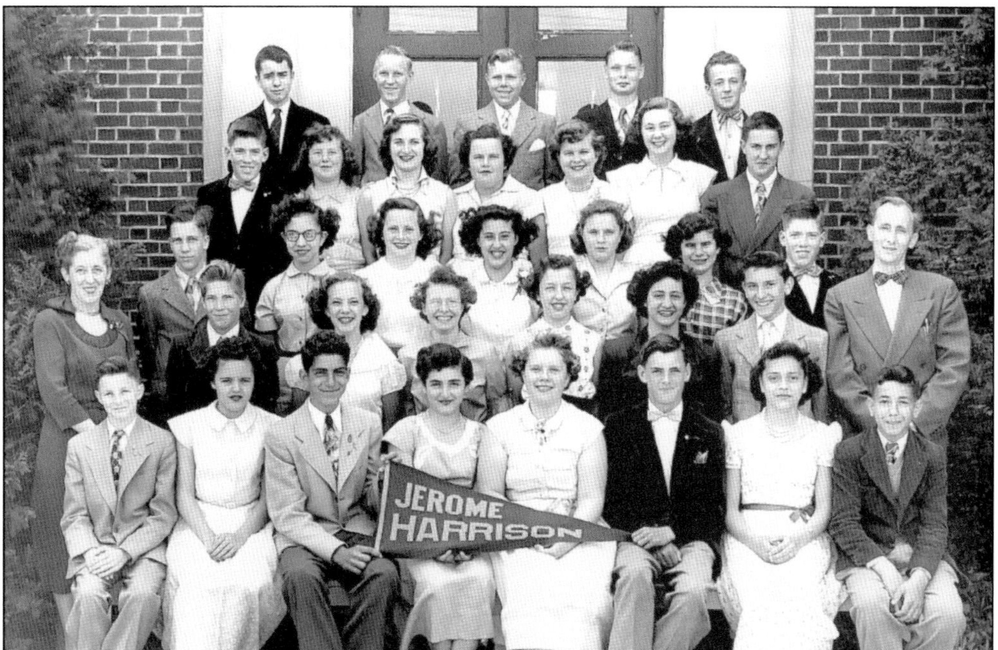

The Jerome Harrison graduates of 1952 pose for a class portrait. The students are, from left to right, as follows: (first row) William Bennett, Sandra Williams, Richard Harrison, Rosalin Camarota, Carol Bright, Peter Hubbard, Shirley Gagne, and Anthony DeFilippo; (second row) Eleanor Williams (teacher), Leonard Gagne, Elizabeth Hansen, Betsey Page, Joan Riggs, Elaine DiDonato, Louis DiPierdomenico, and Warren Comiskey (teacher); (third row) Thomas Russell, Sylvia Drozdz, Dorothy Wood, Jean Thomas, Joan Reynolds, Joan Fazzino, and Elbert Augur; (fourth row) Joseph Augur, Barbara Dubois, Patricia McNally, Dorothy Neubig, Karen Johnson, Juanita Hall, and Philip Lockwood; (fifth row) Daniel Spencer, Donald Bean, Fred Blomster, Harry Juniver, and Brian Eagan. (Totoket Historical Society.)

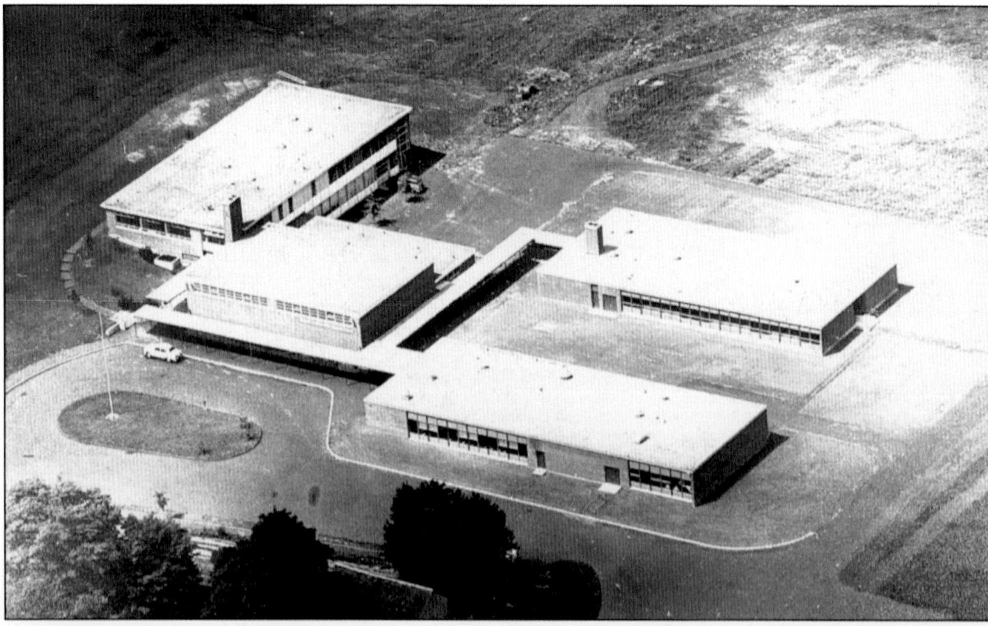

In 1957, a new junior high school was built on Foxon Road (Route 80). The tallest portion, in the middle, is the gymnasium. The library is to the rear. School offices and classrooms were contained in the two-story portion built into the hill. The front wing housed the cafeteria and workshop, and a second wing constructed at a later date contained more classrooms. (Totoket Historical Society.)

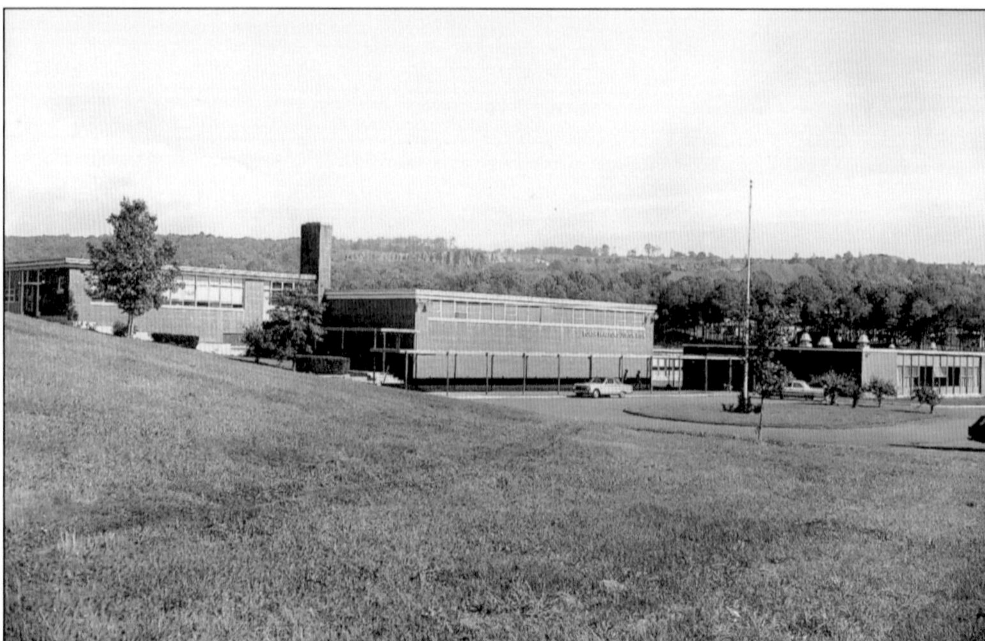

This is a view of the North Branford Junior High School in 1967. The cafeteria was used for town meetings. Before the new church was built on the hill, St. Augustine's held Masses here. When the new intermediate school was built in Northford in 1971, the junior high became the North Branford Intermediate School, housing grades six through eight. (Totoket Historical Society.)

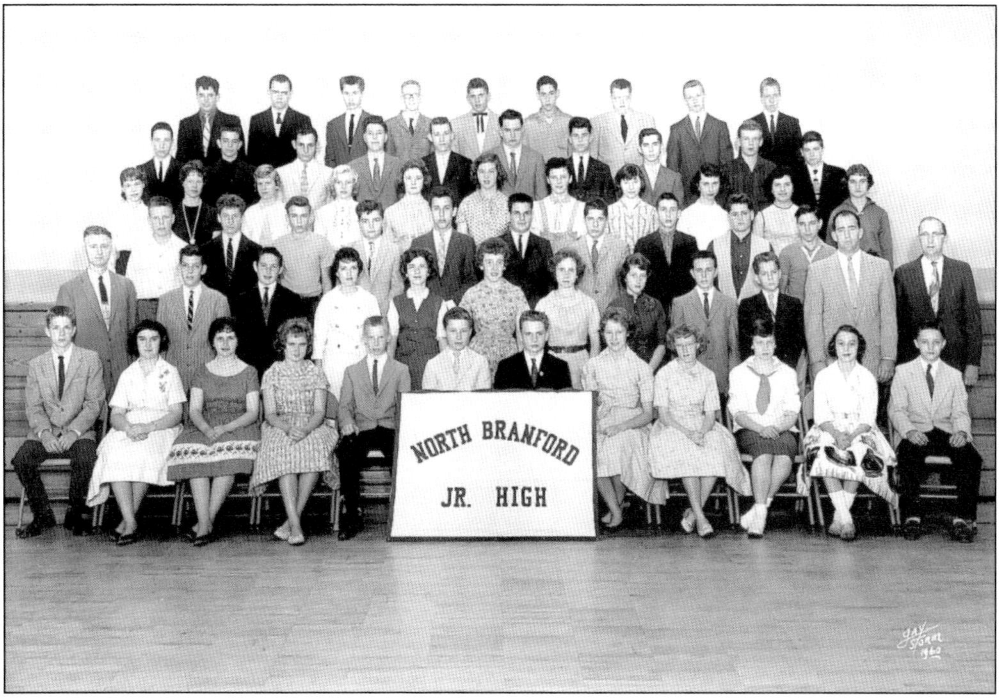

Junior high students pose for a class picture in 1960, a few years after the new junior high school was occupied. (Totoket Historical Society.)

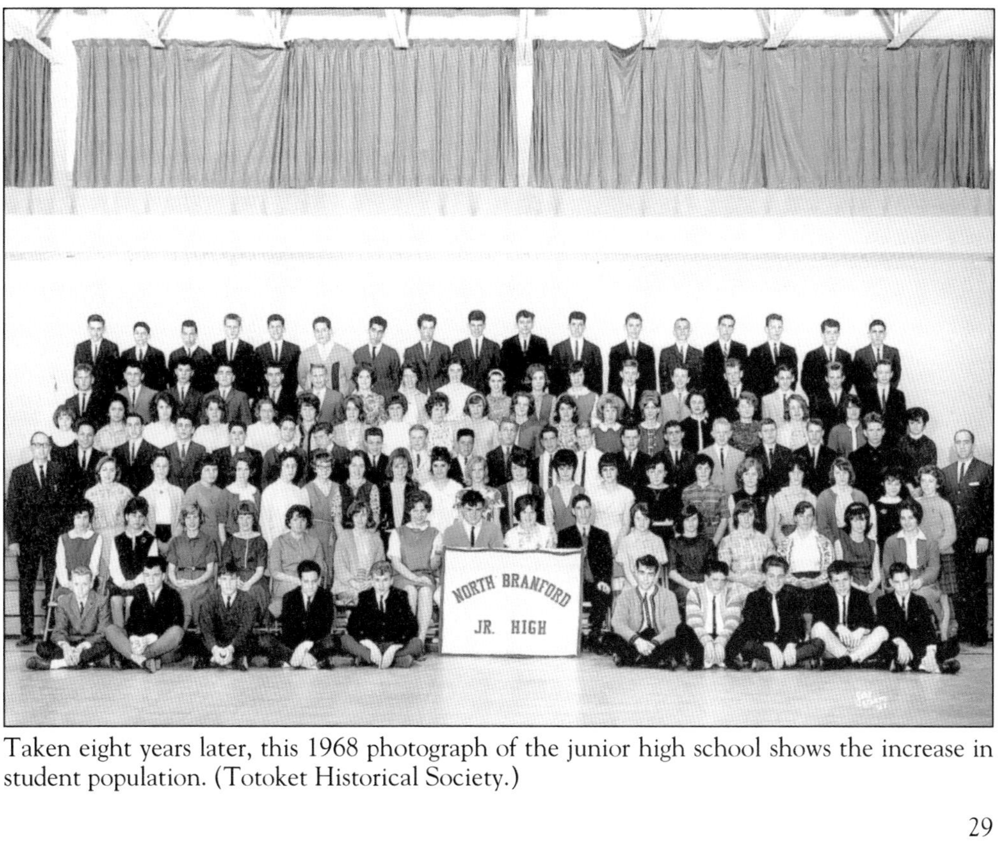

Taken eight years later, this 1968 photograph of the junior high school shows the increase in student population. (Totoket Historical Society.)

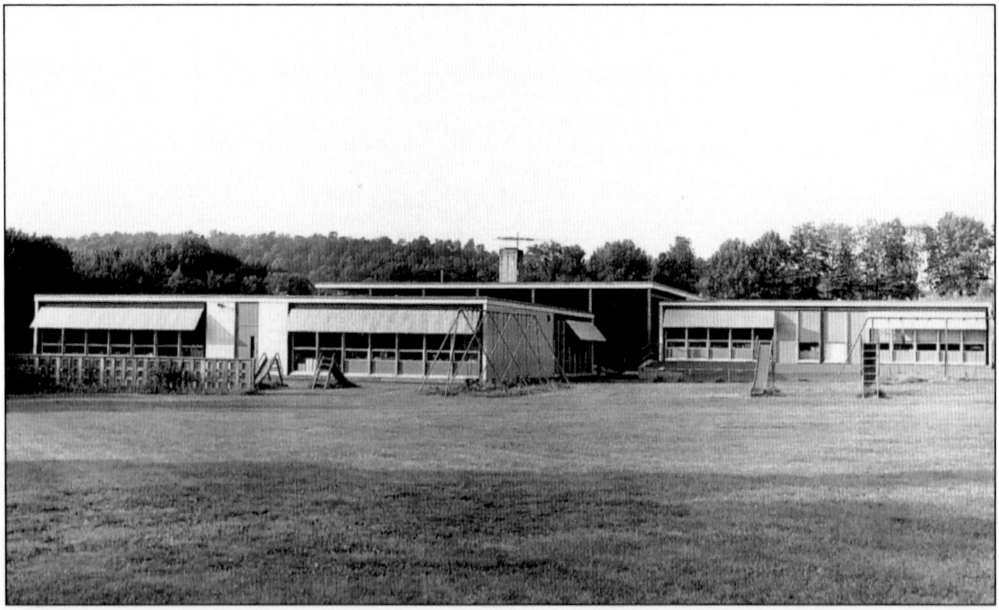

Cedar Lake School with 12 classrooms was built in 1960 on Twin Lakes Road. Four more classrooms were added later. It originally served kindergarten through grade six, later through grade four, when students in the fifth and sixth grades were sent to Jerome Harrison School. When the baby boom began to subside, the school was no longer needed. It was sold in 1980 to General Resistance for industrial use. (Totoket Historical Society.)

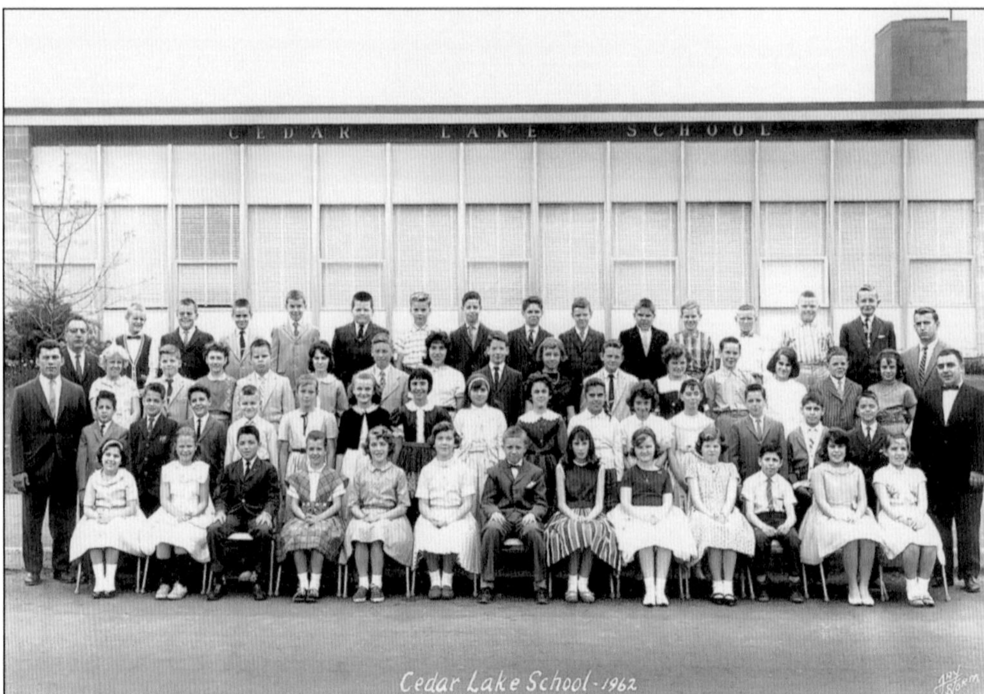

The Cedar Lake School sixth-grade class poses for a picture in 1962 upon promotion to the junior high school. (Wally Anderson.)

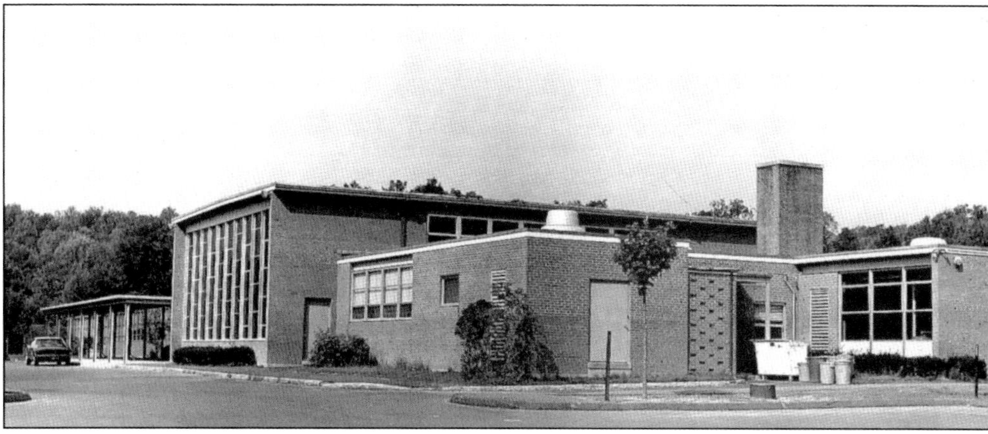

In 1961, a new elementary school was built on Middletown Avenue in Northford. It was named for Stanley T. Williams, a Northford resident who served as chairman of the board of education. He also was the president of the Northford Village Improvement Society in 1925, when it built a community center near William Douglas School. The building was sold when the school expanded in 1952. (Totoket Historical Society.)

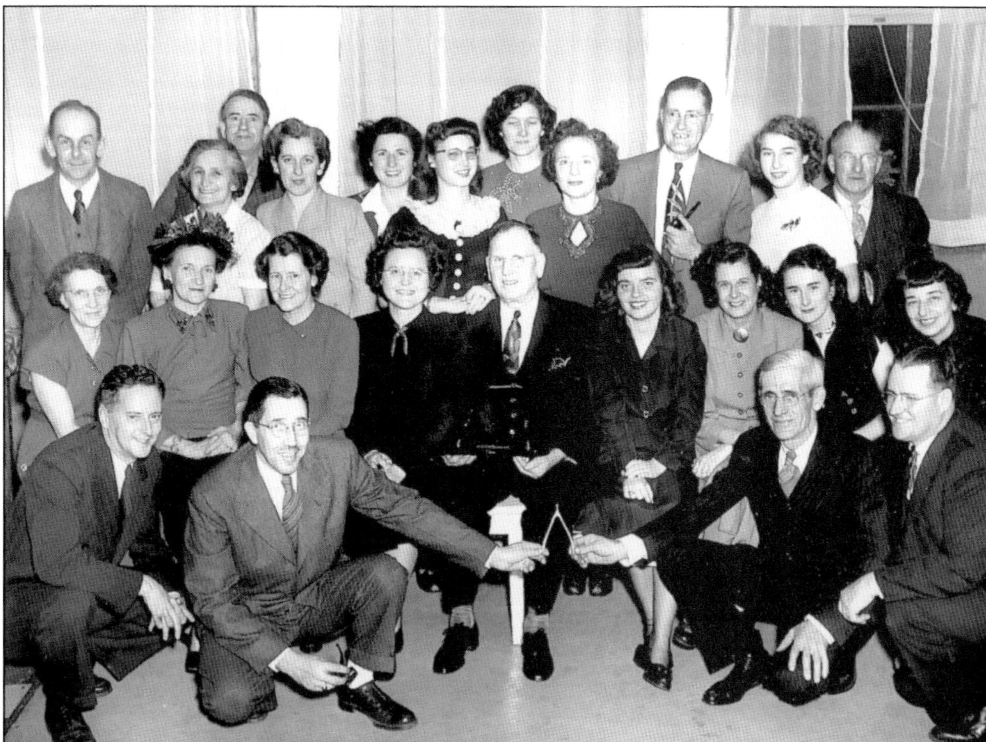

Attendees at the retirement party for Stanley T. Williams pose for this picture. They are, from left to right, as follows: (front row) George Gallagher, Charles Abel, Earl Colter Sr., and Clarence Williams; (second row) Elbertine Hart, Ruth Beers, Ruth Gallagher, Elizabeth Carter, Stanley T. Williams, Barbara Sears, Adele H. Hillman, Martha Johnson, and unidentified; (third row) Charles Jennings, Jennie Bernard, Eleanor Connolly Williams, Carmelita Williams Dillman, unidentified, Mary Bernard, and Alec Hart; (back row) Thomas Bernard, Wilhemina Schuessler, and Haviland Schuessler. (Totoket Historical Society.)

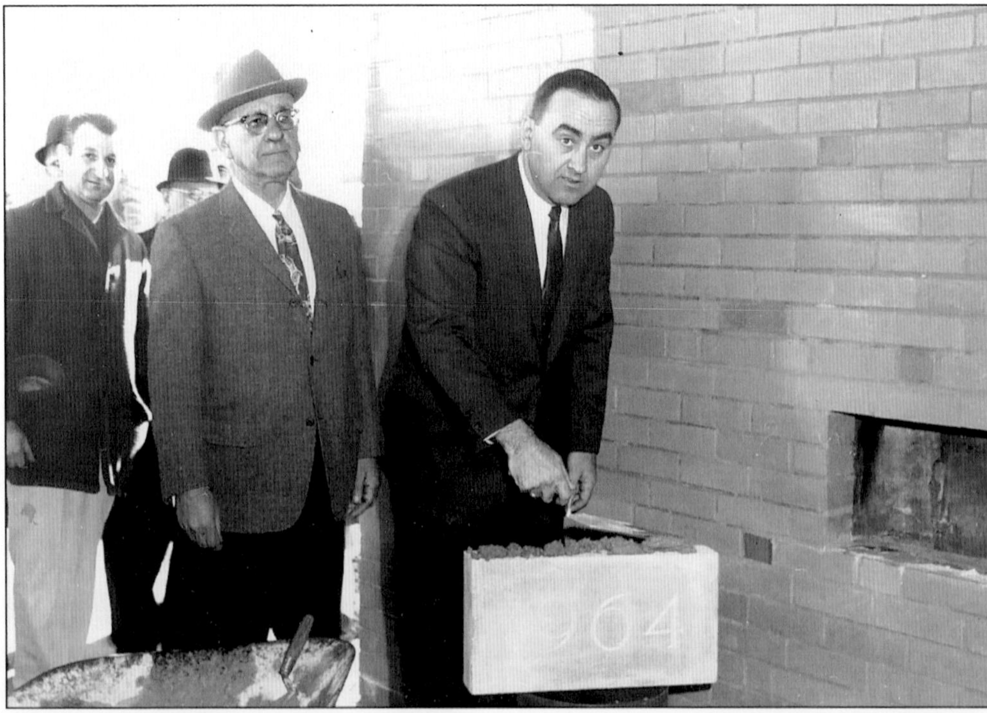

Principal Gene Marra lays the cornerstone for a new high school. It was built on land behind the junior high school with an entrance off Caputo Road. Original plans for the high school included an auditorium, but a vote at a special town meeting eliminated the auditorium, and North Branford did without one until 2003. (Totoket Historical Society.)

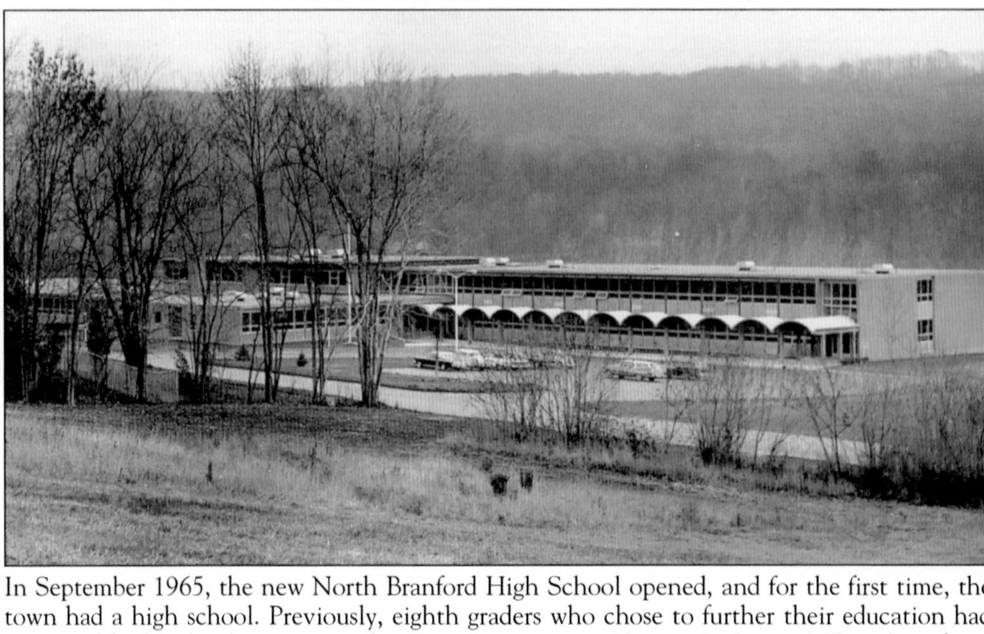

In September 1965, the new North Branford High School opened, and for the first time, the town had a high school. Previously, eighth graders who chose to further their education had to attend high schools in surrounding towns or in New Haven. In June 1965, 103 students graduated, and Gov. John Dempsey spoke at the ceremony. This view shows the brand-new high school. (Totoket Historical Society.)

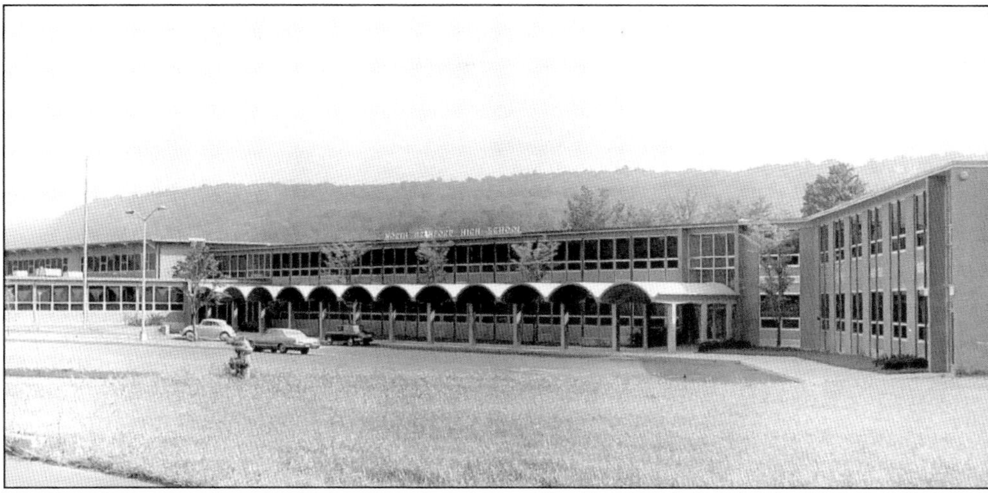

In 1965, the total enrollment in town was 2,515 students with 118 teachers. Expenditure per pupil was $325.29, as compared to the state average of $373.04. Adult education was offered for the first time that year. Compare this 1975 photograph of the North Branford High School to the photograph on the previous page, and note the two-story addition on the left that was built in 1967 and 1972. (Totoket Historical Society.)

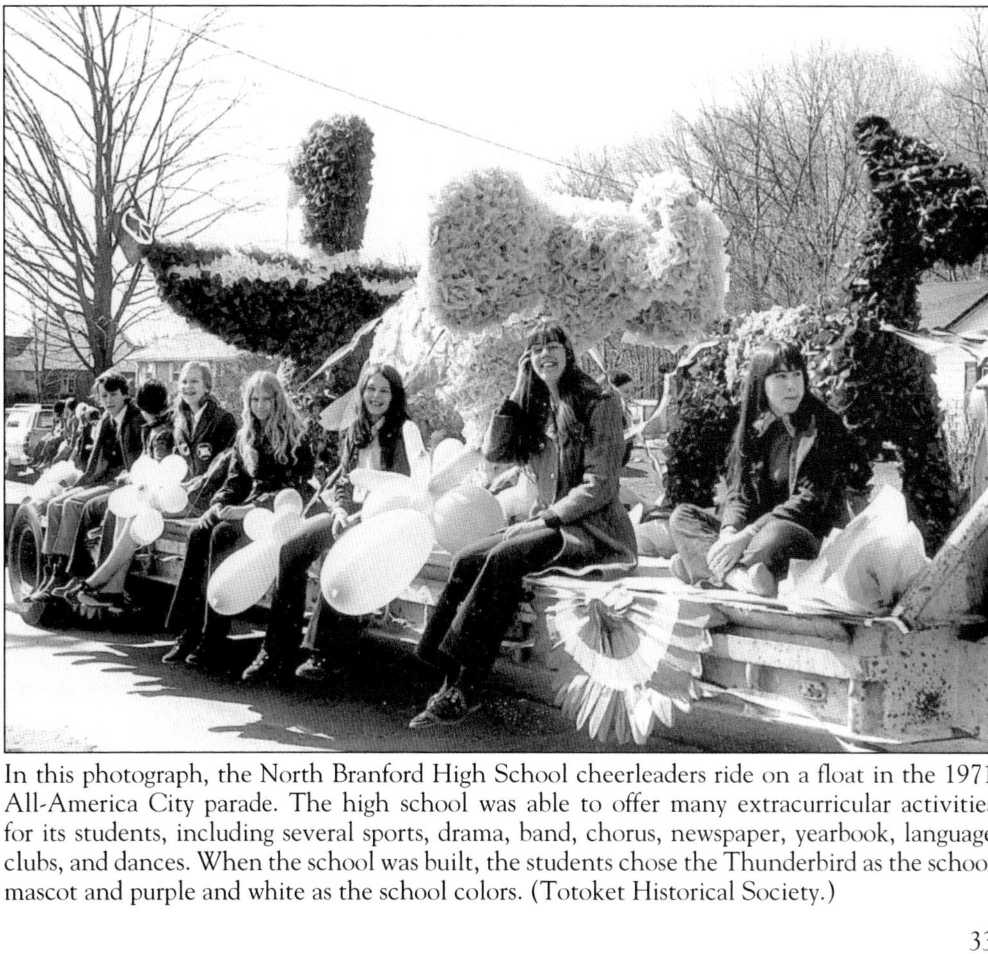

In this photograph, the North Branford High School cheerleaders ride on a float in the 1971 All-America City parade. The high school was able to offer many extracurricular activities for its students, including several sports, drama, band, chorus, newspaper, yearbook, language clubs, and dances. When the school was built, the students chose the Thunderbird as the school mascot and purple and white as the school colors. (Totoket Historical Society.)

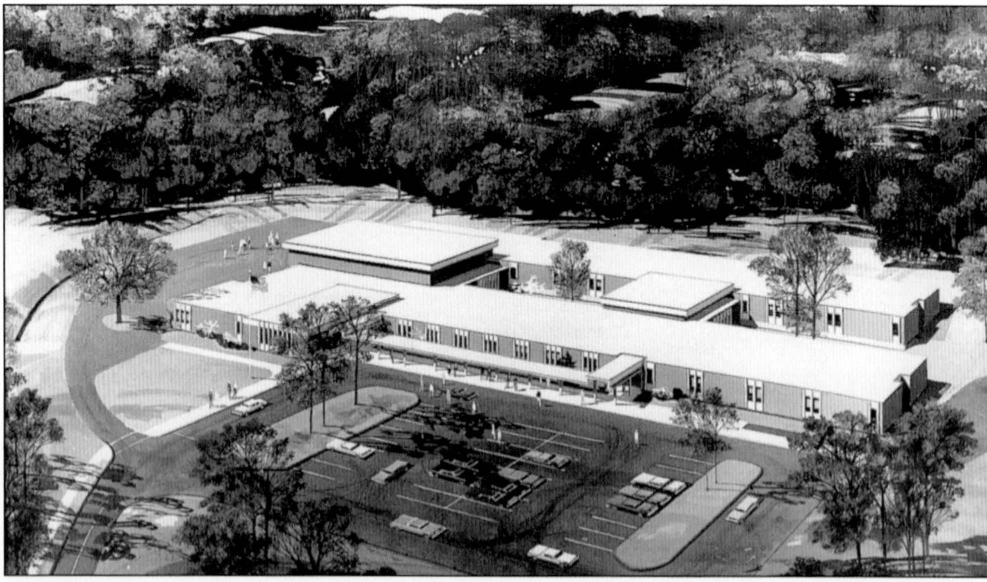

The last school to be built during this 20-year school building spree was the Northford Intermediate School, located next to and to the rear of the Stanley T. Williams School. Occupied in September 1971, it contained classrooms for grades five through eight, a complete cafeteria, a gym, and a library. (Totoket Historical Society.)

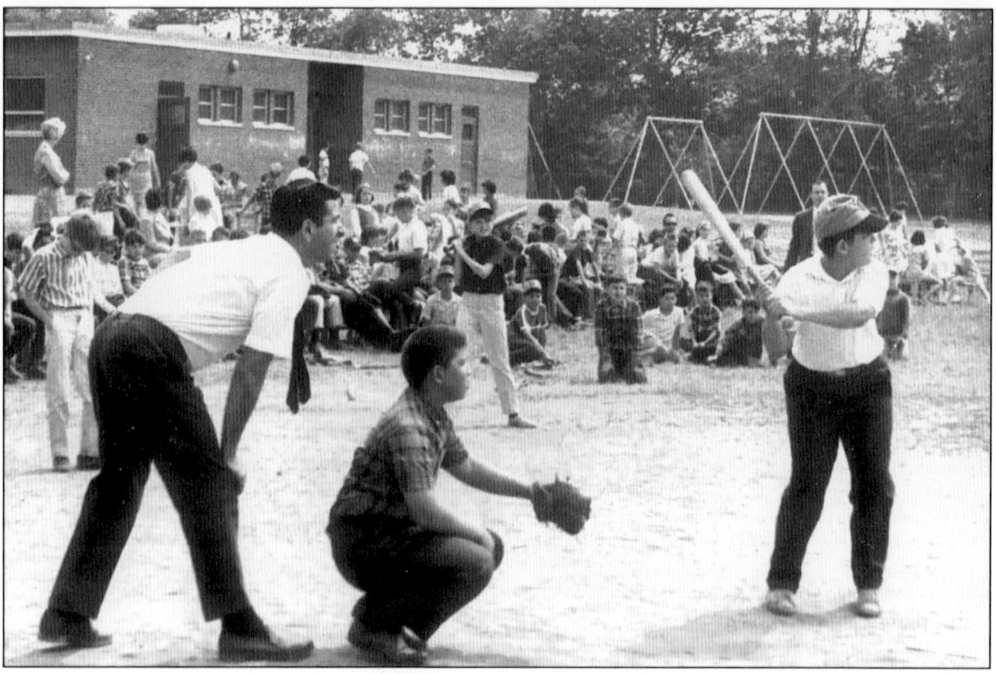

In this photograph, students from the schools at each end of town compete in an interschool baseball game. The teacher umpiring is William Benni, John Foster is at bat, and the catcher is unidentified. There was a historic rivalry between the schools in Northford and North Branford that disappeared when the schools were redistricted in the 1990s and Northford Intermediate School became the Totoket Valley Elementary School. (Totoket Historical Society.)

Three

The Town Government Grows and Grows

With more and more people moving into North Branford and Northford, a need for more governmental services developed. According to the 1950 annual town report, the government provided schools, libraries, a fire department, public works, public health, constable services, and a finance board. Thirty-one years later, the 1981 annual report lists 19 boards and commissions and contains reports from the town manager, the town council, the water pollution control authority, the building department, the purchasing department, the board of education, the board of fire commissioners, the board of tax review, the board of appeals, the conservation commission, the planning and zoning commission, zoning enforcement, the East Shore District Health Department, the economic development commission, the housing authority, the human relations commission, the inland wetlands agency, the jury committee, the library board of directors, the police commission, and the recreation commission. As always, the report contained information on town finances.

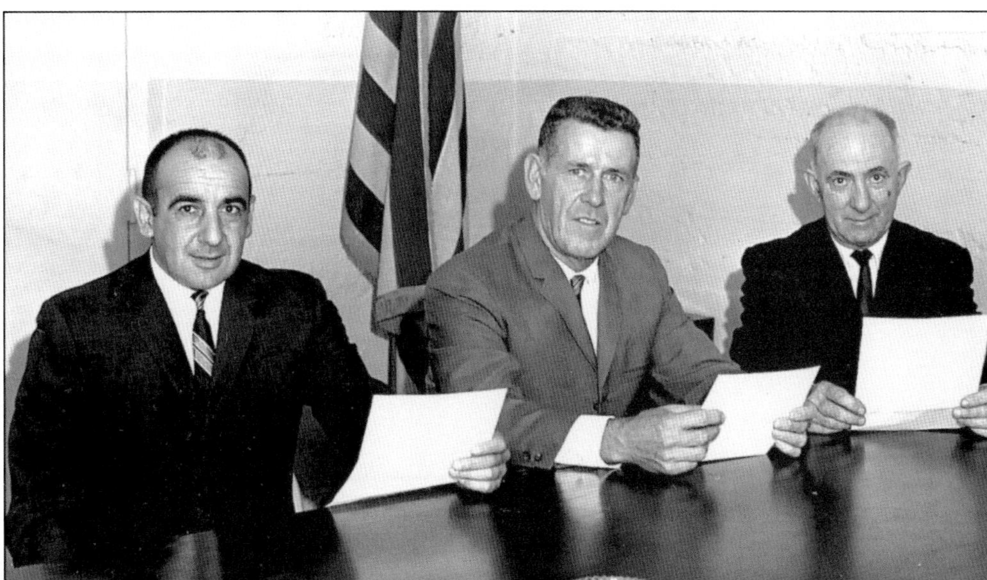

Since the town was incorporated in 1831, three selectmen, elected at an annual town meeting, governed the town. In 1968, the selectmen were Frank Marinuzzi (left), First Selectman John Barrett (center), and John Dwyer. (Totoket Historical Society.)

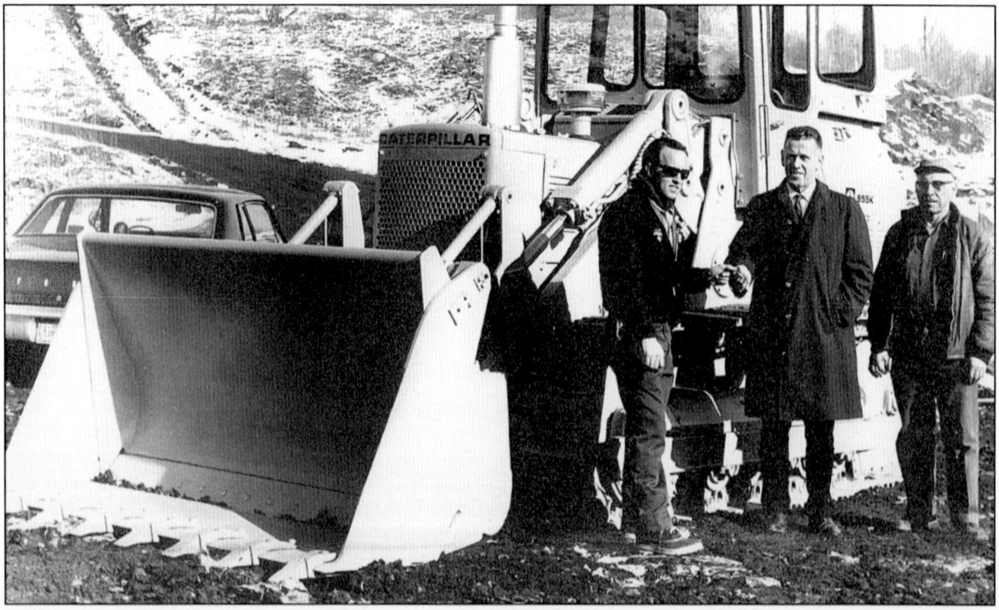

Maintaining the town roads and property has been a major part of the town's public services since the town's settlement. In this 1969 photograph, First Selectman John V. Barrett accepts from a company representative the ignition key to the new and powerful Caterpillar Traxcavator as Charles Smith looks on. This heavy-duty machine was used at the town dump (landfill) as directed by the state for refuse disposal. (Totoket Historical Society.)

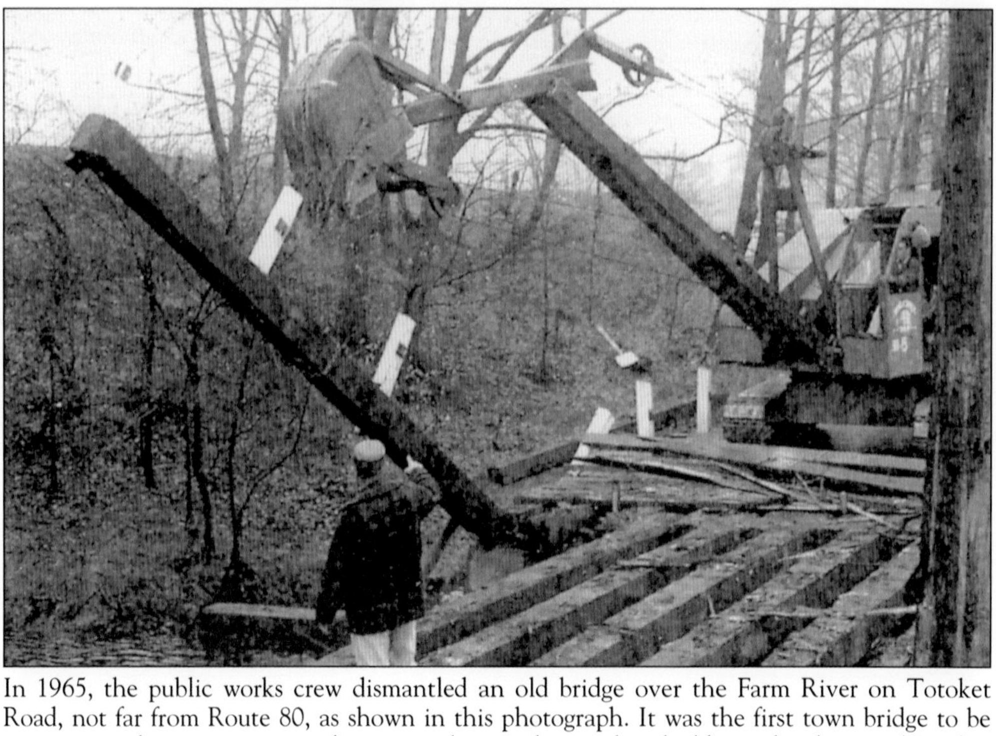

In 1965, the public works crew dismantled an old bridge over the Farm River on Totoket Road, not far from Route 80, as shown in this photograph. It was the first town bridge to be reconstructed using pre-stressed concrete beams that replaced old wooden beams. (Totoket Historical Society.)

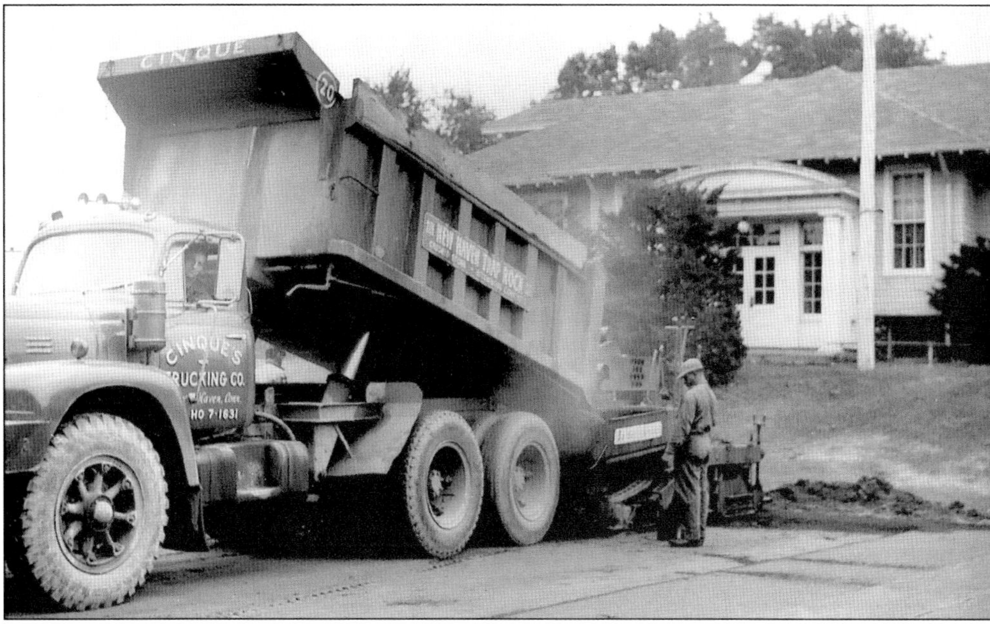

In 1958, basketball courts were constructed in front of Center School to provide a safe place for play. Here, a truck from the Cinque Trucking Company, once located on Middletown Avenue in Northford near the North Haven line, delivers a load of asphalt from the New Haven Trap Rock Company, the town's biggest industry. (Totoket Historical Society.)

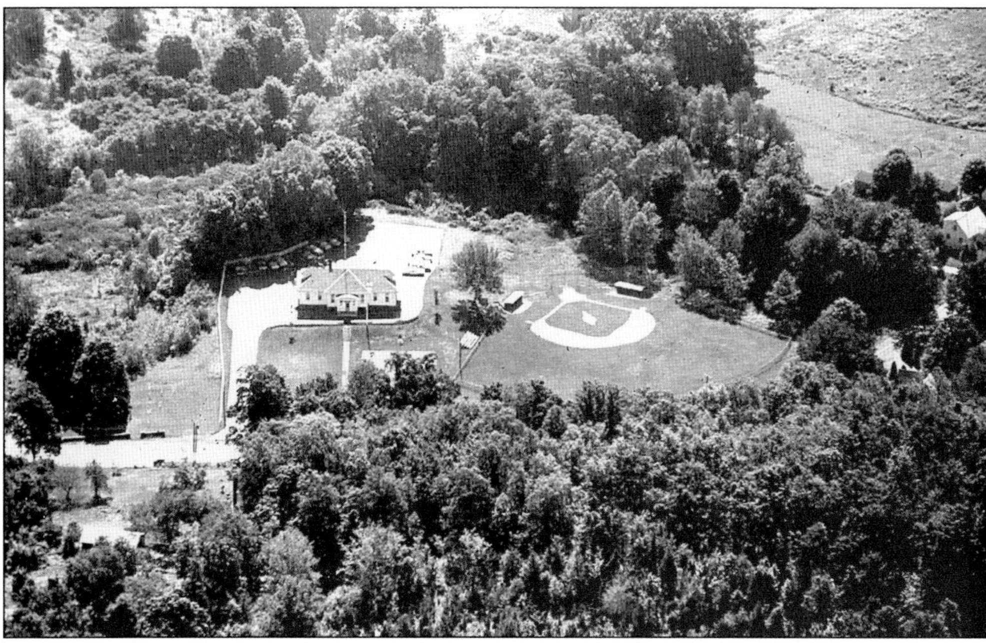

In 1961, Center School became the North Branford Administration Building; the first consolidated public office building in town. A large, two-section vault was installed at the rear of the building, and the school's three rooms became the offices for the selectmen and finance department, the town clerk, the tax assessor, and tax collector. In this c. 1975 aerial shot, the Edward Wall Little League Field can be seen on the right. (Totoket Historical Society.)

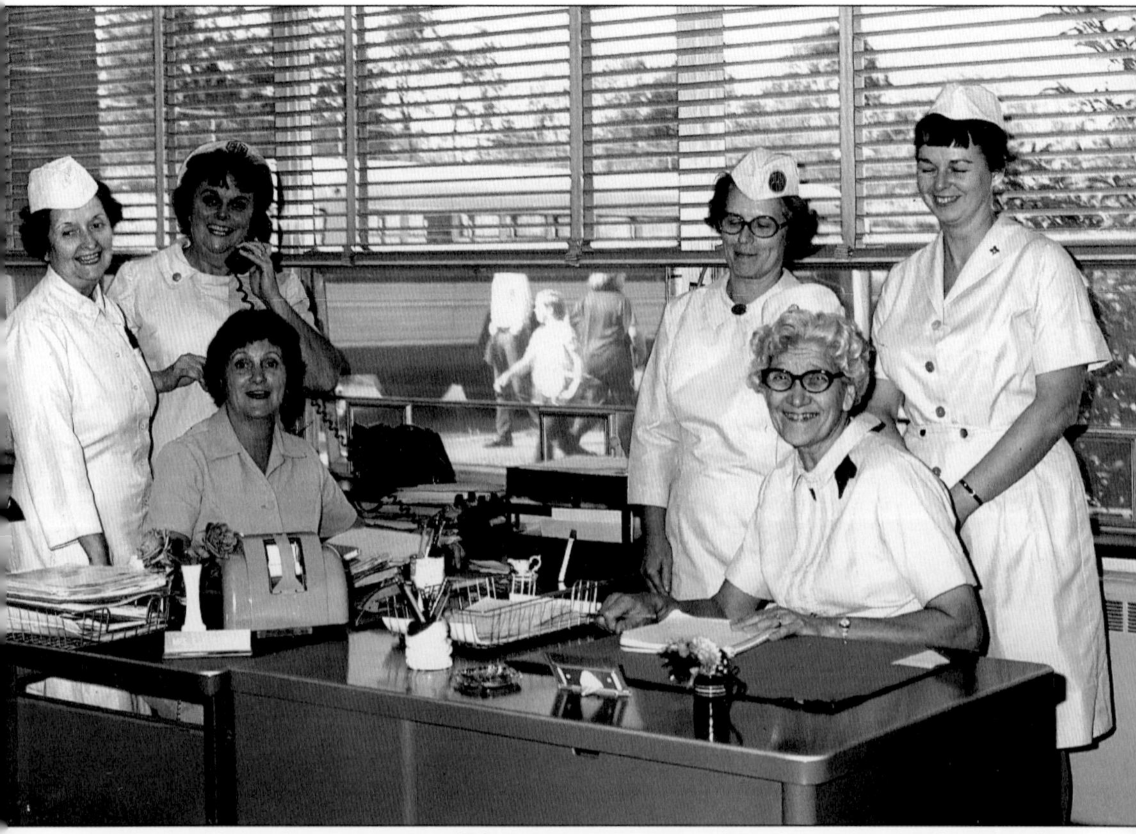

Public health has been a service of the town since 1894, when the town's first health officer was appointed. The schools were inspected for heating, lighting, ventilation systems, and safety; drinking water from wells and ice ponds was tested; and milk from dairy farms was tested. Also, the public health officer was charged with identifying contagious diseases wherever found. In 1944, the town organized the North Branford Public Health Nursing Association. By 1950, it was located at William Douglas School and provided the school health program and home nursing care. Its programs covered child and adult health supervision, maternal care for prospective mothers, control of communicable diseases, securing and caring for all tuberculosis contacts and cases, and cancer control and nursing care. A home visit cost $1. With increased building activity, the health officer became responsible for the inspection of septic systems, making sure that they conformed to state requirements, from 1953 until 1959, when a sanitary inspector was appointed. This 1973 photograph taken at the North Branford High School shows the members of the nursing association. They are, from left to right, Lela Piontek, Marjorie Thompson, Ella Cannon (secretary), Jean McMaster, Virginia Montelius, and Wilhemina Schuessler (director). (Totoket Historical Society.)

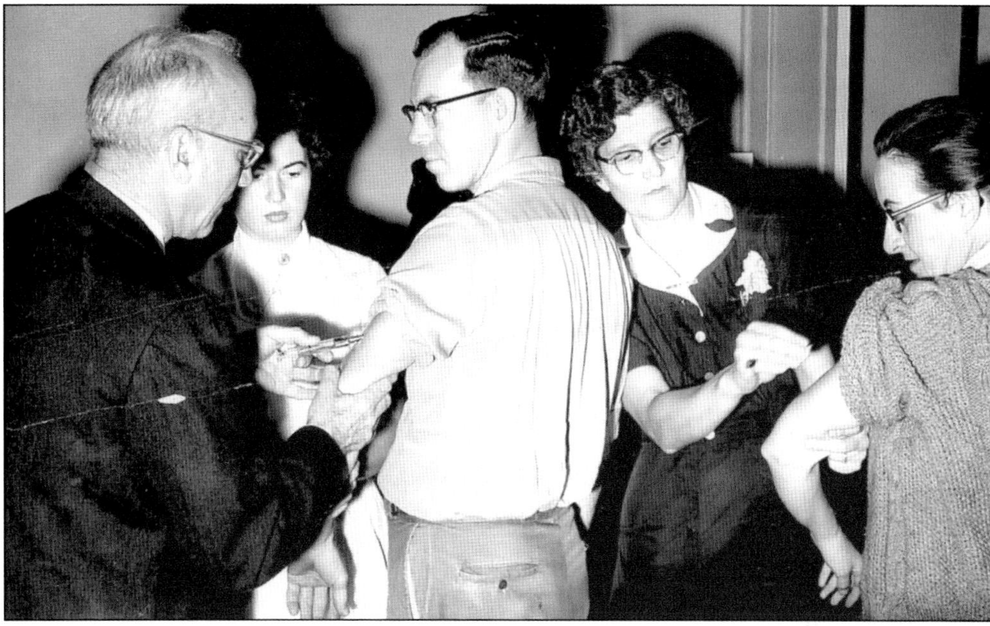

Dr. Sterling Taylor and nurses Peggy Augur Cremins and Wilhemina "Billie" Schuessler administer shots at a public health immunization clinic. The recipients are not identified. Billie Schuessler was the town's first public nurse in 1944 and served until she retired in 1978. (Totoket Historical Society.)

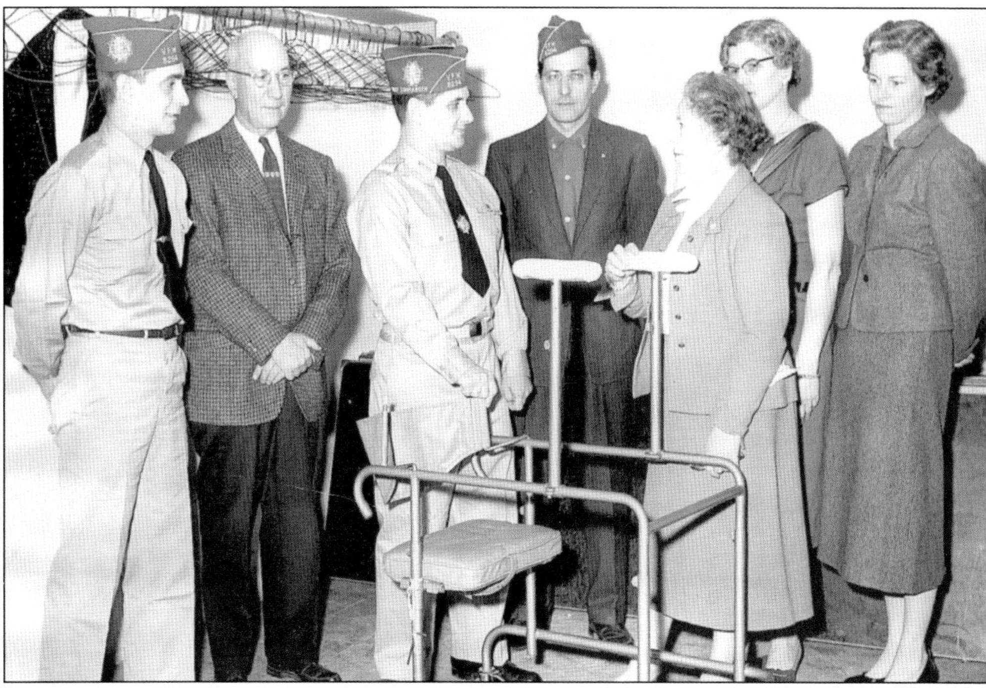

The Veterans of Foreign Wars (VFW) donated an invalid walker to the Public Heath Nursing Association in 1958. Shown here, from left to right, are Adj. Sidney Lloyd, Dr. Sterling Taylor, Comdr. John Williams, Q.M. Fred Peccararo, May Wittmer (president), Billie Schuessler (director), and Lillian Kraft (nurse). (Totoket Historical Society.)

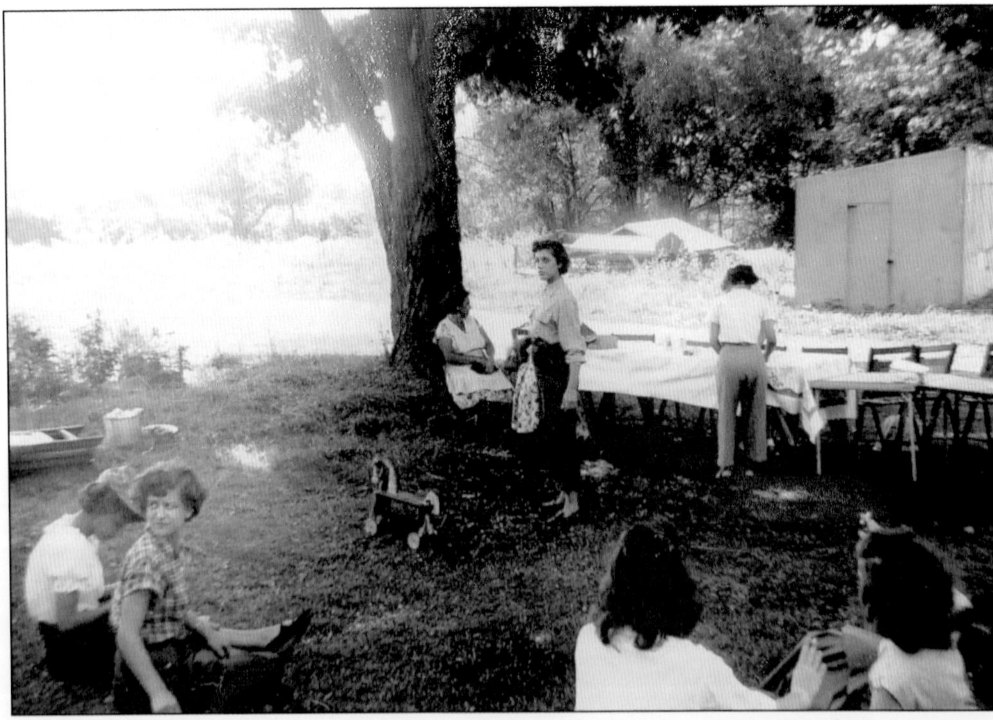

By 1951, a new fire station was needed, as Nathan Harrison's garage on North Street was no longer adequate. The spot chosen to build the new station was next to the Athletic Club barn on Route 80. This view of the site was taken at an August 1951 Rapone family picnic. The square building on the right was a stand for selling fireworks that benefited the fire department. (Grace Marx.)

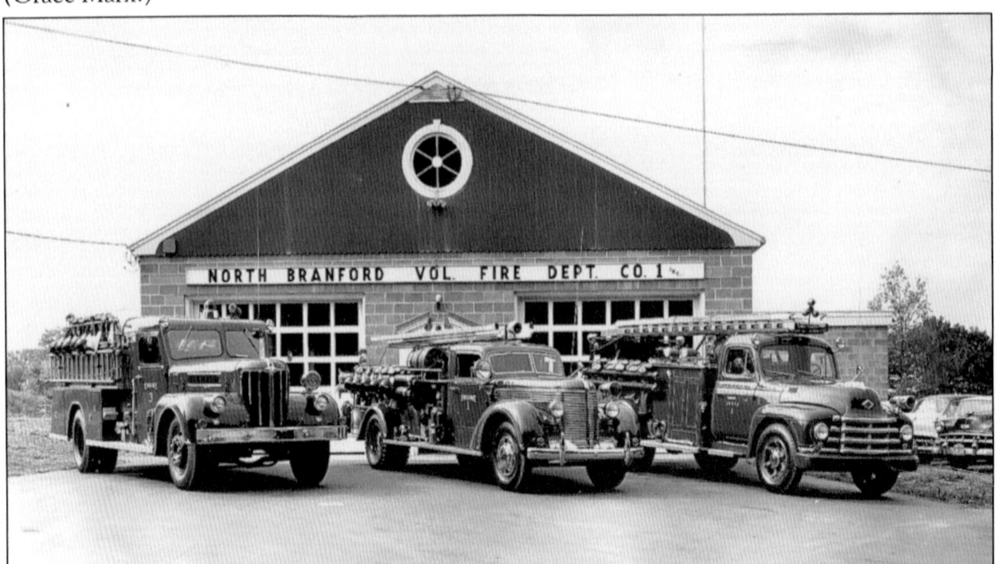

This early photograph shows the newly built North Branford Volunteer Fire Department Company No. 1 firehouse on Route 80. The fire station has tripled its size since then. The Central Shopping Center was built on the property shown at the left side of the photograph. (Barbara Amatrudo.)

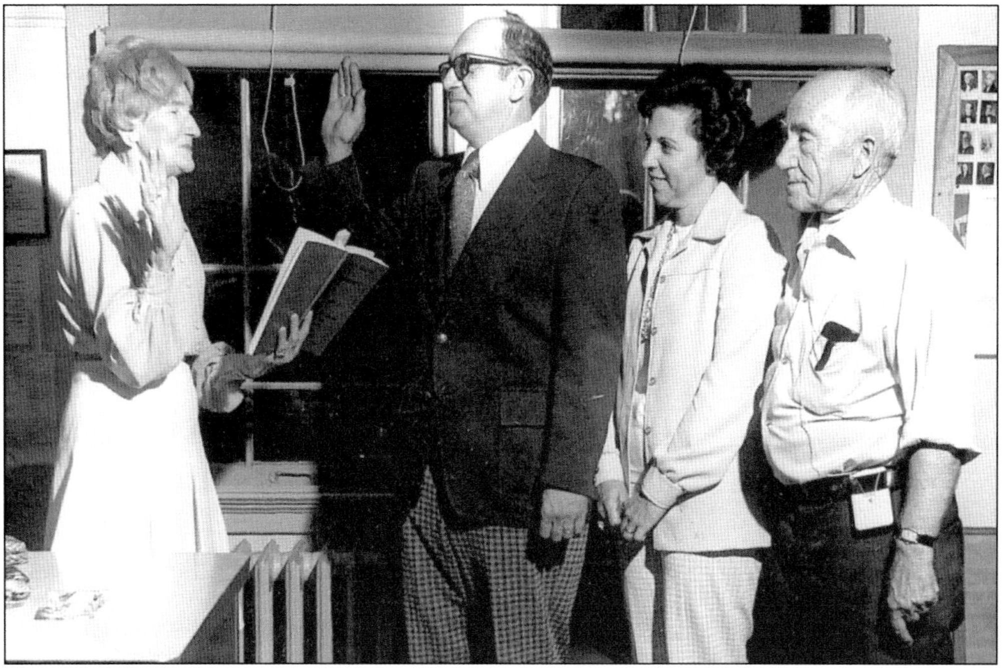

In 1974, Town Clerk Ruth Beers swears in Andrew Amatrudo as chief of the North Branford Volunteer Fire Department in the town clerk's office at the administration building. Looking on is Andy's wife, Barbara, and his father, Michael, a retired assistant chief. (Barbara Amatrudo.)

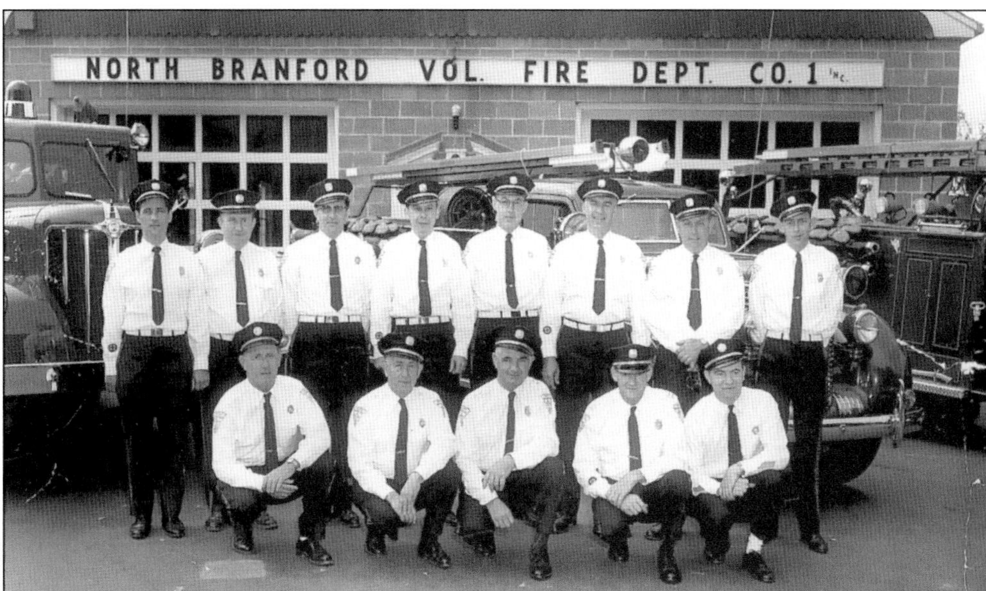

Company No. 1 firemen pose for this *c.* 1965 photograph. They are, from left to right, as follows: (front row) Fritz Vogt, Michael Amatrudo, John Hartigan, Paul Hawkins, and Anthony Daly; (back row) Robert Lanza, Lewis Reid Sr., Andrew Amatrudo, Francis Wagenblatt, Sidney McMaster, unidentified, Thomas Fowler, and John Hindinger. (Totoket Historical Society.)

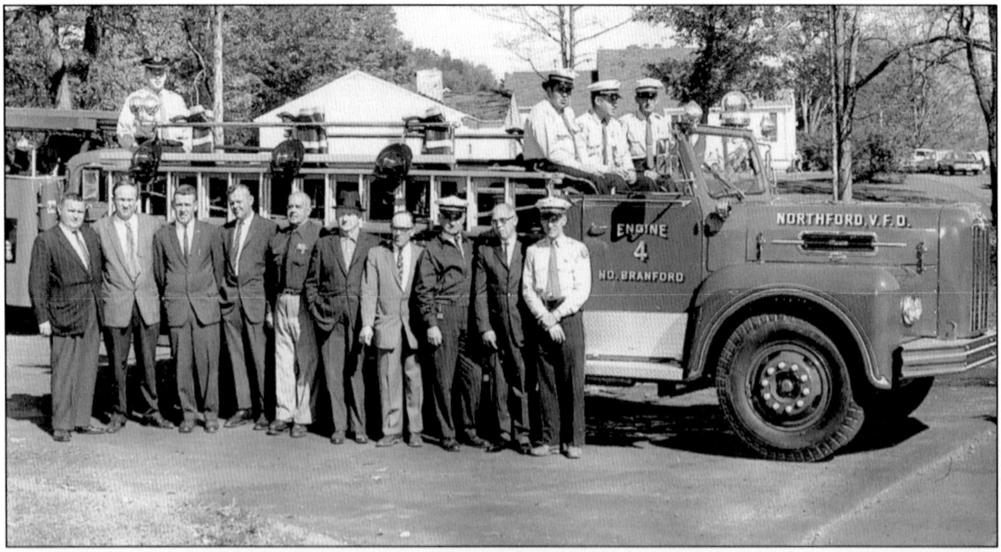

On Sunday, October 13, 1963, town officials and firemen pose in front of the Northford Volunteer Fire Department Company No. 2 firehouse and fire truck. They are, from left to right, as follows: (front row) William Gallogly and Clement Lelasher, fire commissioners; John Barrett and John Moore, selectmen; Charles Leonard, fire commissioner; unidentified; Edward Russell, fire commissioner; John Hartigan, chief; William Lovelace, fire commissioner; and Wilbur Young, fireman; (on truck) Thomas Smith, George Augur, William Neubig, and Pat Sansevero, firemen. (Company No. 2.)

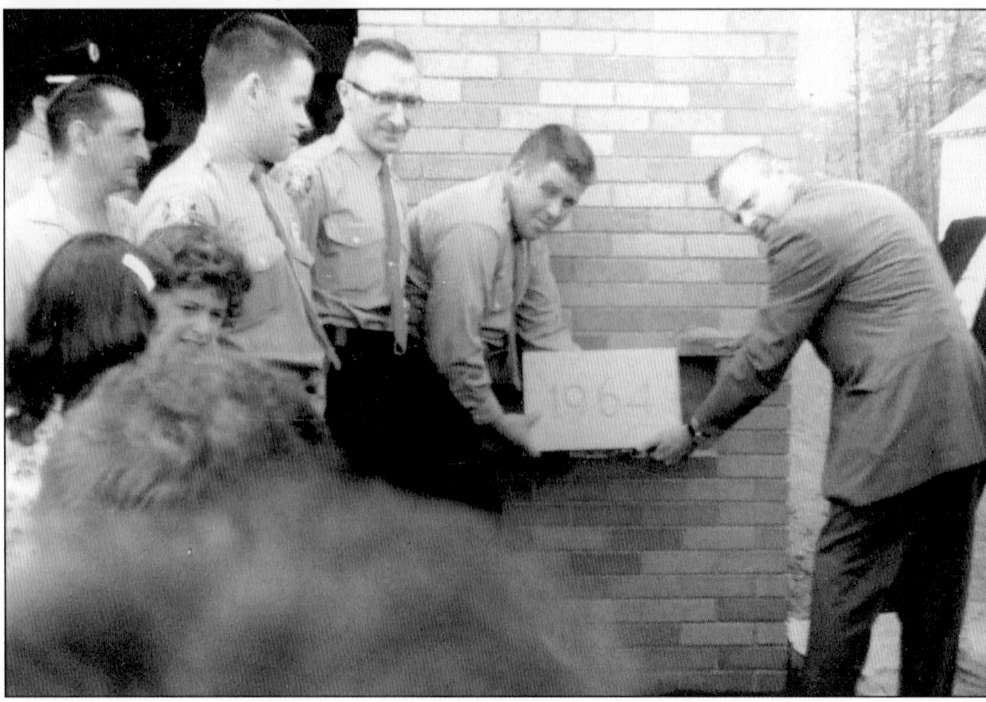

Company No. 2 volunteer firemen ceremoniously set the dated cornerstone (1964) in the wall of their new firehouse on Middletown Avenue in Northford. They are, from left to right, Louis Sacco, William Neubig, Pat Sansevero, George Augur, and Selectman John Moore. (Company No. 2.)

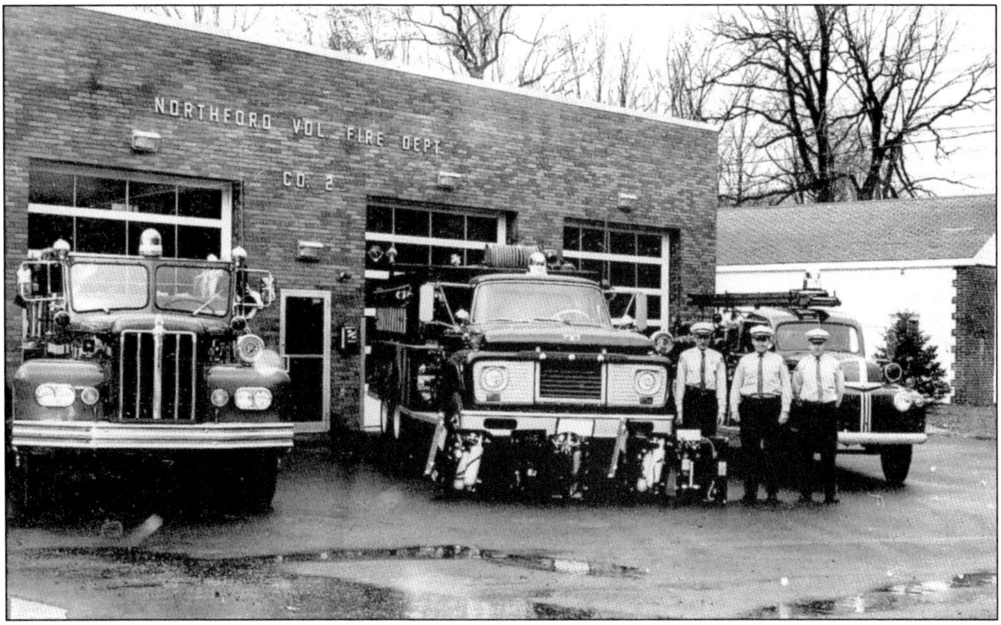

Firemen, fire trucks, and fire apparatus are shown in front of the new three-bay Company No. 2 firehouse. The white building on the right is the original one-bay firehouse built in 1946. The volunteer firemen shown are, from left to right, Pat Sansevero, William Neubig, and Chief Ralph Thomas. (Company No. 2.)

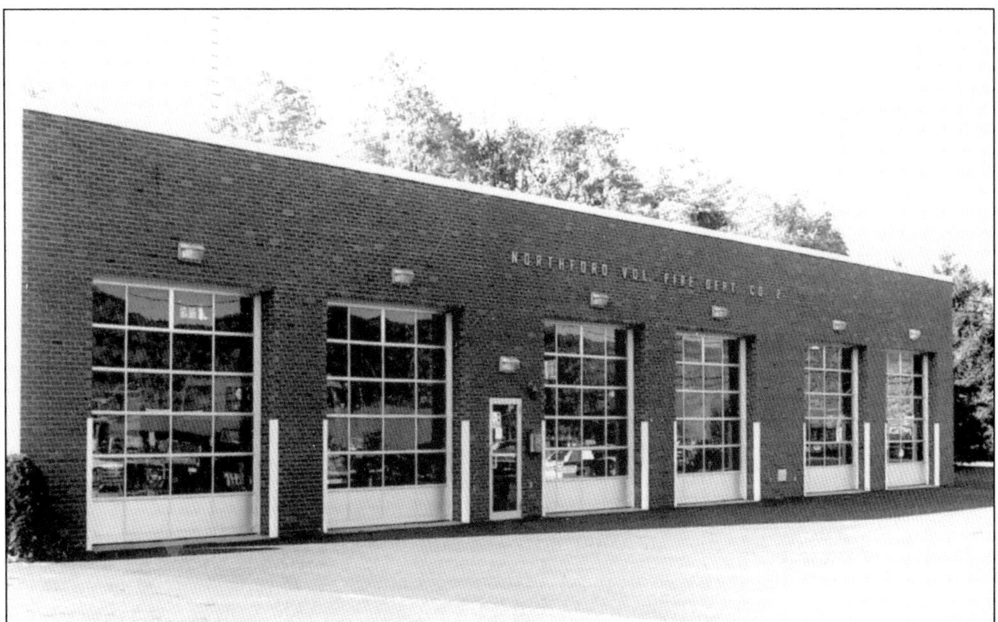

In 1978, two more bays were added to the Northford Volunteer Fire Department Company No. 2 firehouse to accommodate more fire equipment, giving it the appearance it has in 2003. (Company No. 2.)

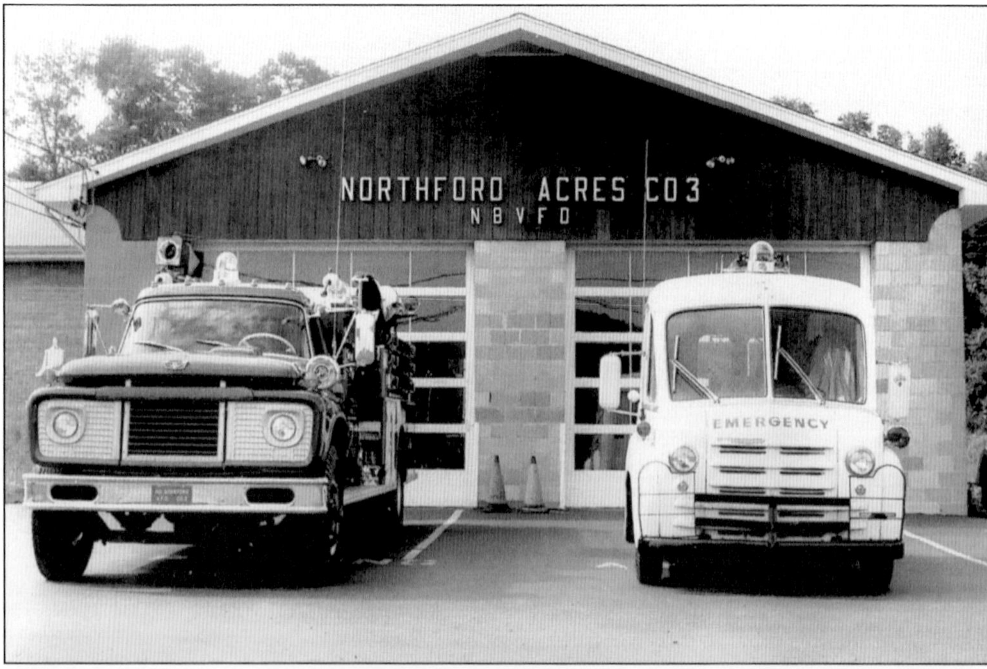

In 1964, another fire company was formed to serve the residents in the northernmost part of town. The Northford Acres, the North Branford Volunteer Fire Department's company No. 3 firehouse with its fire truck and emergency vehicle, is shown in this photograph. (Company No. 3.)

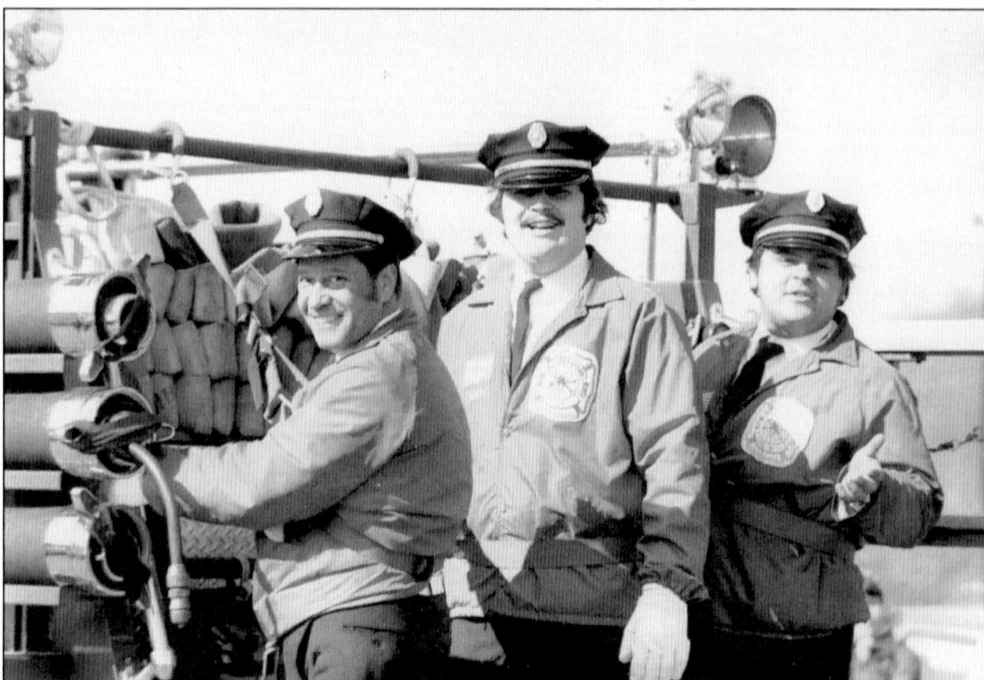

Three volunteer firemen from Company No. 3 pack their equipment and prepare their truck for firefighting readiness. They are, from left to right, Edward Gian, Gordon Gottlieb, and Jerry Deno. (Company No. 3.)

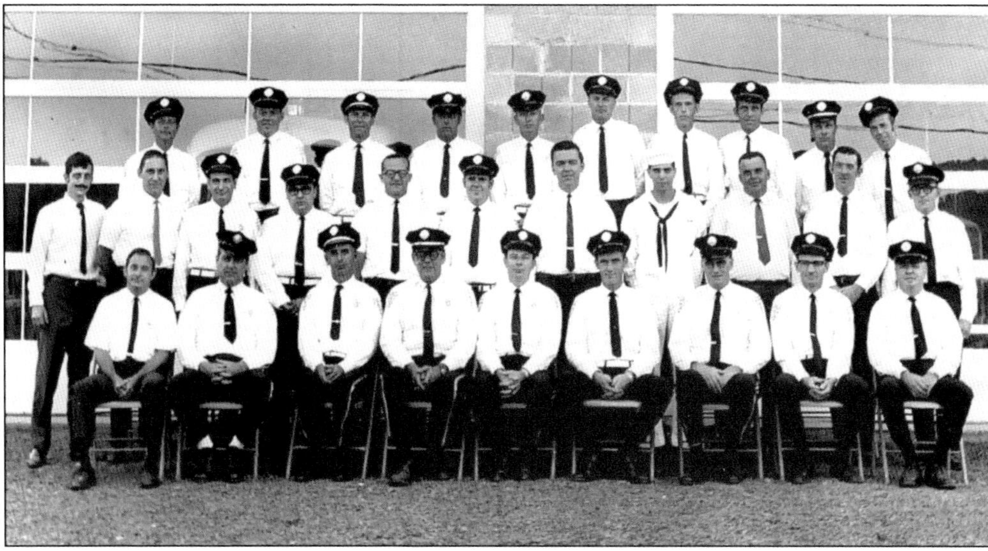

The Northford Acres Company No. 3 firemen pose for this formal photograph in August 1969. They are, from left to right, as follows: (front row) R. Corey, D. Gottlieb, J. Bellonio, E. Manemeit, A. Pokrob, C. Hogan, W. Smith, M. Benham, and L. Jacques; (middle row) ? Migliozzi, ? Eimutis, ? Cusano, S. Varca, P. Mongillo, ? Borchert, J. Carr, D. Cusano, W. Bassett, W. Hogan, and T. Olsen; (back row) W. Reisner, J. Goggins, ? Bica, W. Fiondella, ? Kelly, A. Clark, R. Smith, ? Jones, ? Russell, and ? Flynn. Missing from the photograph is R. Geminell. (Company No. 3.)

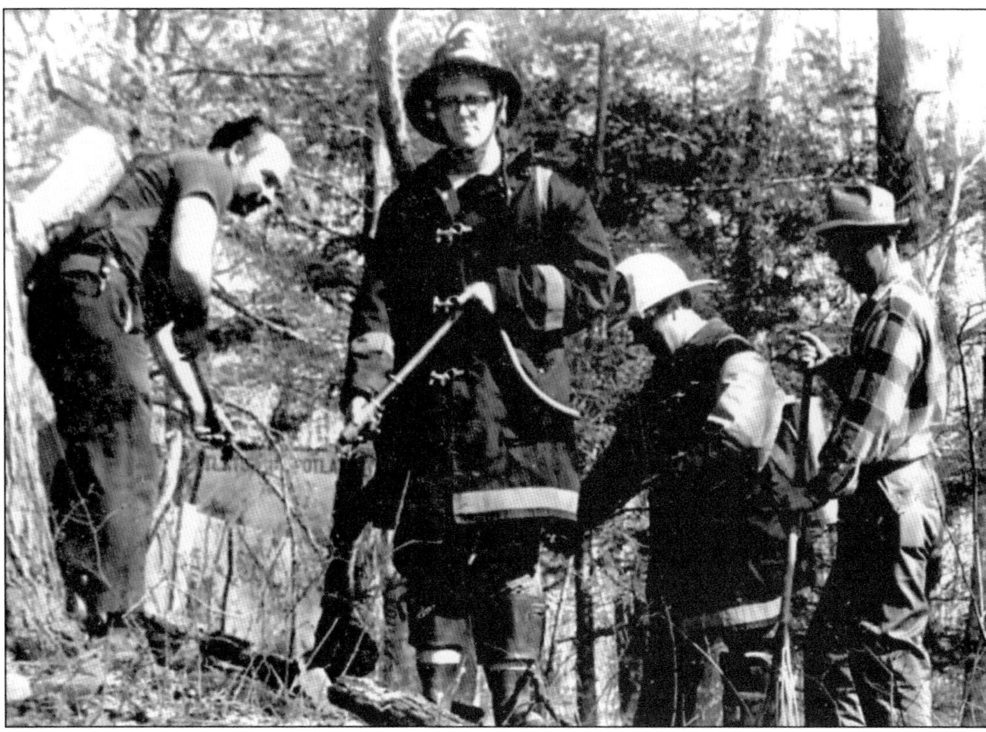

Company No. 3 volunteer firemen fight a woods fire on Mount Pistapaug in Northford. They are, from left to right, unidentified, John Orfice, Ted Olsen, and Joe Bellonio. (Company No. 3.)

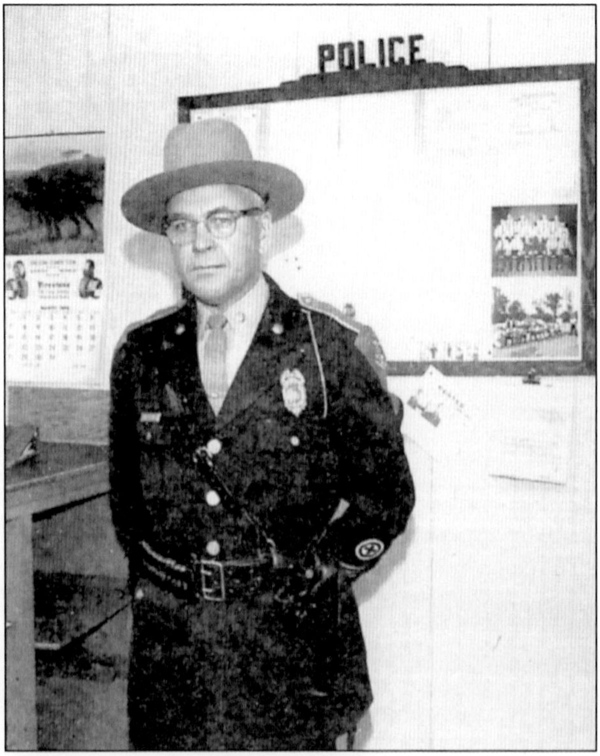

During mid-20th century, public safety in town was the responsibility of a resident state policeman and seven constables elected at the annual town meeting. State Trooper George Baldwin, shown in this photograph, lived on Branford Road and was the resident trooper from 1955 until 1970, when the police department was organized. (Totoket Historical Society.)

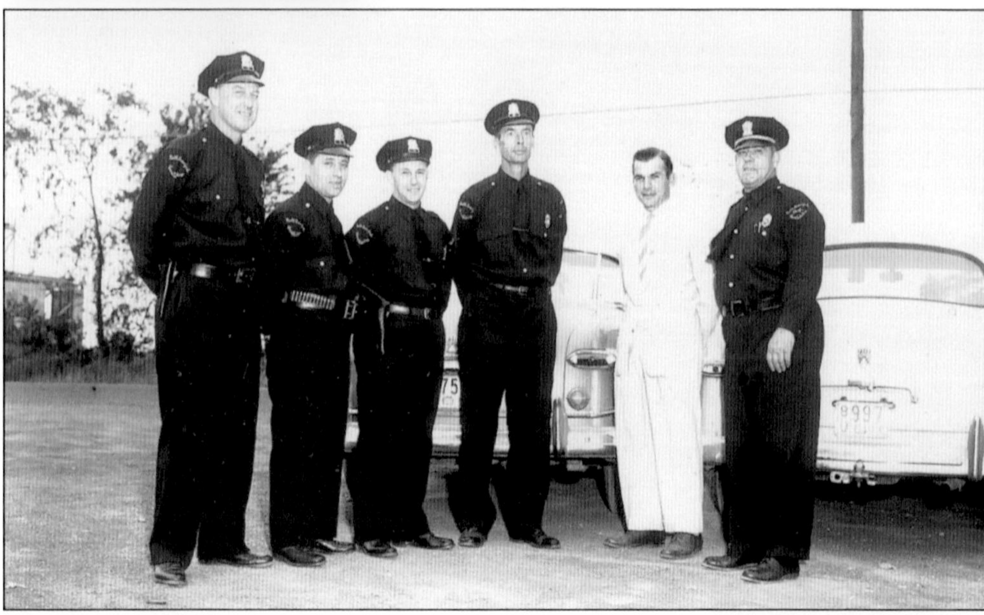

In 1950, the constables began wearing uniforms for the first time, which received "satisfactory comments from the public," according to the 1950 annual town report. Five attended police school conducted at East Haven. They also investigated 216 complaints, found 51 street lights out of order, and handled five instances that electric wires had fallen down. In this 1954 photograph, the uniformed constables are, from left to right, unidentified, Buddy DiDonato, unidentified, Robert Newton, Bud Hill (selectman), and Charles Leonard. (Totoket Historical Society.)

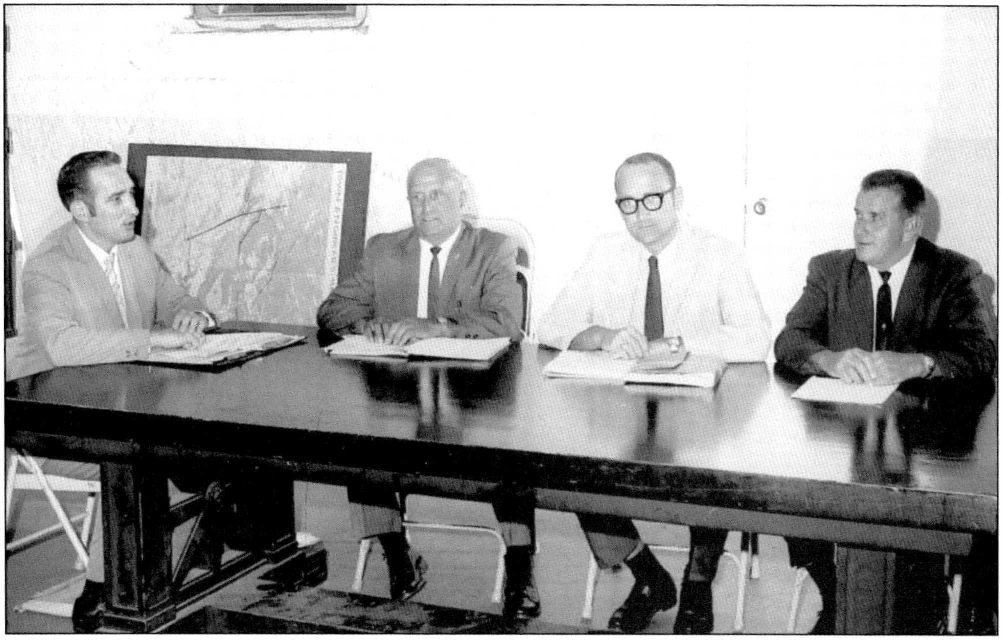

In November 1969, a board of police commissioners was elected to oversee the establishment of a new police force. The commissioners pictured here are, from left to right, Howard F. Krom, Chairman Michael J. Torello, Peter H. Tveskov, and Charles E. Strickland. Commissioner John E. Moore was not available when the photograph was taken. (Totoket Historical Society.)

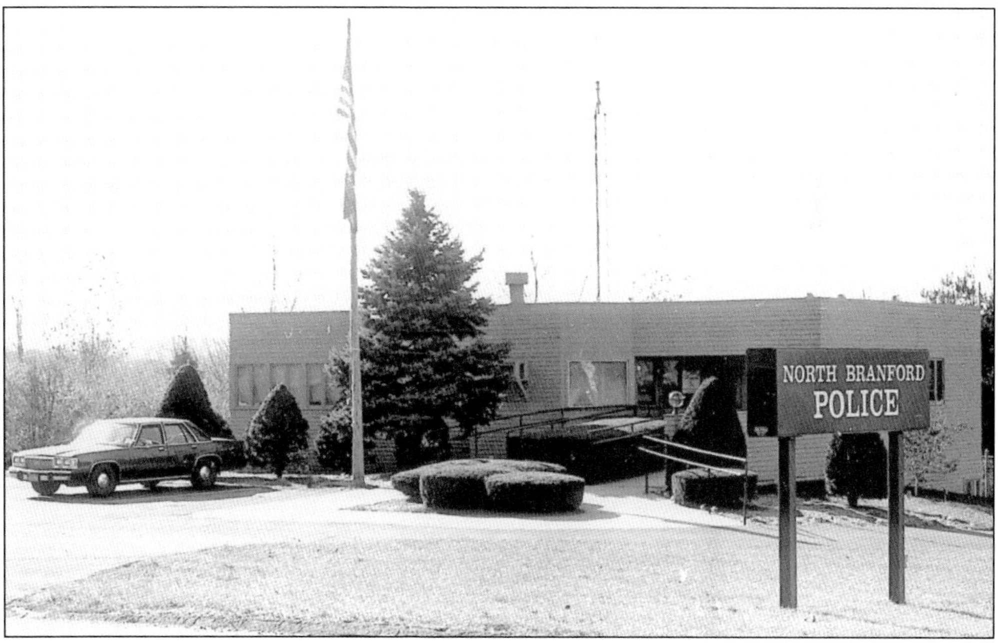

The commissioners set up physical and educational standards for policemen and proceeded to hire nine men. Frank Stomboli was appointed chief of police and the new police force began operating out of the basement of the administration building on June 1, 1970. The first police station, shown in this photograph, was built on Forest Road in 1975. It has since been renovated and enlarged. (North Branford Police Department.)

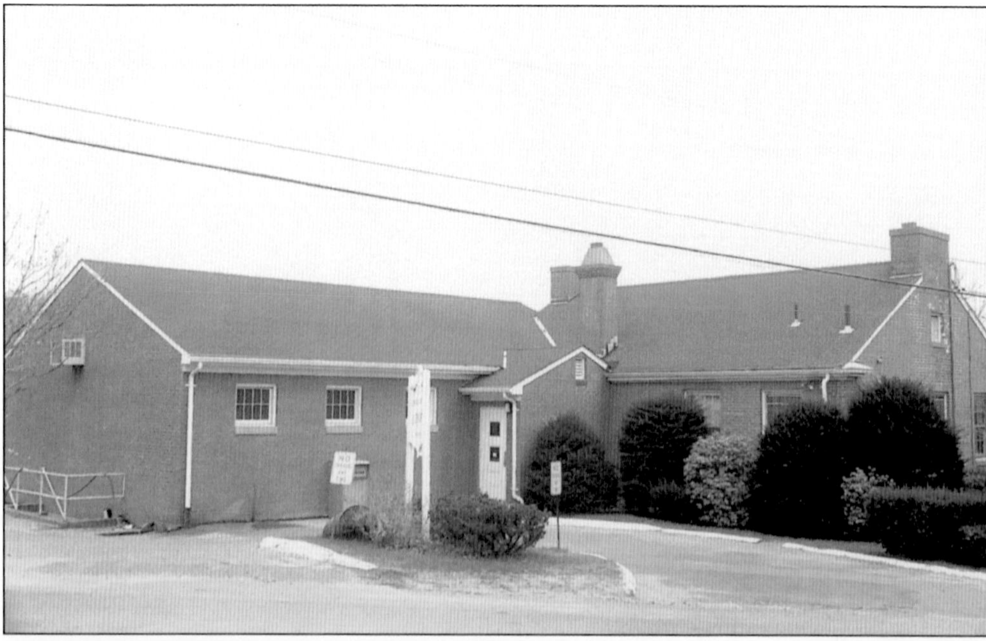

There were two libraries in town in 1950. In 1957, using funds left to the town by Clara Smith (the daughter of Edward Smith), the Edward Smith Memorial Library was built to replace the one in the Little Red School House in Northford. In 1965, the library was expanded with a wing built on the back, as shown in this photograph. (Totoket Historical Society.)

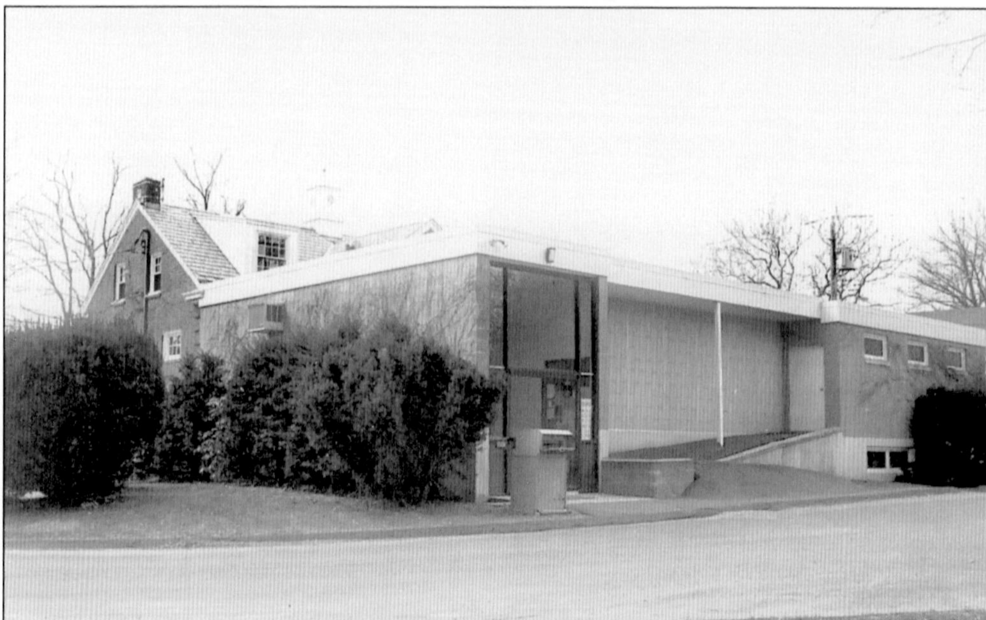

In 1967, the Charles Atwater Memorial Library also was expanded by a large concrete block addition on the back of the original brick building. The adult section was located on the main floor, and the children's department was in the basement. The ramp shown in the photograph was built for trucking the books in and later became the handicapped access. (Totoket Historical Society.)

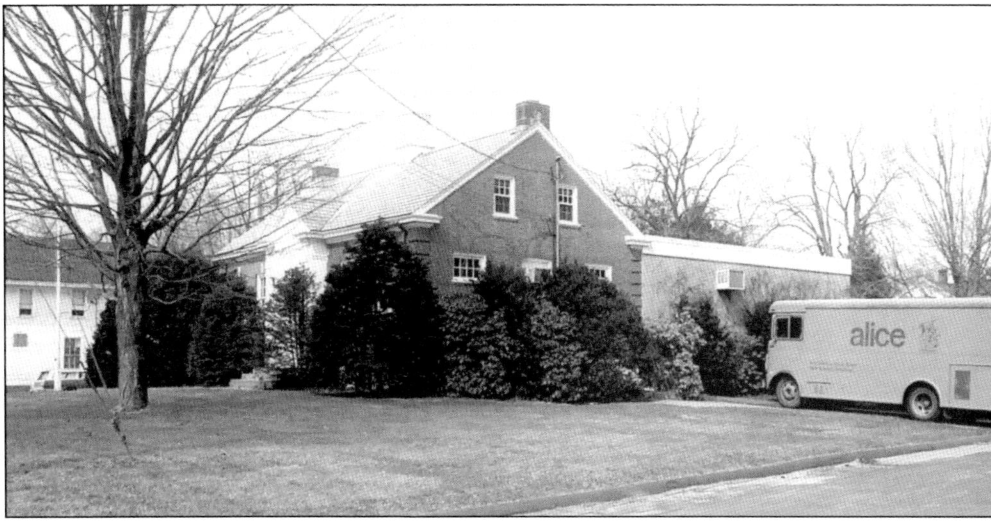

Shown parked next to the Charles Atwater Memorial Library is Curious Alice, a large orange bookmobile that traveled around town providing library service to all of the various neighborhoods from 1974 to 1980. (Totoket Historical Society.)

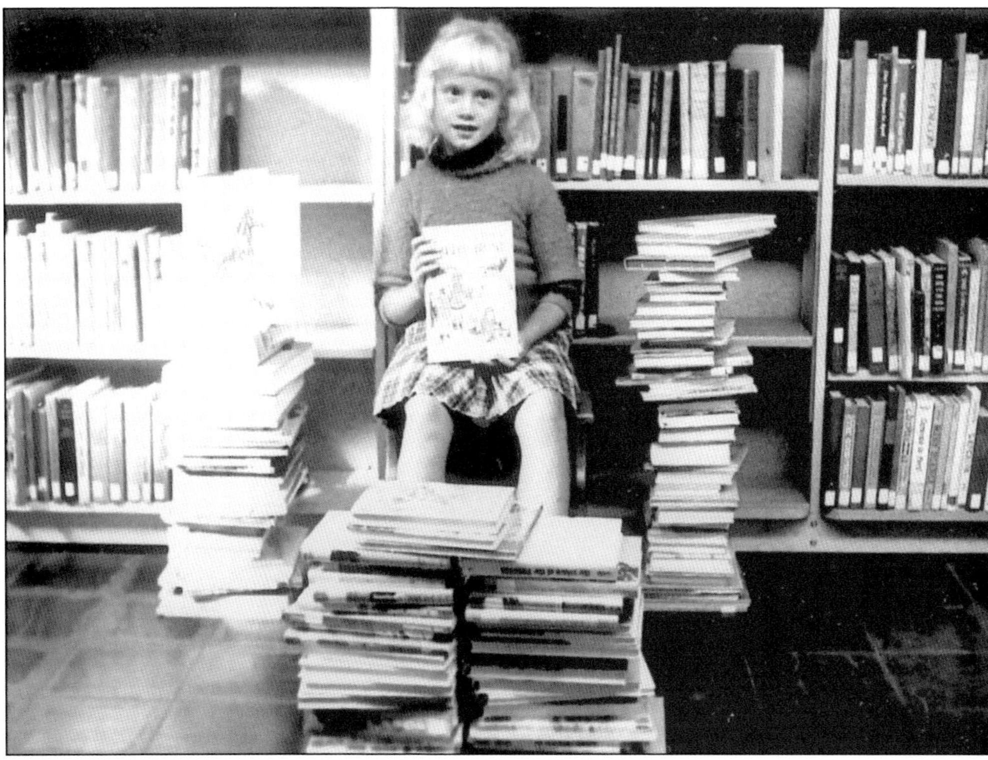

There has always been a close relationship between libraries and other town organizations since the Congregational church housed the town's first public library. Various town service organizations have raised funds, landscaped buildings, donated books and services, and conducted story hours for the libraries at both ends of town. Here, a little girl shows off a donation of children's books from the North Branford Women's Club. (North Branford Women's Club.)

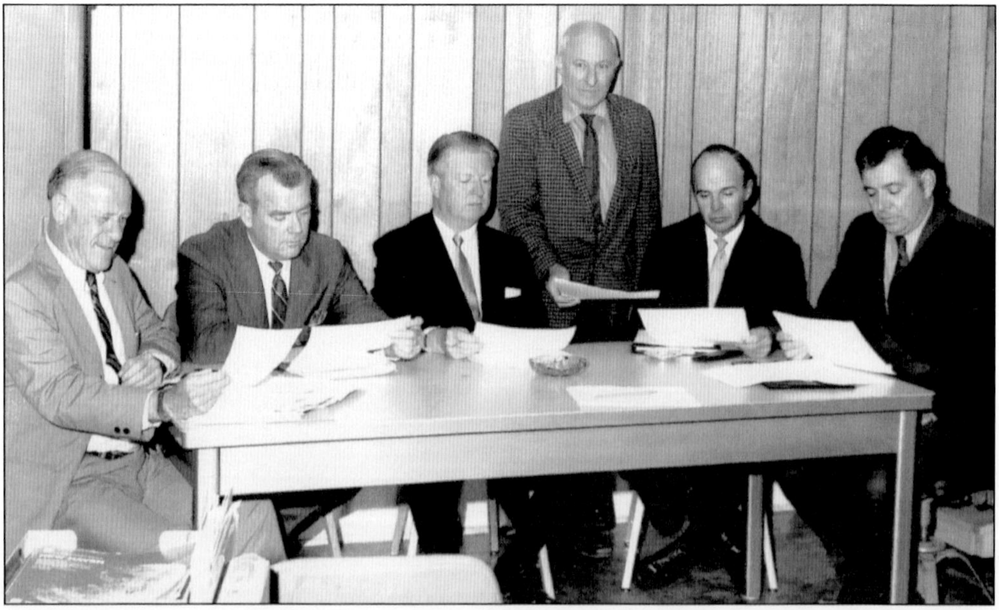

A board of finance, first elected in 1931, was responsible for preparing the annual budget. It was then submitted by the selectmen to the annual town meeting for approval. Ellsworth Foote served as chairman of the finance board from 1932 to 1963. In this 1968 photograph, the members of the board are, from left to right, William Carter, Timothy Ryan, Charles Seefahrt, Erwin Petry, Raymond Blanchet, and Carl Negro. (Totoket Historical Society.)

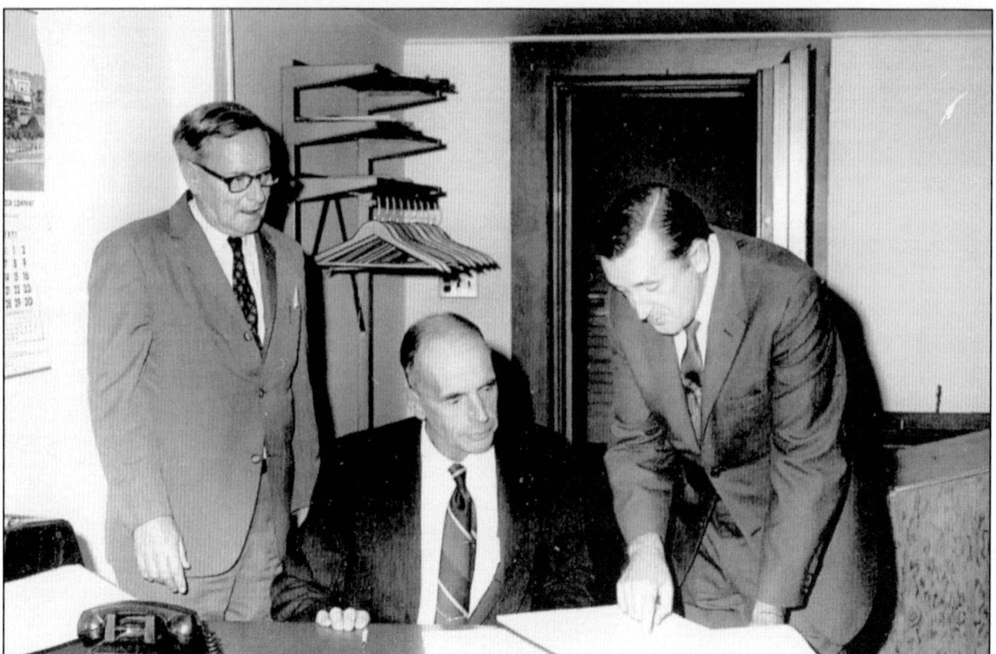

The board of assessors, elected at the annual town meeting, determined the value of real estate and personal property for taxation purposes. In 1971, the board members were, from left to right, George Gallagher, Robert Newton, and Joseph Lemmon. Robert Newton served as the town assessor for 50 years, from 1954 to 1984. (Totoket Historical Society.)

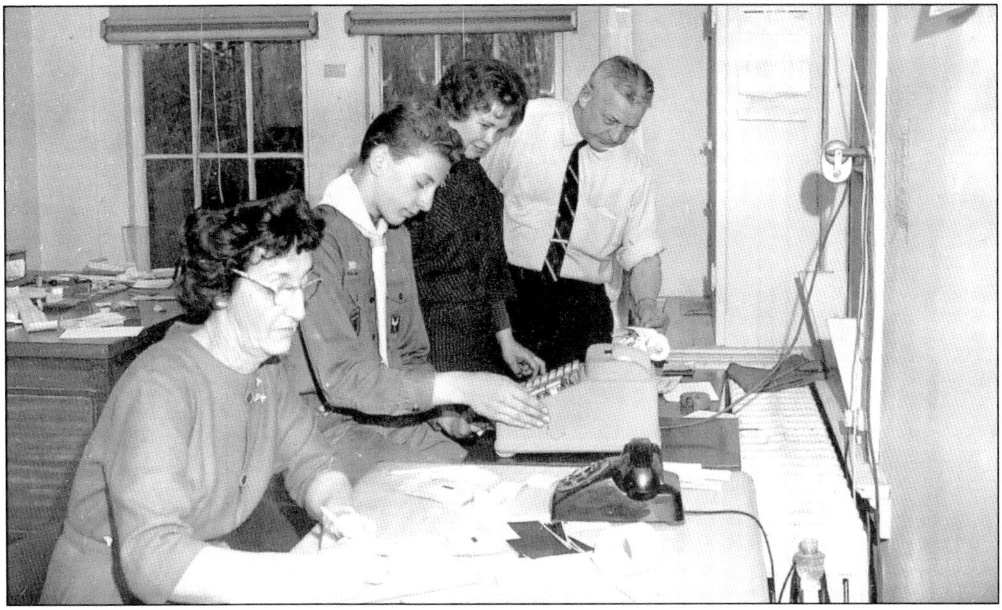

The tax collector's office was located in a small office that was part of one of the original classrooms on the south side of the administration building. In this photograph, Boy Scout Charles Ferucci is shown how taxes are calculated. Also pictured, from left to right, are Virginia Lovelace (secretary), Karen Johnson, and Edgar Johnson (tax collector). (Totoket Historical Society.)

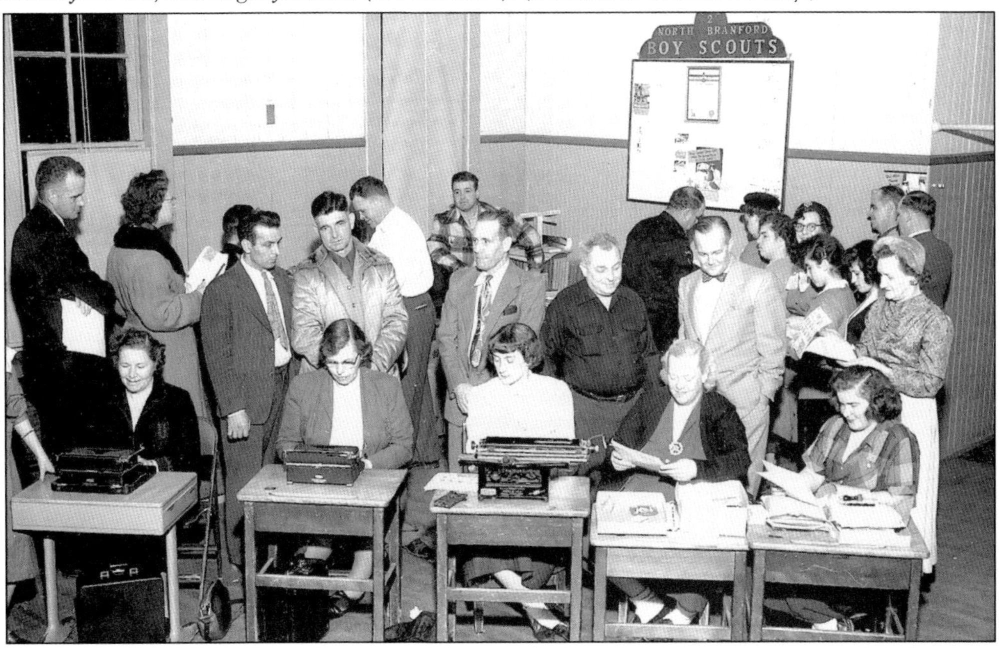

Since World War II and especially during the Cold War, civil defense procedures were planned in case of an emergency or attack. This January 19, 1952, photograph shows a civil defense registration. The volunteers are, from left to right, as follows: (front row) May Wittmer, Carrie Doody, ? Brais, Leila Bretton, and Helen White; (back row) Tony Rapone, John Hartigan, Daniel Doody, ? Bretton, Haviland Schuessler, and Ruth Beers. Vincent Lupone is by the door. (Totoket Historical Society.)

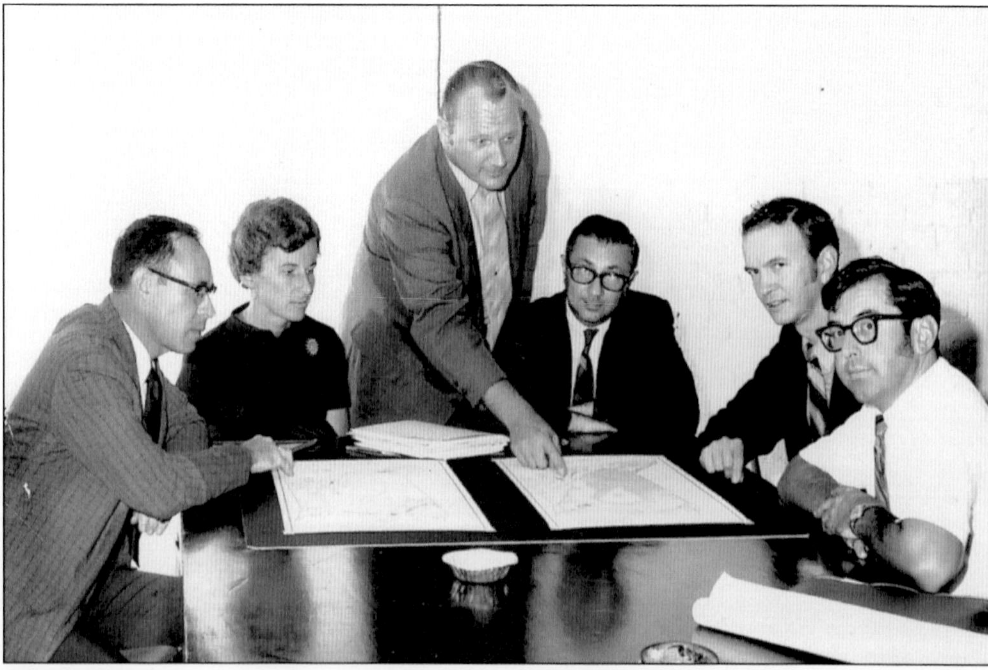

Although the town was growing quickly, it took several years before there was any attempt at planning and zoning. In 1955, a vote at a special referendum adopted provisions in general state statutes relating to zoning, and a planning commission was appointed. In this 1969 photograph, members of the planning and zoning commission are, from left to right, Gordon McGuire, Dorothy McCluskey, Henry Sondergaard, Anthony D'Addetta, David Wight, and Maurice Raymond (alternate). (Totoket Historical Society.)

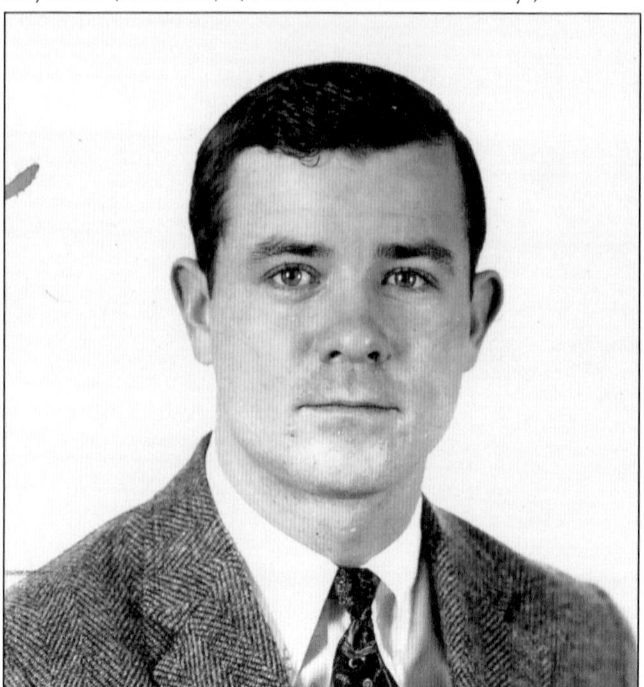

The planning commission adopted the comprehensive plan of development for the town in May 1961. In 1968, under the federal Community Development Act, the town developed a Community Development Action Plan (CDAP) that was coordinated by Frank Connolly, who was hired for this purpose. Connolly later served as town manager from 1990 to 2001. (Totoket Historical Society.)

Dorothy McCluskey served on the town's first conservation commission, created in 1965. Under her chairmanship in 1970, the commission developed a town-wide conservation plan. Later, McCluskey served as a state representative in the General Assembly and was instrumental in the formation of the South Central Connecticut Regional Water Authority, a public corporation encompassing 17 municipalities, which purchased the privately owned New Haven Water Company in 1980. (Totoket Historical Society.)

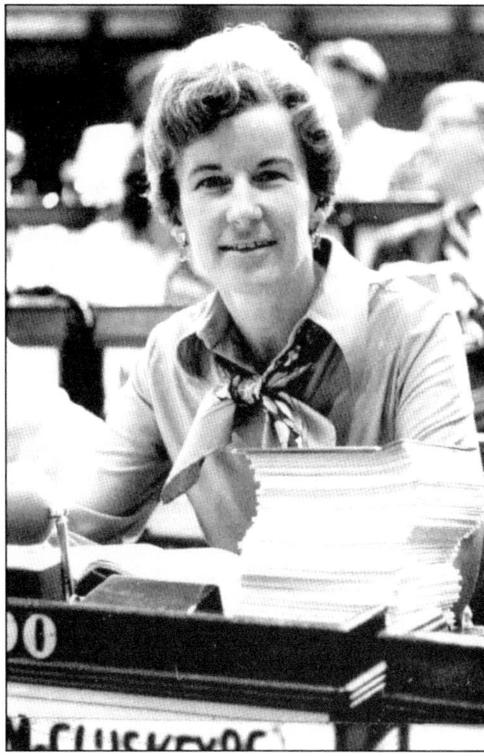

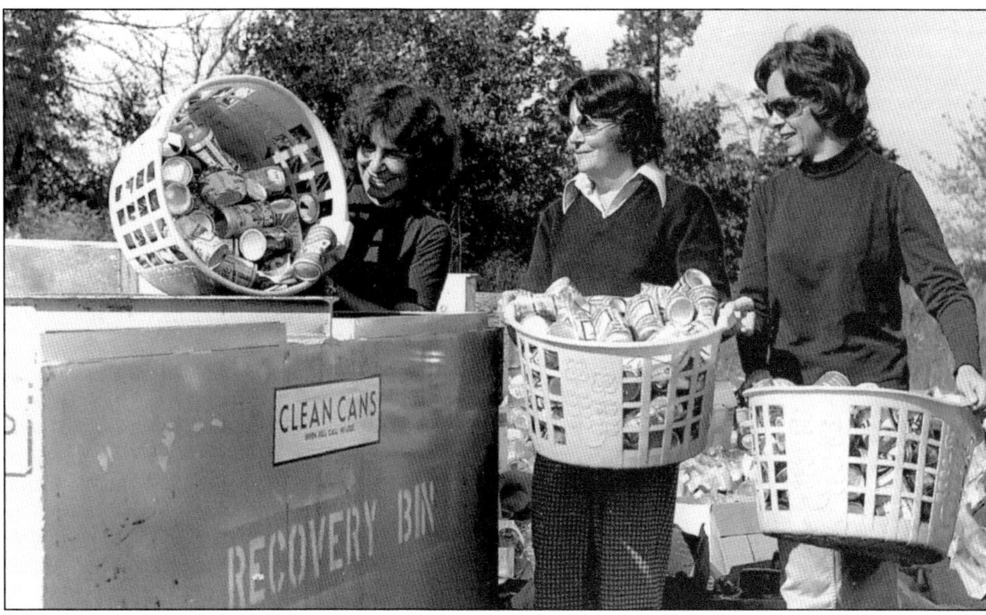

Recycling began in 1971 as a volunteer service under the guidance of the conservation commission and has now become an important town service. At first, residents brought their glass and aluminum containers to the public works department on Forest Road. The glass bottles were dumped into metal barrels and were crushed by hand with heavy metal tampers. In this photograph, volunteers ? Schabel, Janet S. Gregan, and Lorane Black collect aluminum cans for recycling. (Totoket Historical Society.)

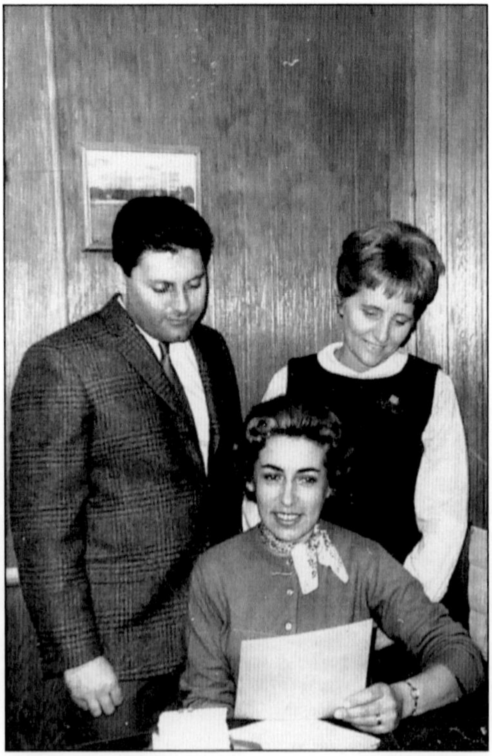

In 1956, residents at a town meeting voted to create a recreation commission to oversee recreational needs. Stephen Lenzi, George Crosson, Frank Marinuzzi, Ed Wall, and Irene Petry were appointed as its first members. Eight years later, in December 1964, Alphonse DeRuccio, shown here on the left, was hired as director of the recreation department. Joyce Budrow (center) and Janet Rau (right) worked at the Over 60 Drop-In Center. (North Branford Parks and Recreation Department.)

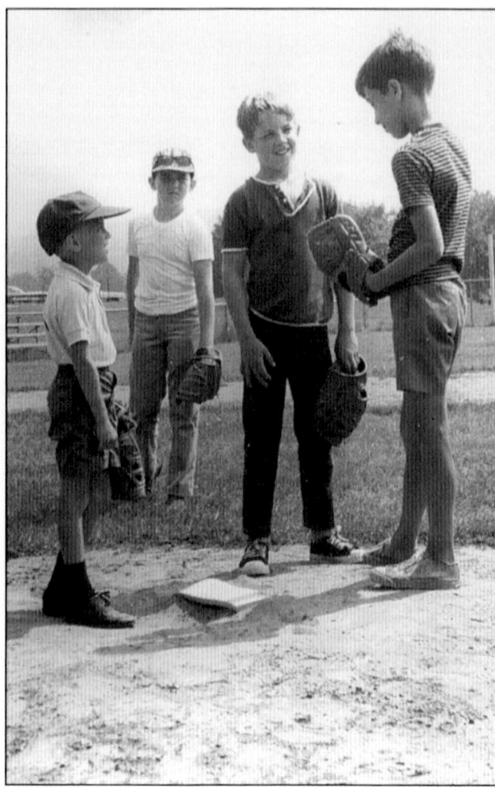

At first, the recreation commission was mainly concerned with recreational facilities: baseball fields and basketball and tennis courts. As the town's recreational needs began to grow, various programs were offered, such as the Summer Playground program at the town's elementary school. Shown in this 1965 photograph are, from left to right, Henry Schmitz, Jim McKeown Jr., Danny Gorham, and Joseph Labagnara playing baseball at the Stanley T. Williams School. (Totoket Historical Society.)

Another recreation department program, the Over 60 Drop-In Center for the town's senior citizens, was initiated in 1965. Recreational activities and lunch were offered at North Branford Hall. As one of their first service projects, members of the North Branford and Northford Women's Clubs assisted at the center. This building, first a school then a community hall, was completely renovated in 1986 for recreation offices and the senior citizen center. (Totoket Historical Society.)

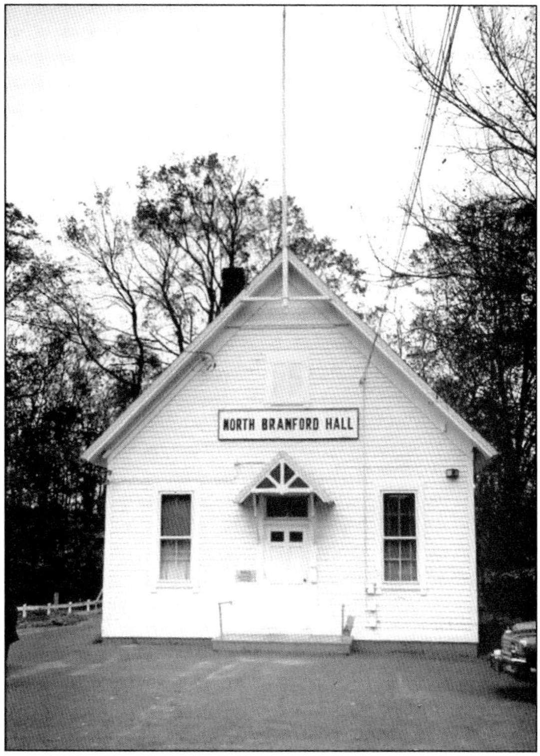

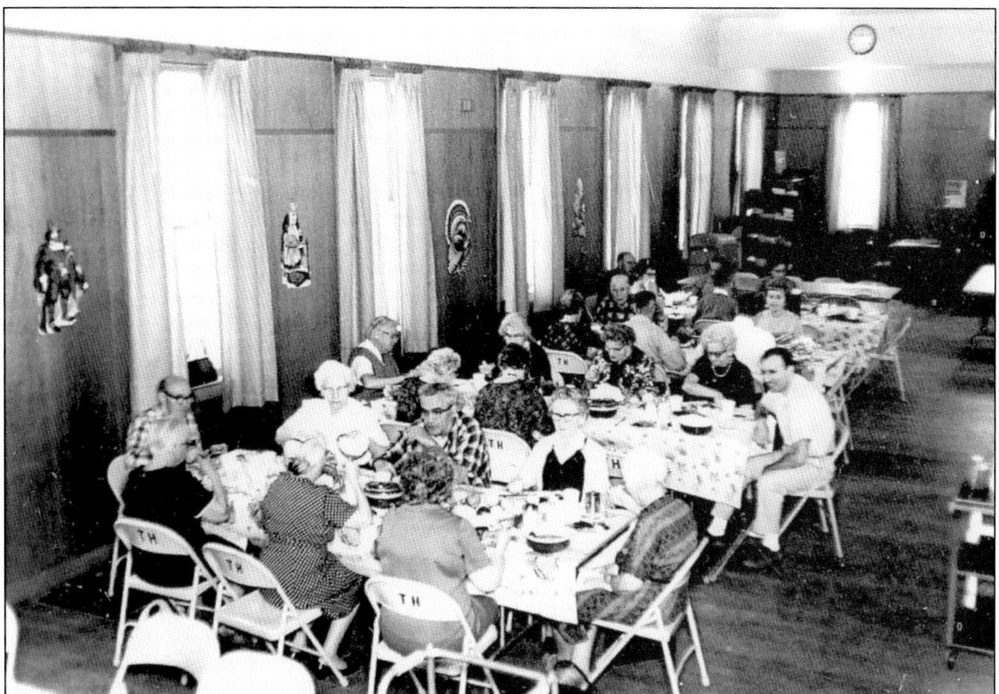

A Thanksgiving dinner is served at the Over 60 Drop-In Center at North Branford Hall on Wednesday, November 27, 1968. (North Branford Parks and Recreation Department.)

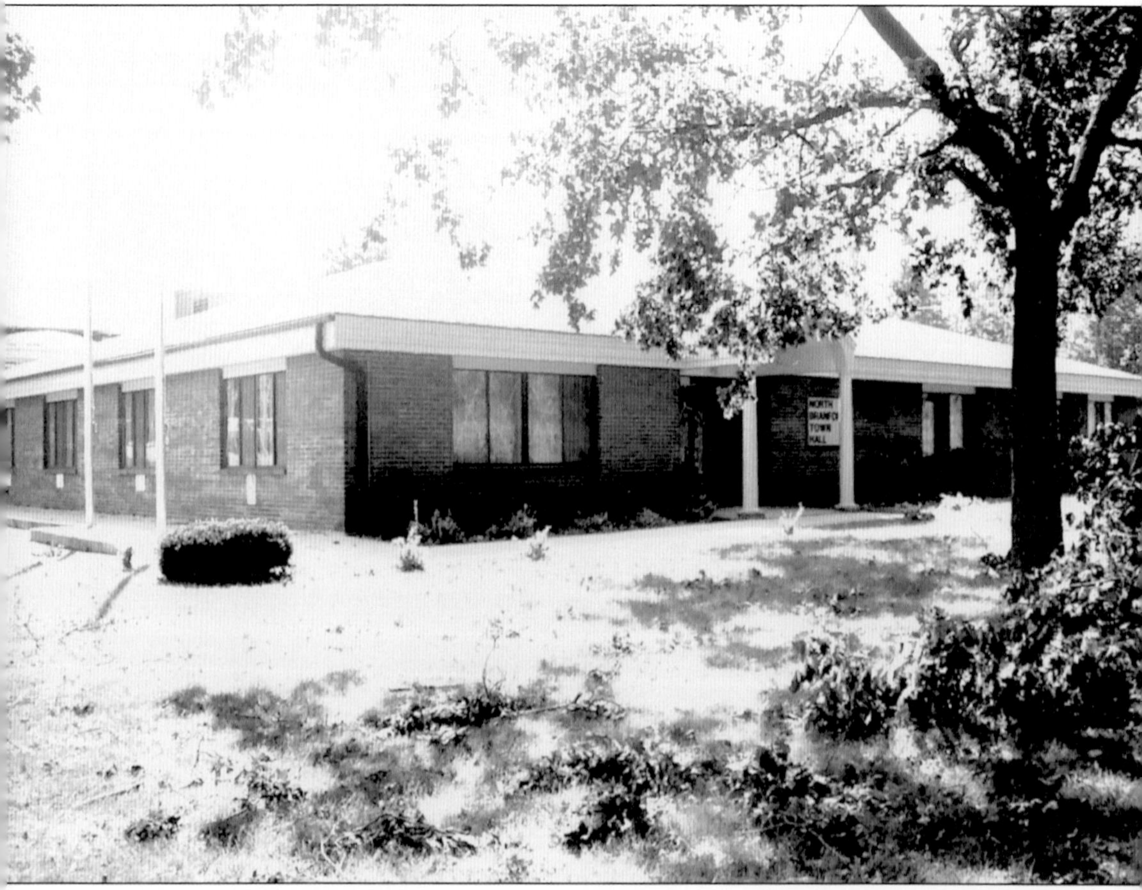

North Branford saw a change of government in 1971. The change began in January 1969, when the selectmen appointed a charter revision commission. The commission recommended a town council–town manager form of government, but the selectmen rejected their recommendation. In March 1970, the League of Women Voters, which had worked with the charter revision commission, began holding public meetings about the proposed change, and a citizens group, the Citizens for Council-Manager Government (CCMG), was formed. These two organizations urged the selectmen to put the matter to a vote. Residents who were against the proposal formed their own organization, the Concerned Citizens of North Branford. The league and CCMG finally succeeded in having the question put to the voters, and a referendum was held in March 1971. It brought out an unprecedented 67 percent of voters, and the new charter was approved by a 1,731 to 1,547 vote. Nine years later, as shown in this photograph, a new town hall with offices for all the new government departments was built in front of the old administration building. (Totoket Historical Society.)

Four

The Churches Add More Space

As more people moved into North Branford and Northford, the five existing churches began to need more room for their congregations and church schools. There were so many children enrolled in the North Branford Congregational Church Sunday school that classes had to meet across the street at North Branford Hall and at the Charles Atwater Memorial Library. Zion Episcopal Church, located next to its cemetery on Route 80, had no room at all to expand. The two Northford churches, St. Andrew's Episcopal and Northford Congregational, also needed to expand their facilities. But it was the population boom of people in the Roman Catholic faith that was the most phenomenal. St. Augustine's little church with a seating capacity of 198 could no longer contain enough people or schedule enough Masses to satisfy the community's needs. Mass was celebrated in the cafeteria of the newly built junior high school from 1959 until a new church could be built. Mass was offered for Northford residents at first in the Northford Community Center and later at the Northford Congregational Church until a new church, the Chapel of St. Monica's, could be erected.

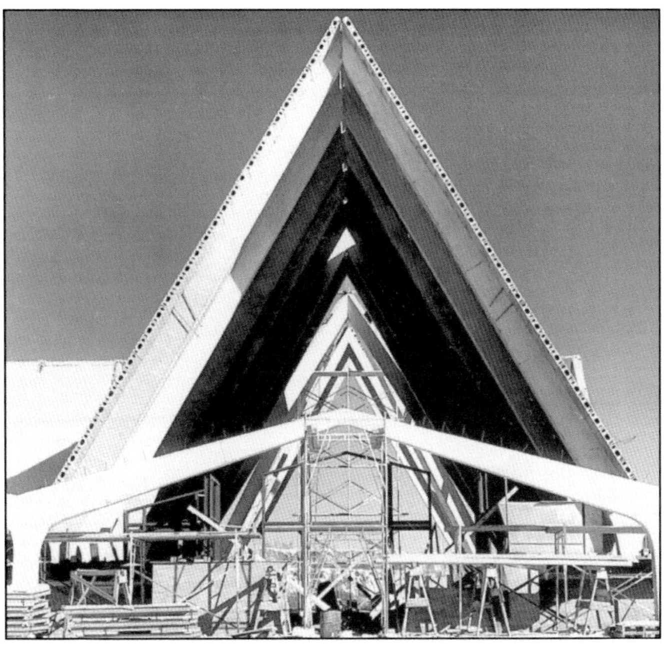

Ground for the new St. Augustine's Roman Catholic Church was broken on April 9, 1961. Carrie and Daniel Doody and Joseph Spezzano donated 15 acres of land, and another two acres was purchased from Frederick Dudley to provide frontage on Caputo Road. This photograph shows the construction of the beautiful, new, contemporary church high on the hill. (St. Augustine's.)

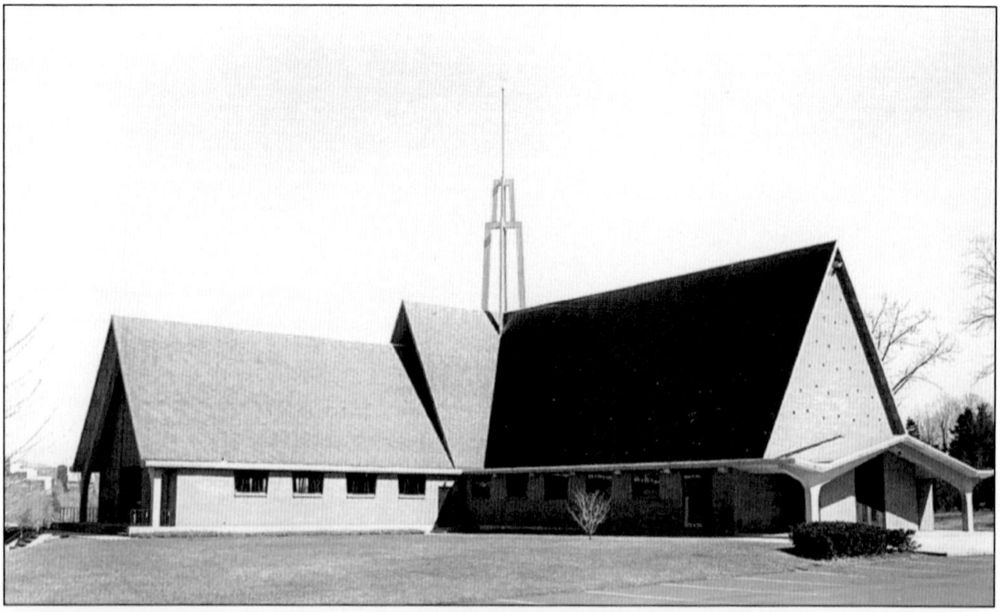

St. Augustine's Catholic Church was dedicated on August 11, 1962, with the archbishop presiding over the colorful ceremonies. When this church was completed, there were 500 Catholic families in the parish, and by 1967, there were 800 families. In this photograph, the crusher on the hill at the New Haven Trap Rock Quarry can be seen on the left. (Totoket Historical Society.)

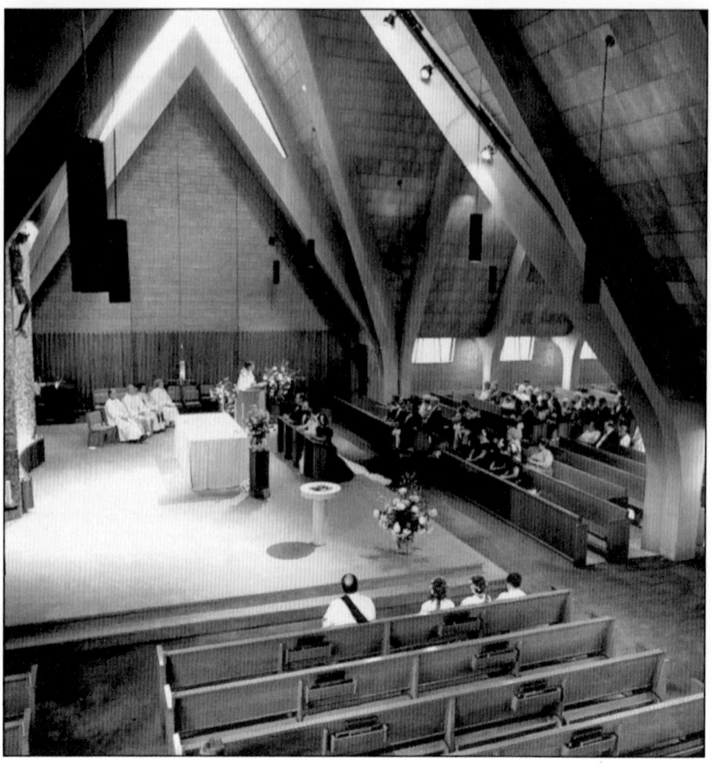

This photograph, taken from the choir loft, shows the interior of St. Augustine's during a 1967 wedding ceremony. The design incorporates a cruciform plan and is almost entirely constructed of masonry, making the church virtually fireproof. The church is built on two levels with easy access to both. The designers, the architectural firm of Davis, Cochrane, and Miller, won an award for excellence for the design of the church. (St. Augustine's Roman Catholic Church.)

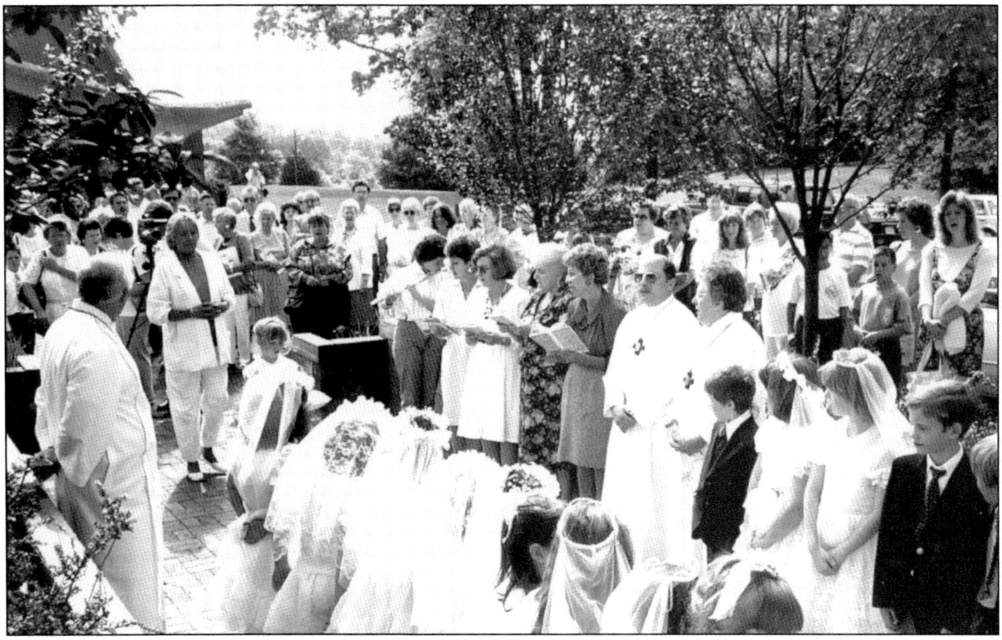

The beautiful site of St. Augustine's allows a wonderful setting for special occasions both indoor and outdoor. In this photograph, a May crowning to honor the Virgin Mary is being held outside the church building. (St. Augustine's Roman Catholic Church.)

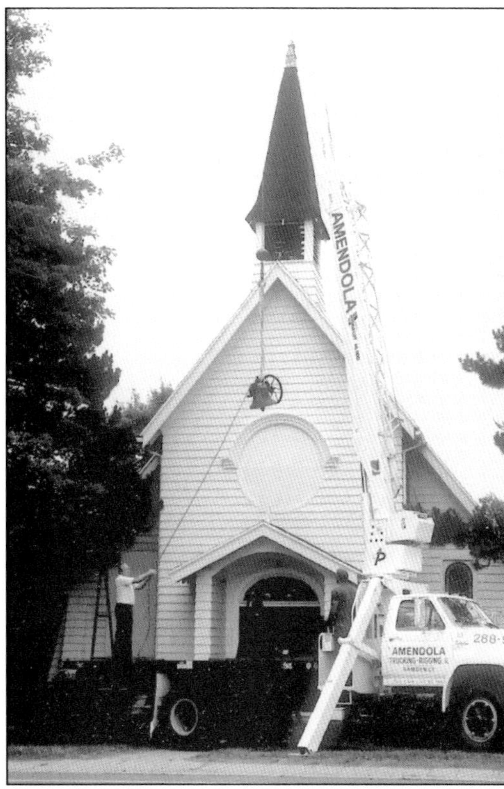

After years of being used for community functions and storage, the original St. Augustine's on Branford Road was sold at the recommendation of a special study committee that determined that it was unfeasible to move the building to the Caputo Road property. Here, the bell, named St. Monica after St. Augustine's mother, is being removed from its steeple by the Amendola Trucking and Rigging Company before the building is sold. (Totoket Historical Society.)

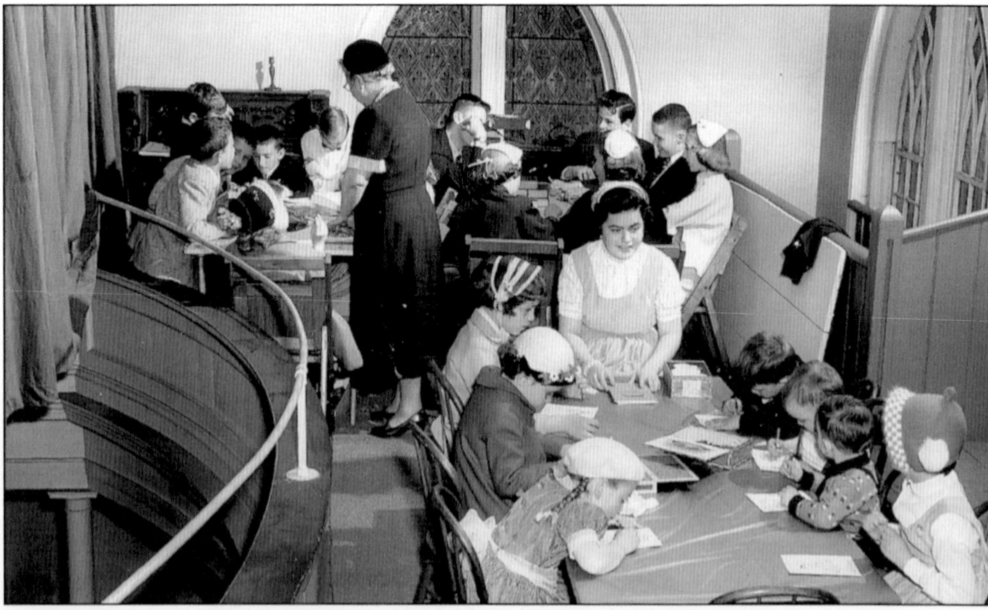

Zion Episcopal Church's original location at Foxon Road between its small cemetery and the North Branford Town Hall site was truly cramped for space. There was no room on the property to expand, even to offer restroom facilities. Parishioners stepped out of the front door onto the busy Route 80 highway. This photograph shows the balcony being used for a church school class. (Zion Episcopal Church.)

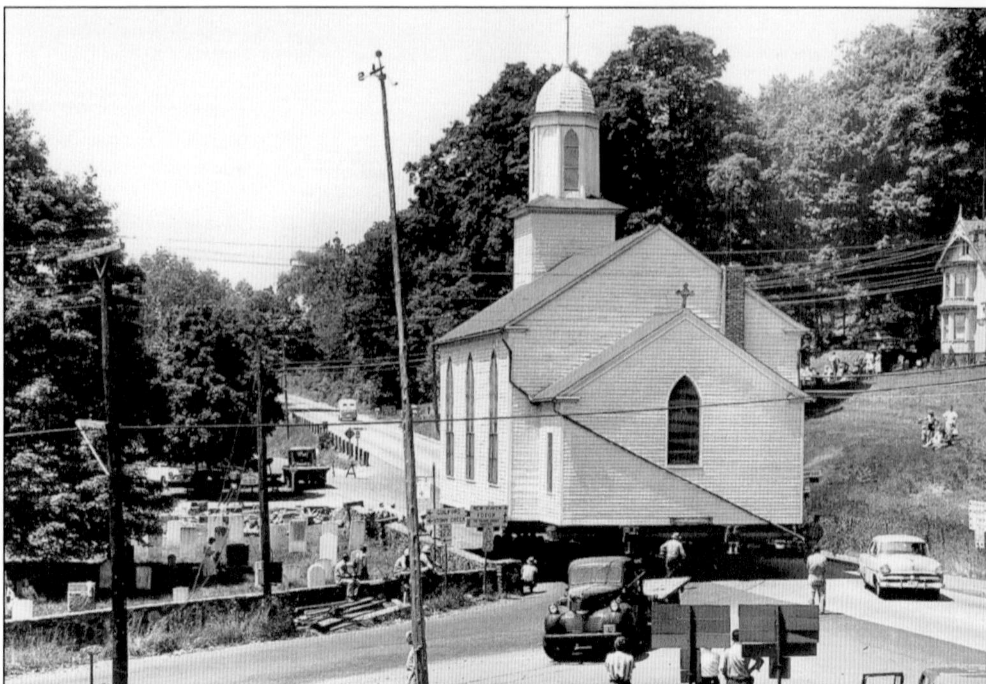

The solution to providing the needed space for Zion Episcopal Church was to pick up the entire edifice and move it 1,000 feet around the corner to a new location on Notch Hill Road. The move in the summer of 1957 drew spectators from all around the area. (Zion Episcopal Church.)

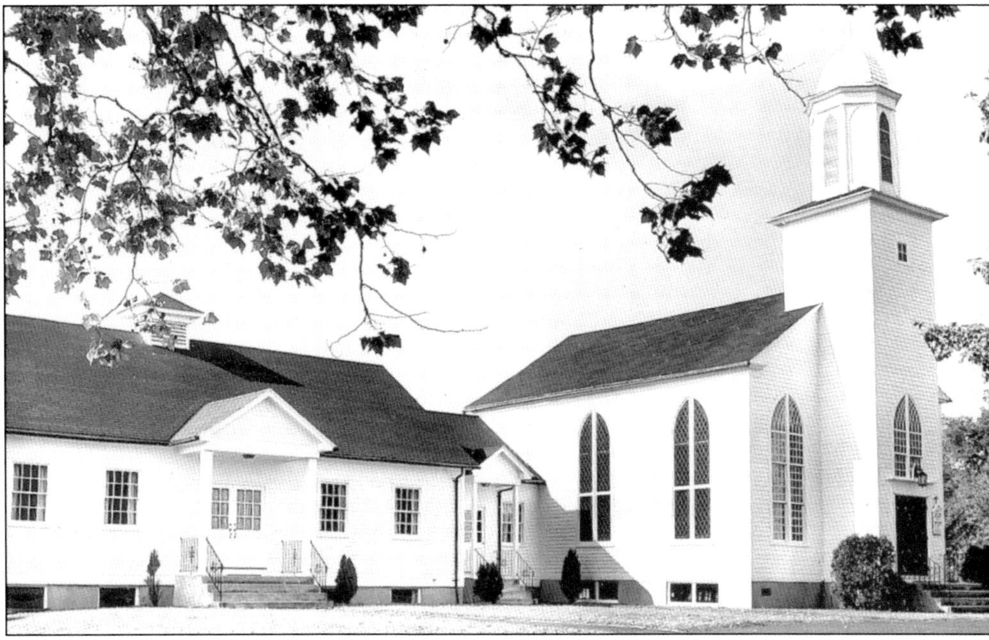

A new parish hall with classrooms, a meeting hall, kitchen, and restrooms was built onto the old Zion church building. The construction of this church began in 1818 and took many years to complete. It is the oldest public building in town. Notch Hill Nursery School has been located here for many years. (Zion Episcopal Church.)

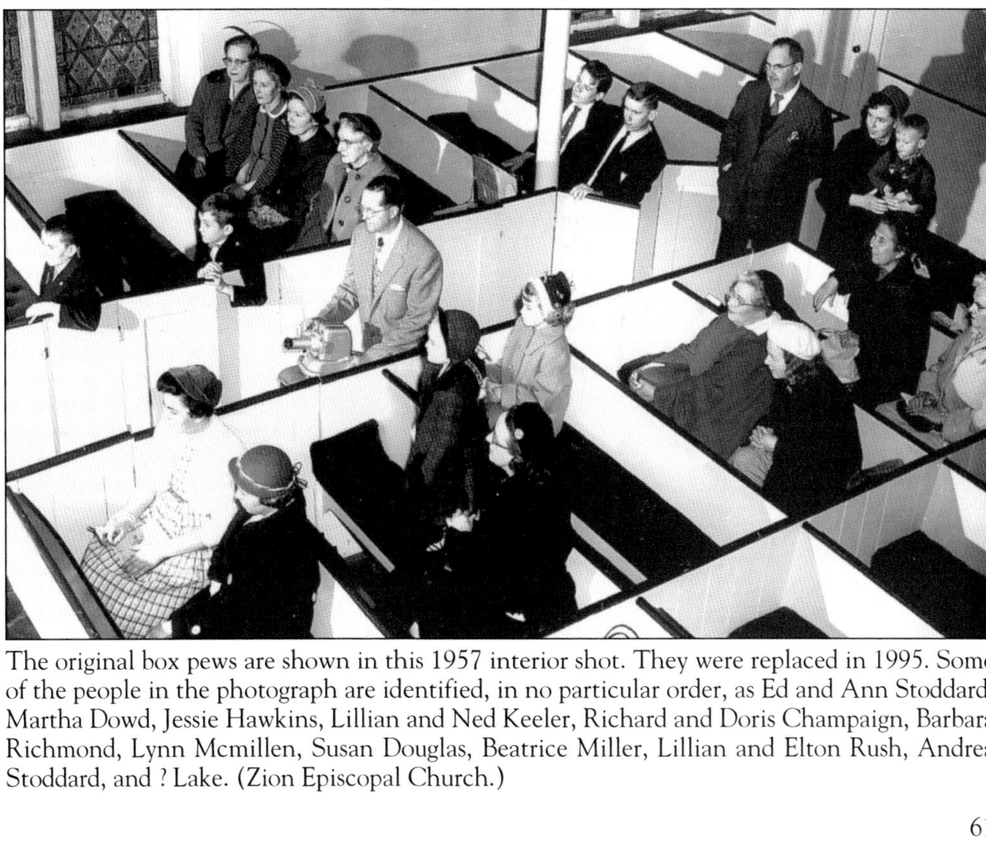

The original box pews are shown in this 1957 interior shot. They were replaced in 1995. Some of the people in the photograph are identified, in no particular order, as Ed and Ann Stoddard, Martha Dowd, Jessie Hawkins, Lillian and Ned Keeler, Richard and Doris Champaign, Barbara Richmond, Lynn Mcmillen, Susan Douglas, Beatrice Miller, Lillian and Elton Rush, Andrea Stoddard, and ? Lake. (Zion Episcopal Church.)

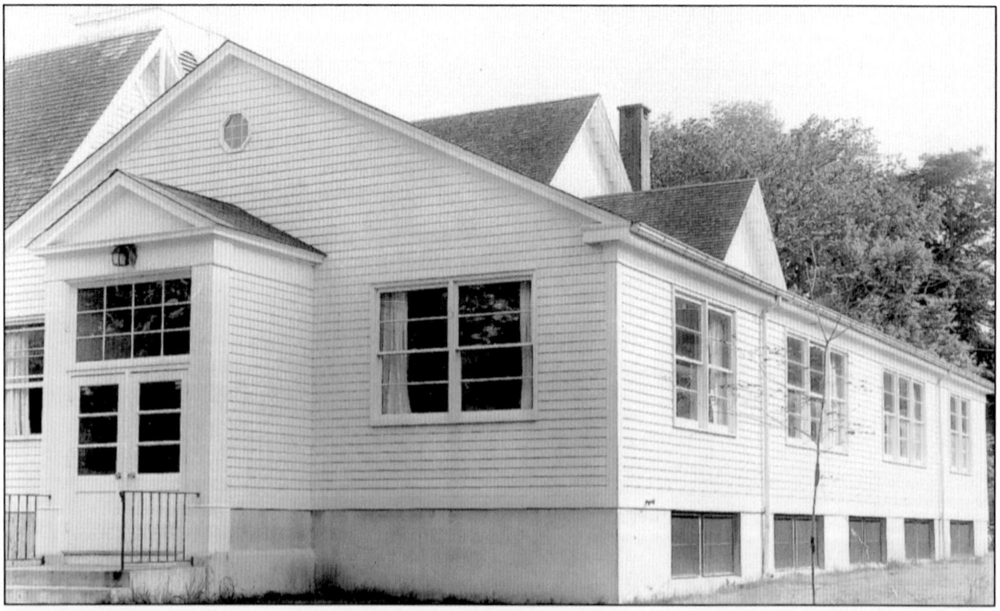

The North Branford Congregational Church added a parish house in 1961 to provide for meeting and church school needs. The new addition was built on the back of the 1909 church building and joined the church to the chapel. The chapel, built in 1887, had to be moved forward. Classrooms are on the main floor, and a meeting hall is in the basement. A new kitchen was built under the chapel. (North Branford Congregational Church.)

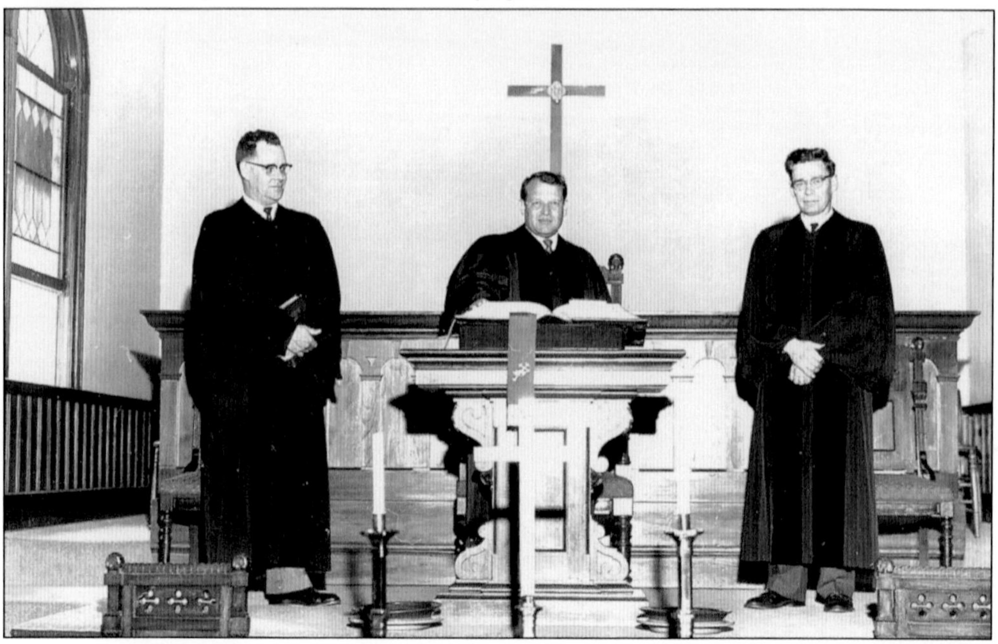

This photograph was taken at the June 25, 1961, dedication service for the new parish hall. The ministers are, from left to right, Rev. Robert Lane (minister at that time), Rev. John DeSousa, and Rev. A. Lee Holcutt (former pastor). The original raised choir loft and pulpit can be seen with the communion table at floor level. This pulpit recess area was renovated in 1972. (North Branford Congregational Church.)

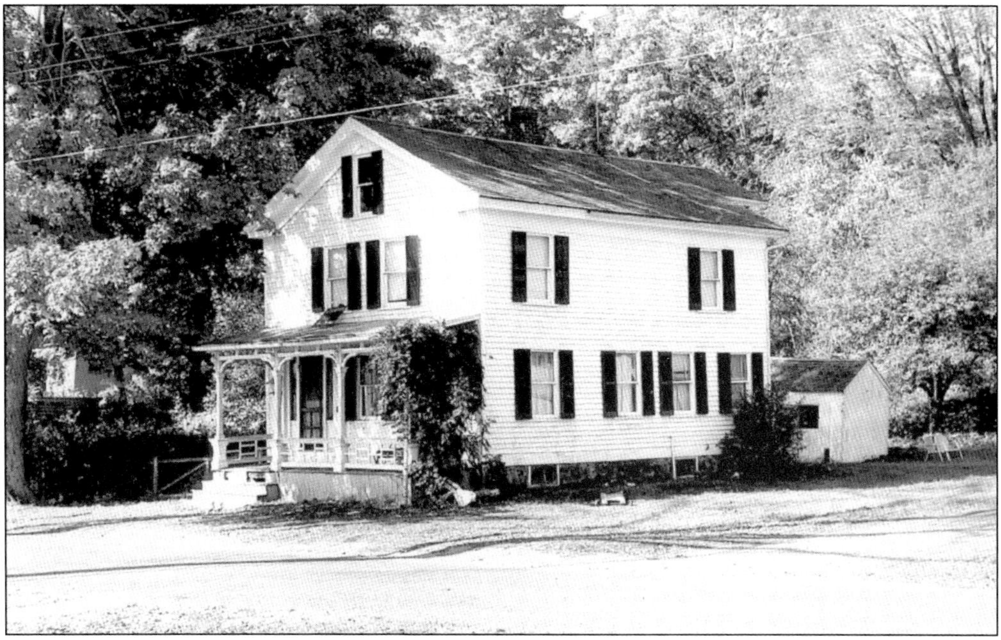

This house stood on Church Street where the present Congregational church parking lot is located. The Grosvenor House was acquired by the church and rented for a while. In the early 1970s, when the house needed many repairs, it was decided to demolish it and pave the grounds. Remnants of the fence can be seen today. (North Branford Congregational Church.)

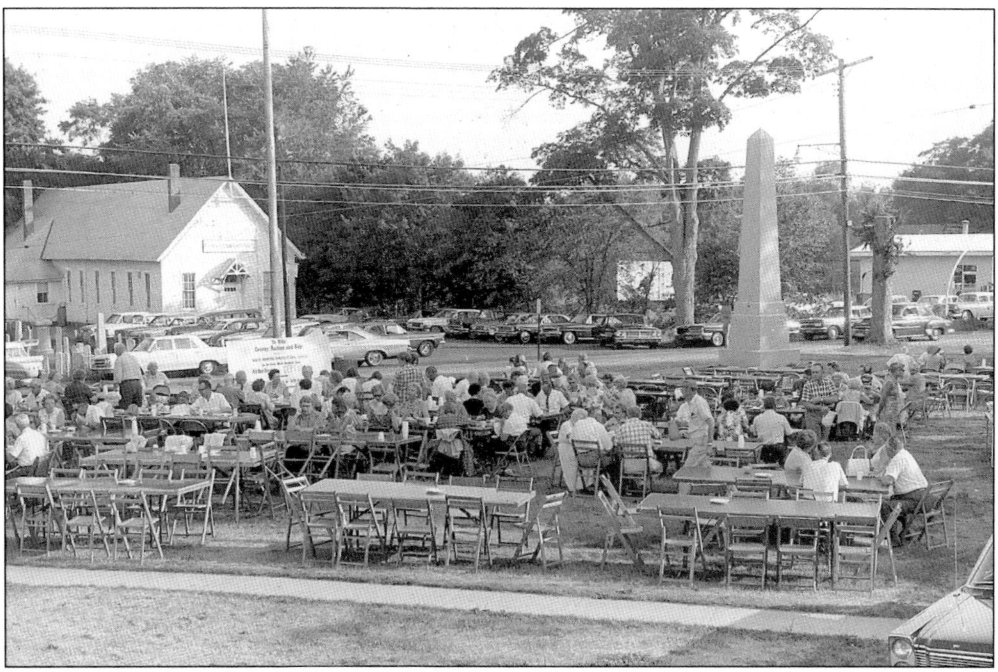

To raise funds to pay off the debt incurred when the parish hall was built, members of the North Branford Congregational Church held a very popular chicken barbeque for several years in the mid-1960s. This photograph shows the tables set up for the August 1966 supper on the green by the Civil War monument. (North Branford Congregational Church.)

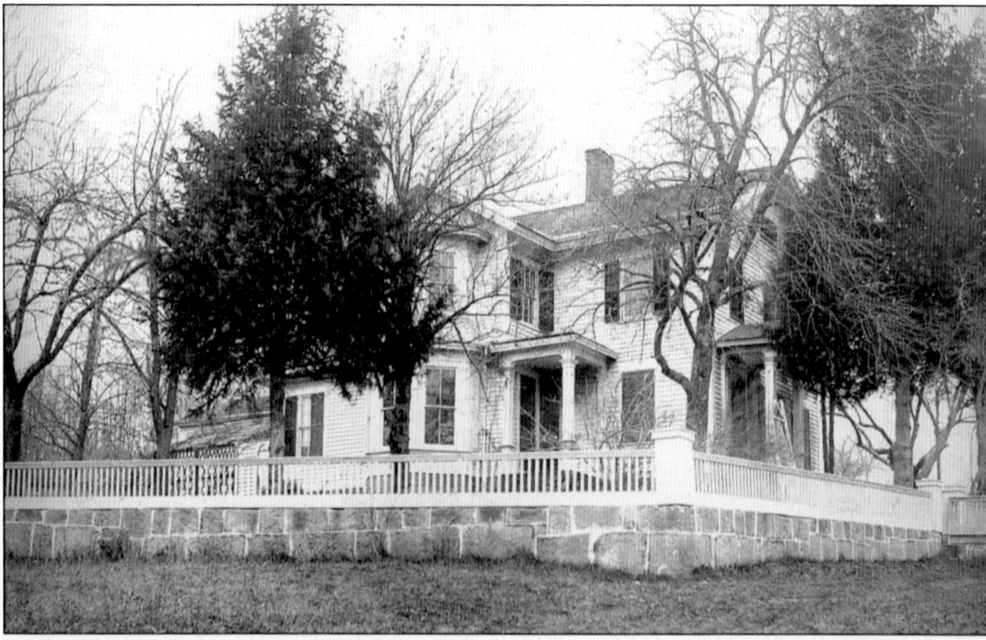

The Northford Congregational Church purchased the house next door in 1957 for a parish house. The house was originally built for Northford manufacturer Thomas A. Smith *c.* 1860 and later became the home of Stanley T. Williams. This photograph shows the house as it looked in early 1900s. (North Branford Congregational Church.)

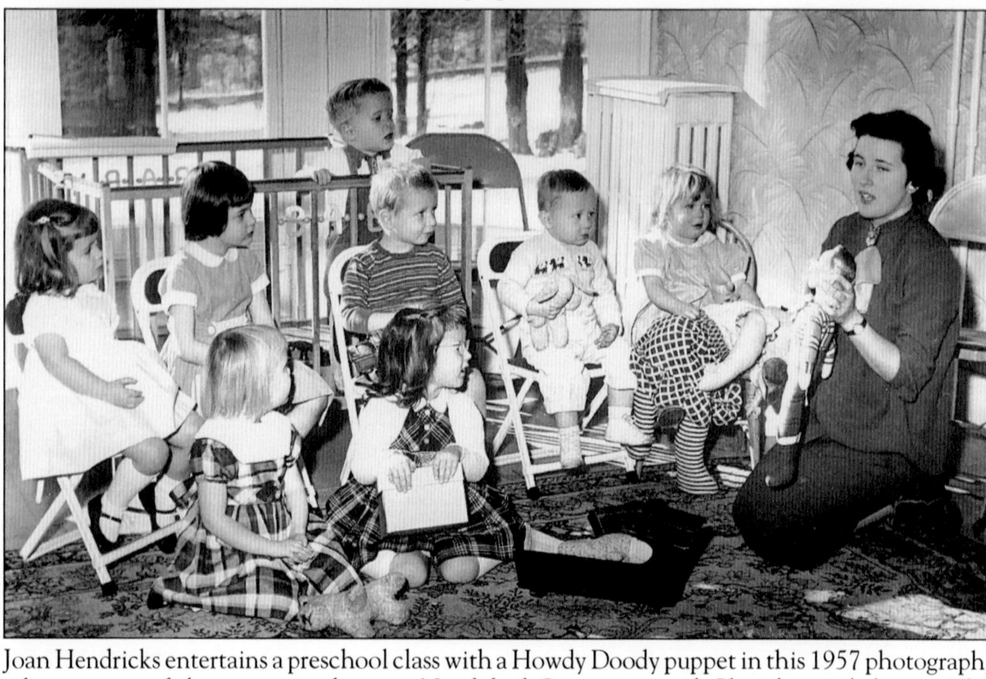

Joan Hendricks entertains a preschool class with a Howdy Doody puppet in this 1957 photograph, taken in one of the rooms in the new Northford Congregational Church parish house. The children, from left to right, are as follows: (front row) Alice Anderson and Betsy Hendricks; (back row) Lisa Hendricks, Cindy Batty, unidentified, Ricky Burke, and unidentified. In the crib is Paul Hendricks. (North Branford Congregational Church.)

A view of the Northford Congregational Church steeple taken *c.* 1975 shows the detail in the brownstone construction as designed by famous architect Henry Austin. The church was built on the site of the original meetinghouse in 1845. A disastrous fire occurred in 1906, destroying the interior and steeple. The steeple was rebuilt shorter than the one designed by Austin. The side balconies were not replaced after the fire. (Northford Congregational Church.)

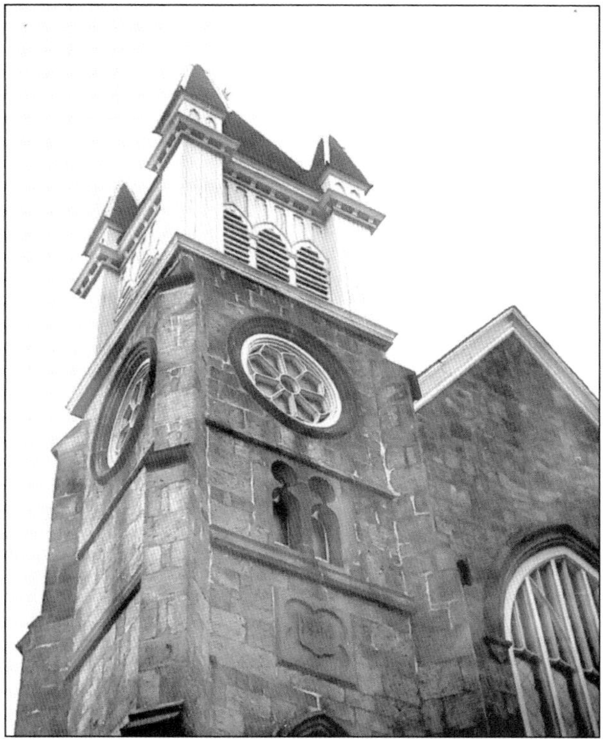

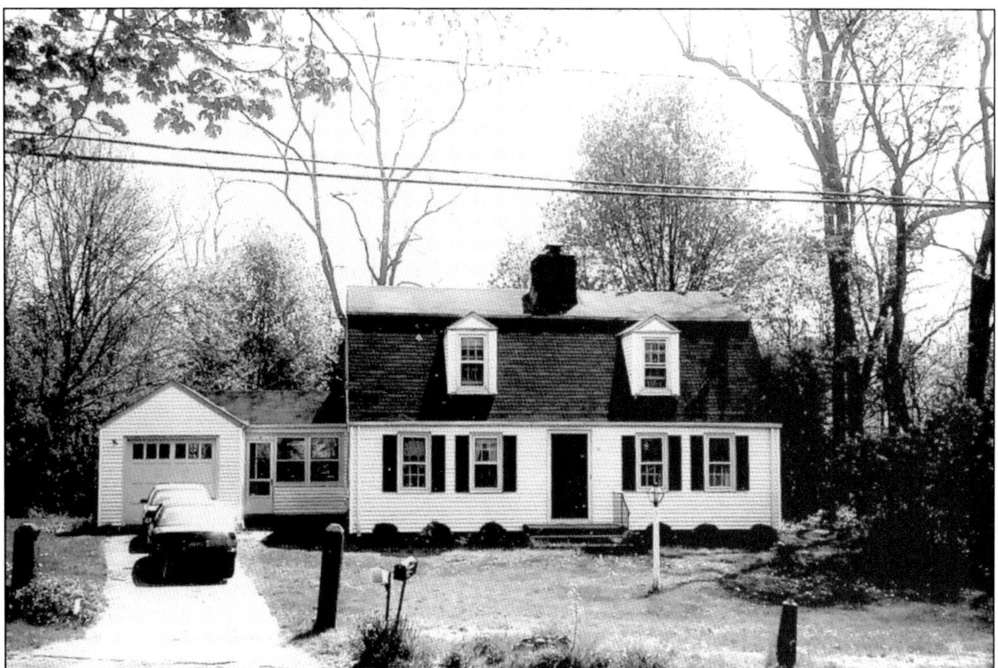

The Northford Congregational Church parsonage, located across Old Post Road from the church, replaced the old parsonage destroyed by fire in 1944. It was this spectacular fire that inspired the formation of the Northford Volunteer Fire Department Company No. 2 in June 1944. (Northford Congregational Church.)

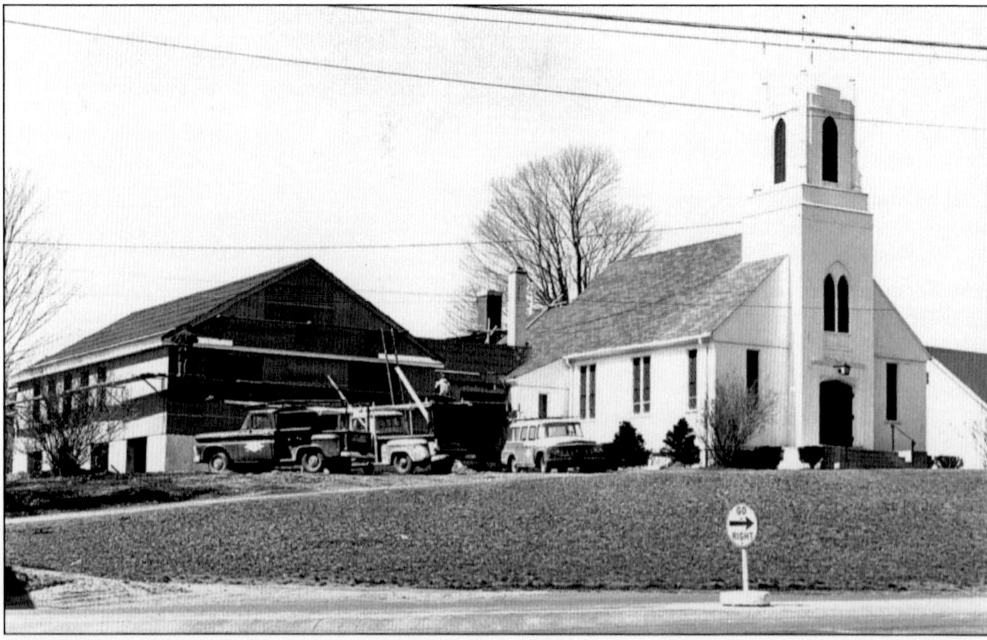

A parish house was added to St. Andrew's Episcopal Church in Northford, and this photograph shows its construction in 1965. The first St. Andrew's Episcopal Church was located on Old Post Road on the site of the Area Community Education Services School, the old William Douglas School. (Totoket Historical Society.)

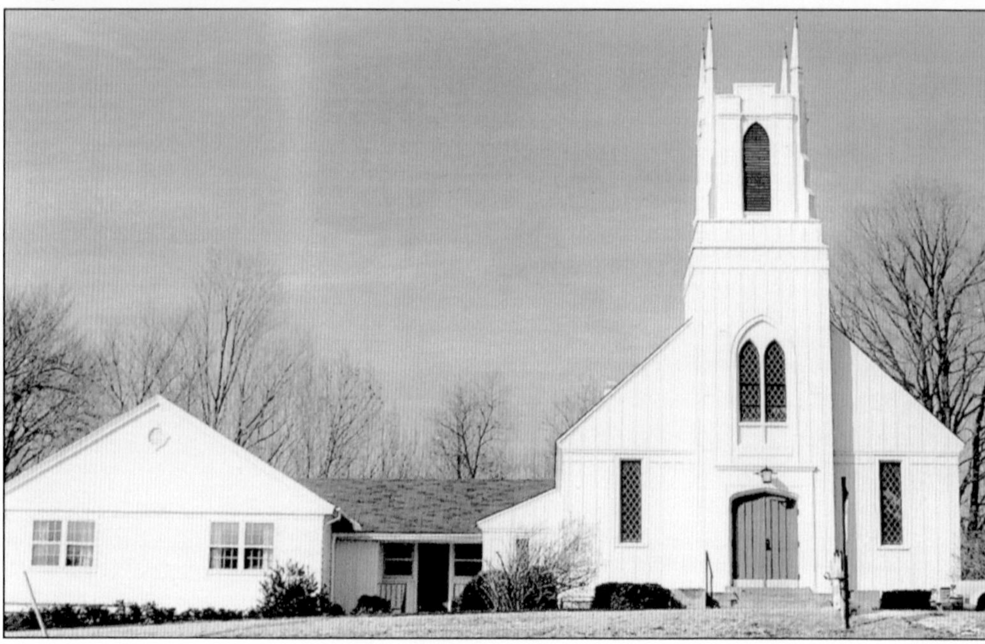

The original Gothic-style St. Andrew's Church, built in 1845 on this site, was destroyed by fire in 1938. While the present church building was being constructed, services were held in the Warham Williams house for two years. The house served as a rectory and later as a parish house after being purchased in 1866 by St. Andrew's. The house was sold when the new parish hall was built. (Totoket Historical Society.)

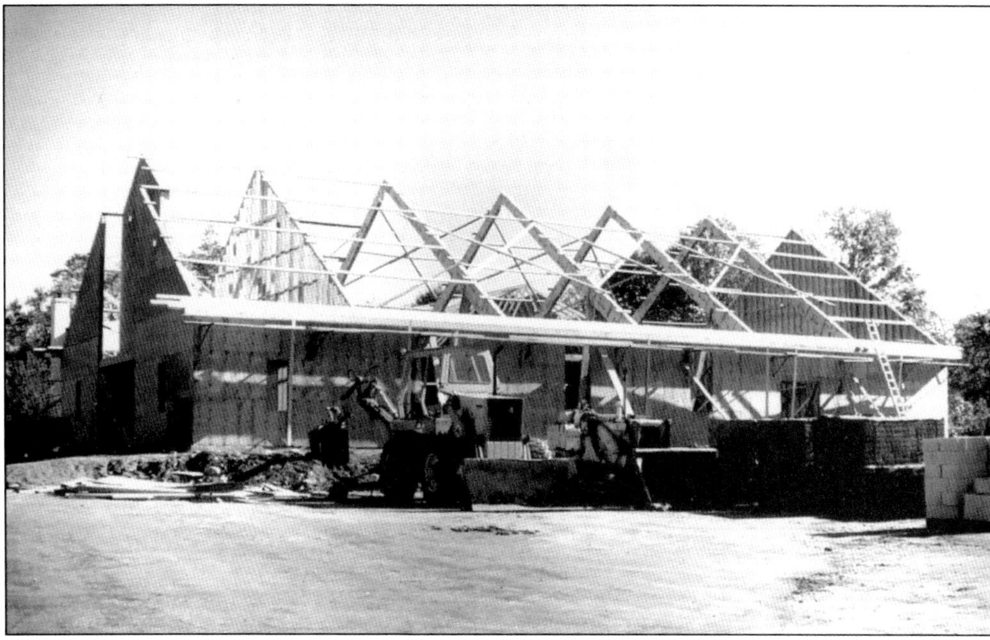

This is a photograph of the new St. Monica's Catholic Church being constructed in 1978. It was located to the south of the original 1951 chapel, which had canted, wood sheathed, corncrib-styled walls. The chapel was reconstructed to compliment the new-style church connected to it and now houses a recreation hall, classrooms, and a kitchen. (Carl Battista.)

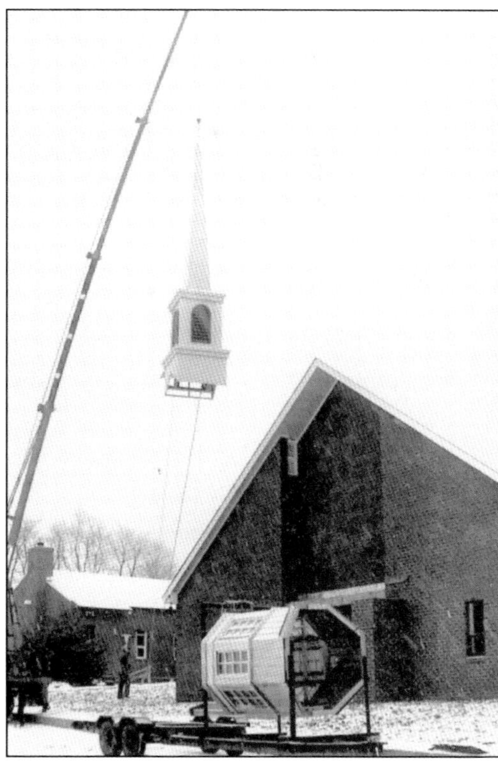

The steeple is lifted to the top of the new church. St. Monica's was a mission church of St. Augustine's until 1964, when the new parish was established. Fr. Stephen Vitka was the first pastor. (Carl Battista.)

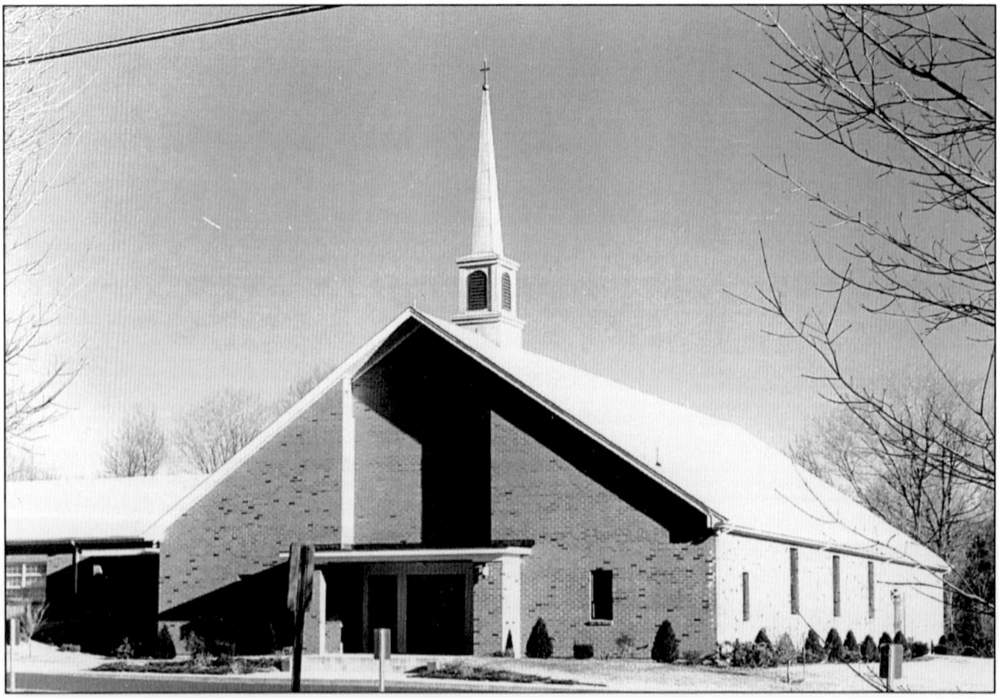

The new St. Monica's Catholic Church is shown in this photograph two years after its dedication. (Totoket Historical Society.)

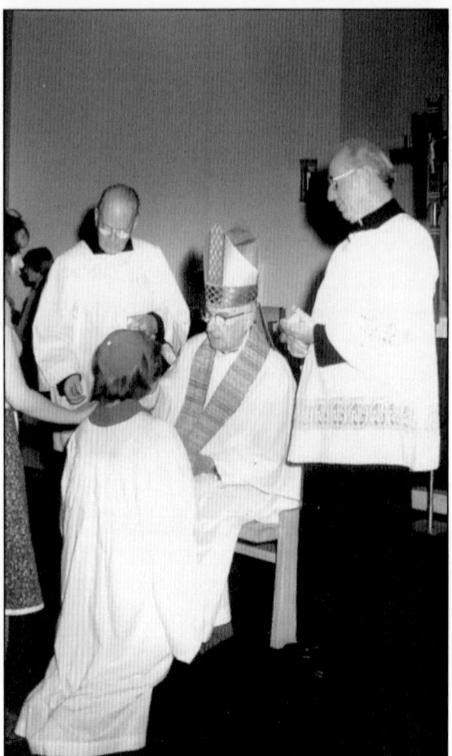

This photograph shows a confirmation ceremony, the first one held in the new St. Monica's Catholic Church. Fr. William J. Reilly is on the right. Father Reilly was pastor of St. Augustine's during the time when both new Catholic churches were built. (Carl Battista.)

Five

Commerce and Industry Come to Town

The New Haven Trap Rock Quarry and the New Haven Water Company were the two biggest taxpayers in North Branford in the mid-20th century. The three general stores and two gasoline stations, sufficient in 1950 to serve the town's 1,207 residents, were no longer able to supply the needs of the burgeoning population as time progressed. Shopping centers were developed in both ends of town, and several strip malls with various commercial establishments began to appear along the major highways. In 1964, an economic commission was appointed to help bring industry to town to supplement the tax base. Several industrial sites were identified, and major industries moved in.

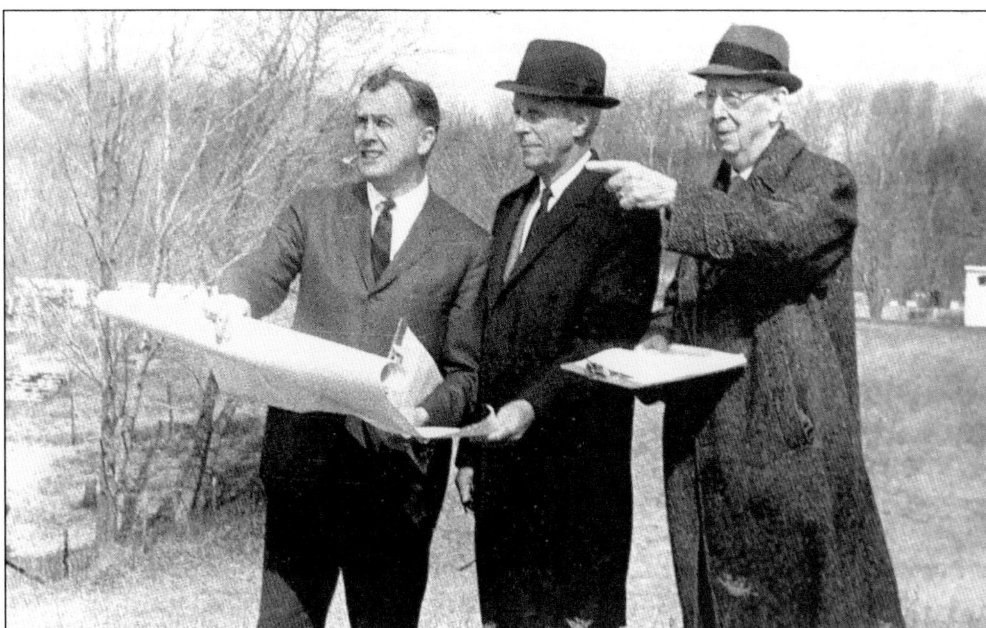

Pictured in this March 19, 1966, photograph, from left to right, are George W. Heston of the First New Haven National Bank; C. Forbes Sargent, former president of the Sargent Company; and Earl Arnold, North Branford industrial coordinator. They are looking over property on Route 139 destined for industrial use. Today, many industrial buildings are located there. (Totoket Historical Society.)

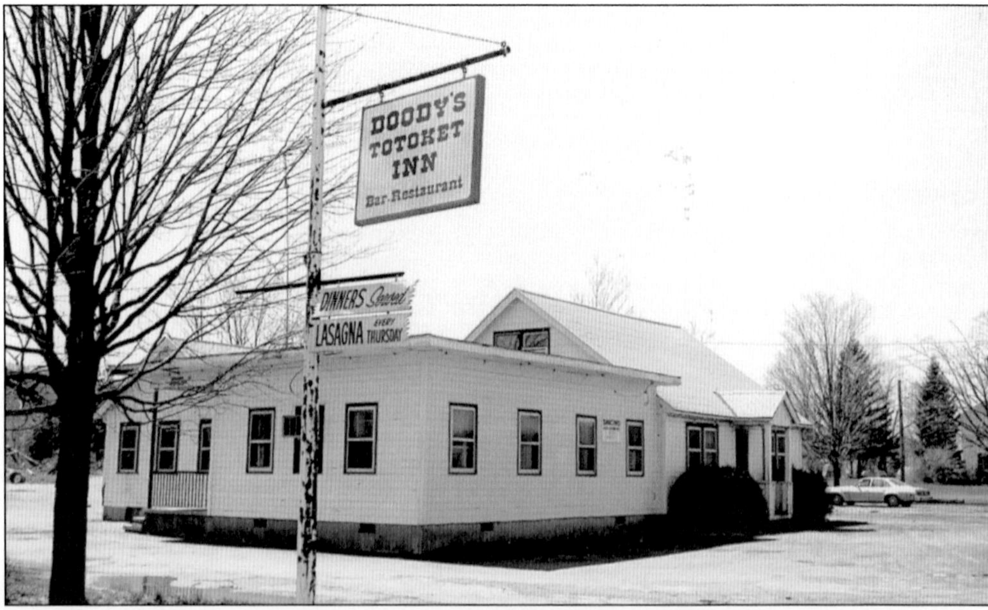

In 1933, after Prohibition was repealed, the Doody brothers opened a tavern on their Route 80 property. It had the first liquor license in town. It is now a full restaurant, Doody's Totoket Inn, run by their grandchildren, John Doody and Susan Doody Duhamel. The restaurant is a local institution and meeting place for numerous local organizations. The North Branford Lions Club, no longer in existence, was chartered there. (Totoket Historical Society.)

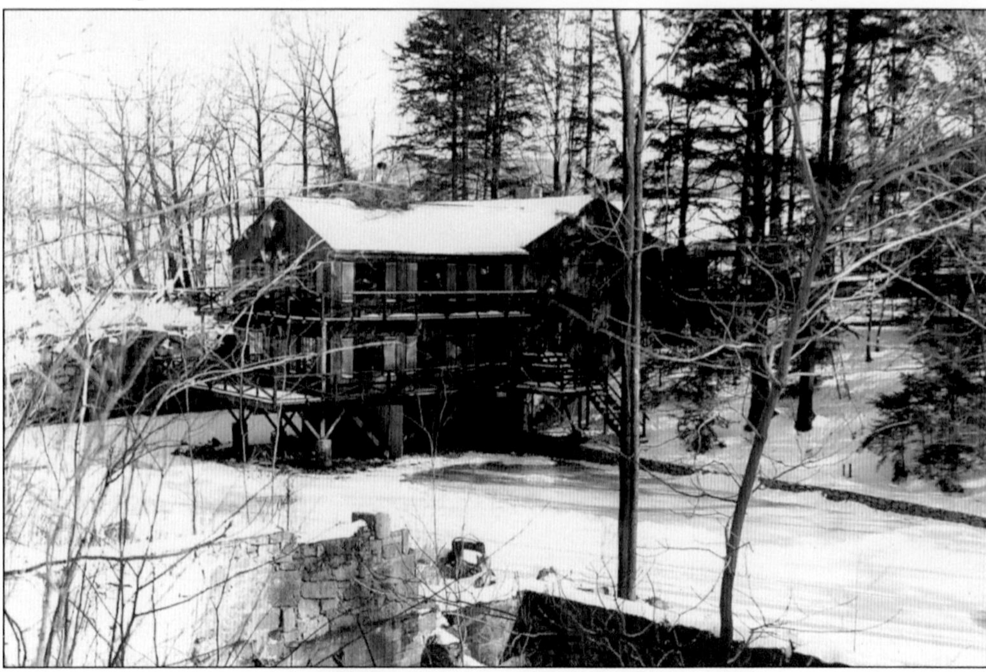

In 1969, a new restaurant, the Mill Pond Taverne, was built at the old dam on the Farm River, where a 19th-century manufacturing complex was originally located. In this photograph, the remains of the Maltby Mill can be seen in the foreground. The old industrial site was placed on the National Register of Historic Places in 1998. (Totoket Historical Society.)

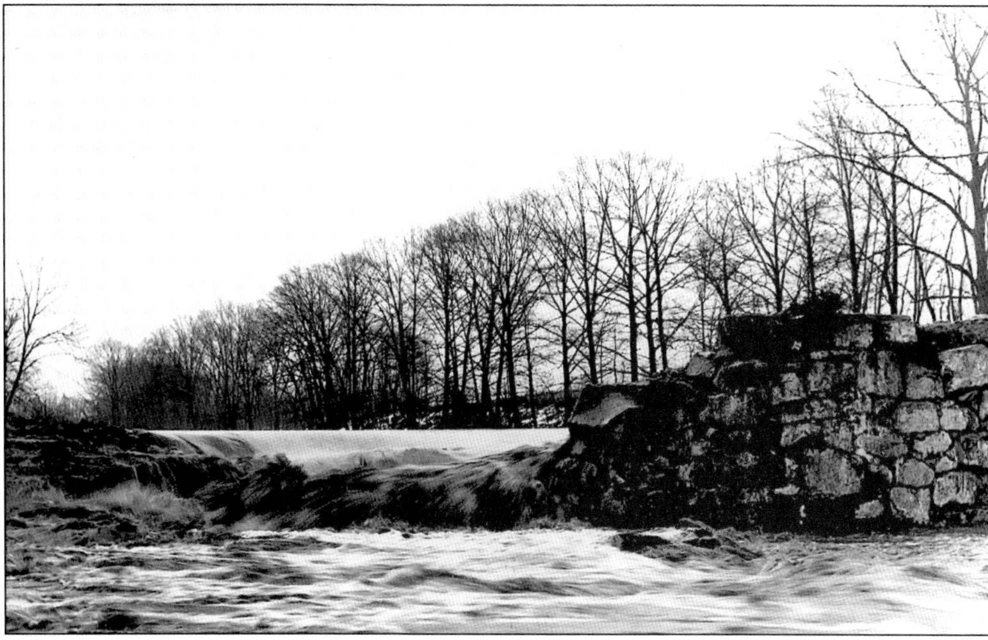

As the Mill Pond Taverne restaurant was being constructed in June 1968, a disastrous flood occurred caused by several days of steady rain. The flood took out the old dam and the large millpond that stretched along this section of Middletown Avenue (Route 17). (Totoket Historical Society.)

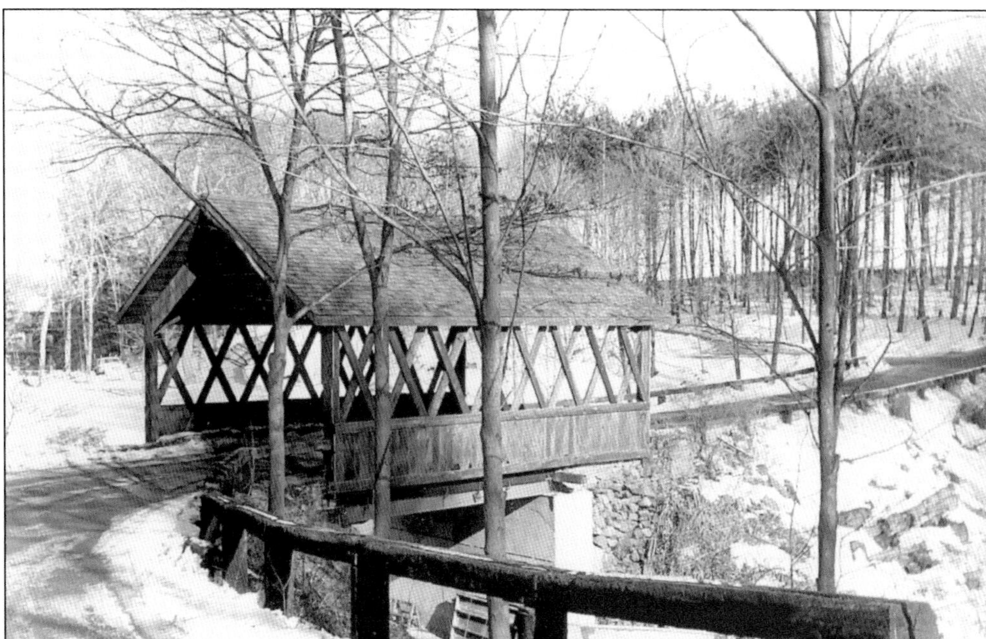

This covered bridge was built in 1969 over the Farm River as the entrance to the Mill Pond Taverne from Middletown Avenue. The restaurant can be seen on the left. The bridge was a local attraction but fell into disrepair and was taken down. The restaurant was sold and is now the RiverRun at the Millpond. (Totoket Historical Society.)

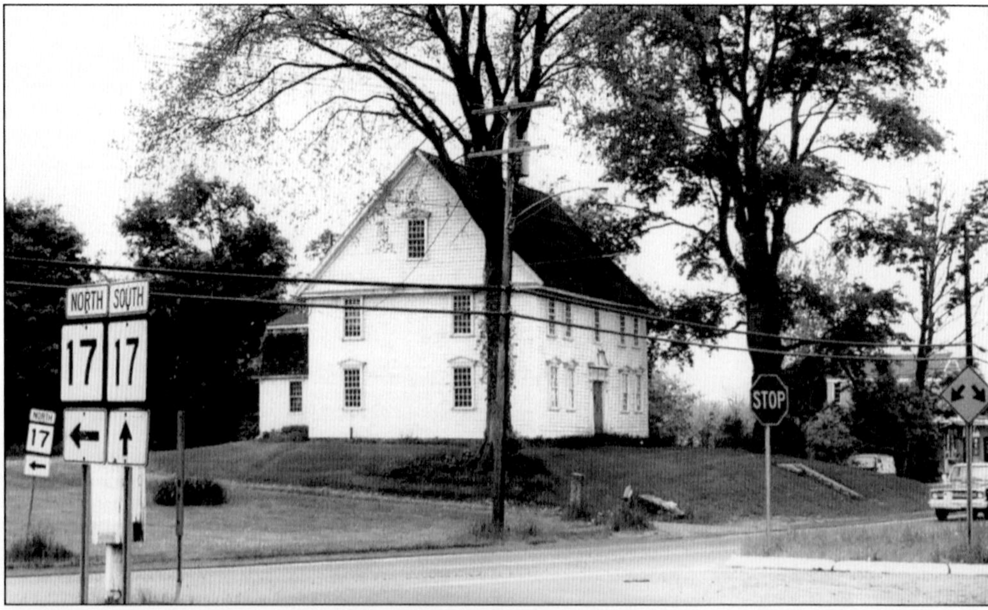

The Warham Williams house, built in 1750 for the first minister of the Northford Congregational Church, stood in the center of Northford. It was one of the best examples of Colonial architecture in town. It was a private residence for many years and later became the St. Andrew's Episcopal Church rectory. After the 1938 church fire, it was used for Sunday worship services until the new church was built. (Totoket Historical Society.)

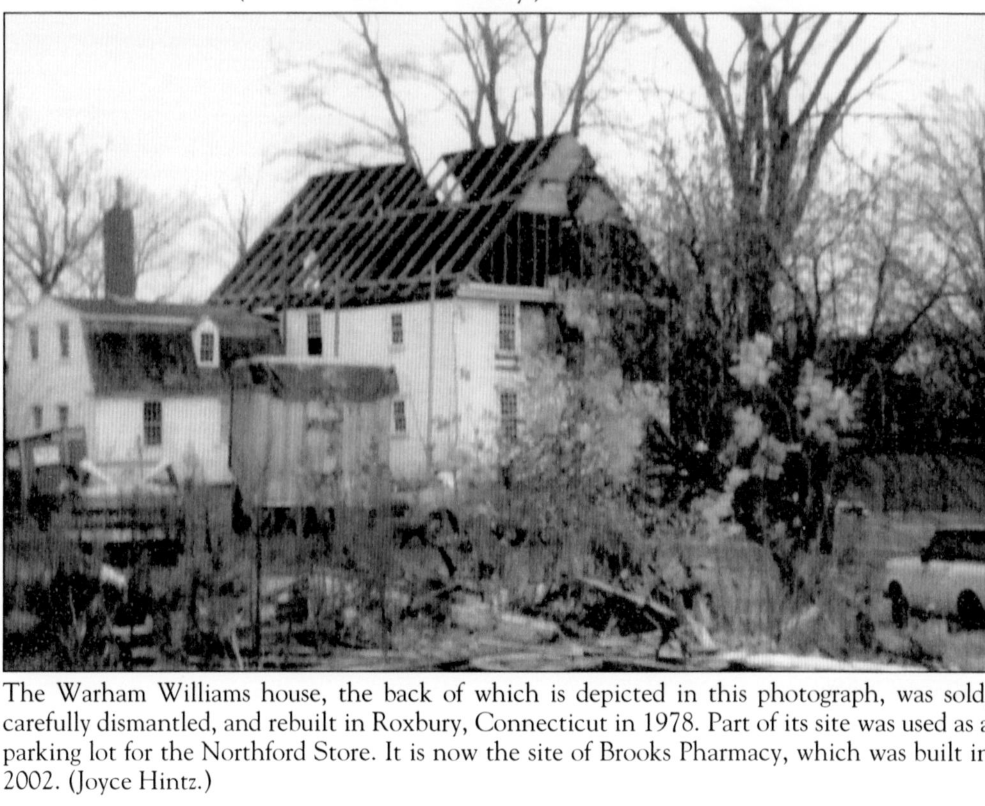

The Warham Williams house, the back of which is depicted in this photograph, was sold, carefully dismantled, and rebuilt in Roxbury, Connecticut in 1978. Part of its site was used as a parking lot for the Northford Store. It is now the site of Brooks Pharmacy, which was built in 2002. (Joyce Hintz.)

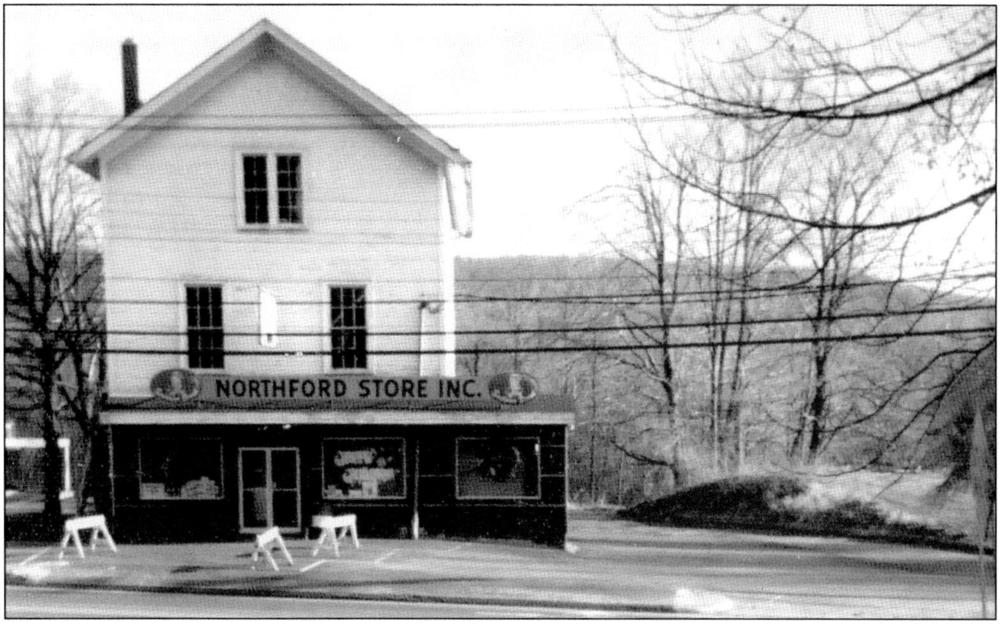

The Northford Store, one of the three stores in town, was built in 1871 by an association of residents founded for the purpose of raising funds to erect in the village center, near the churches, a building suitable for a store and a public hall. In the 1950s, a brick entrance replaced the porch on the original three-story building. (Joyce Hintz.)

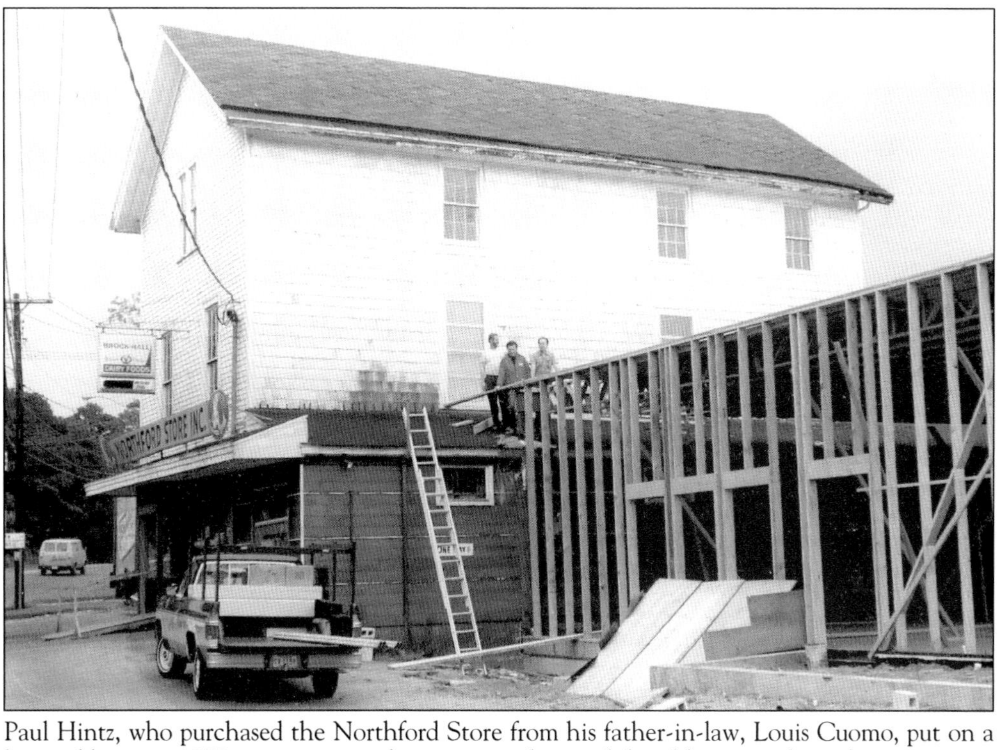

Paul Hintz, who purchased the Northford Store from his father-in-law, Louis Cuomo, put on a large addition in 1978 to create a modern supermarket, and the old store took on the appearance it has today. Louis Cuomo had purchased the store from Ed Johnson in 1961. (Joyce Hintz.)

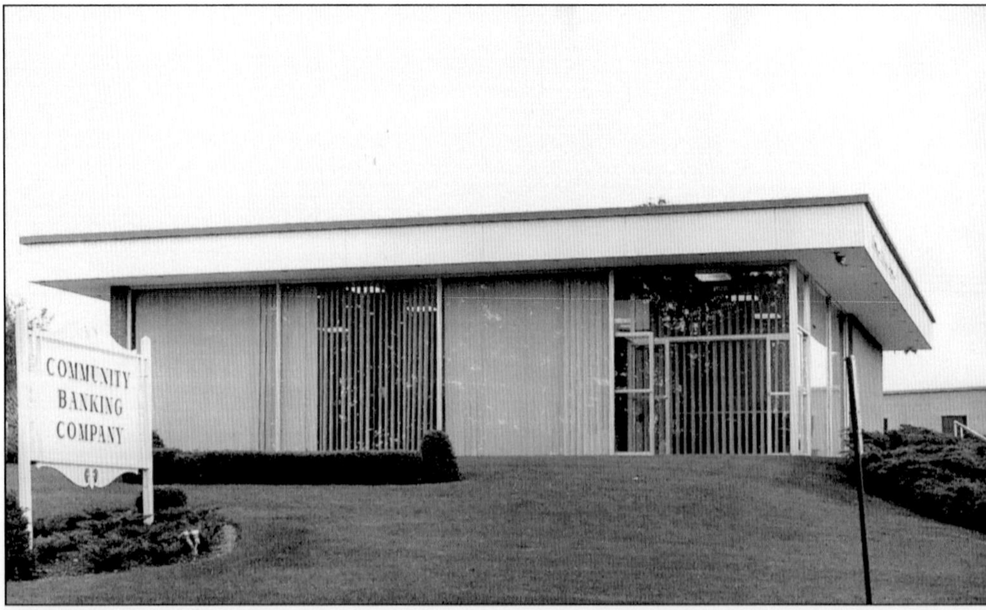

With the growth in population and more commercial and industrial activity, there was a need for banking facilities. This bank on Branford Road (Route 139) near the shopping center was built for the North Branford Bank and Trust Company, a company formed by some town residents. It later became the Community Banking Company, as shown in this photograph, and now is a branch of Fleet Bank. (Totoket Historical Society.)

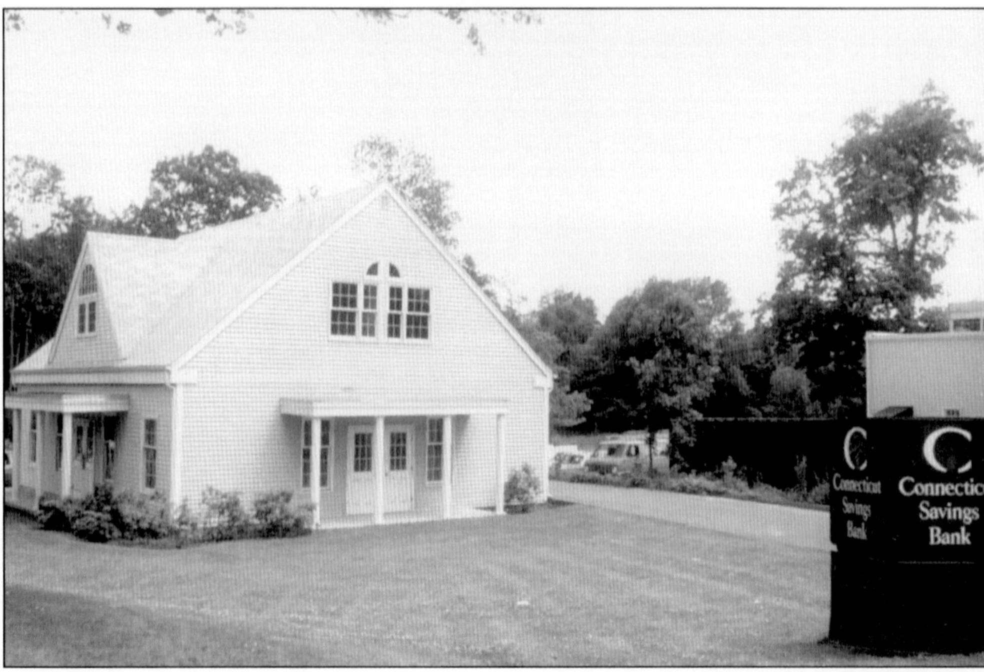

The Connecticut Savings Bank was built in the Northford section of town on the site of the Dobbs house. For several years, the walkout basement of the Dobbs house served as the Northford post office. The bank has changed owners many times. Recently, it was a branch of the Union Trust and is now, in 2003, owned by Wachovia. (Totoket Historical Society.)

In 1970, the old Stevens house and the Elizur Foote house located on Foxon Road across from the Charles Atwater Memorial Library were purchased so the site could be used for a shopping complex. This photograph shows the Stevens house being moved down Route 80 to its new site on the corner of Clear Lake Manor Road. The Foote house was moved to North Street. (Totoket Historical Society.)

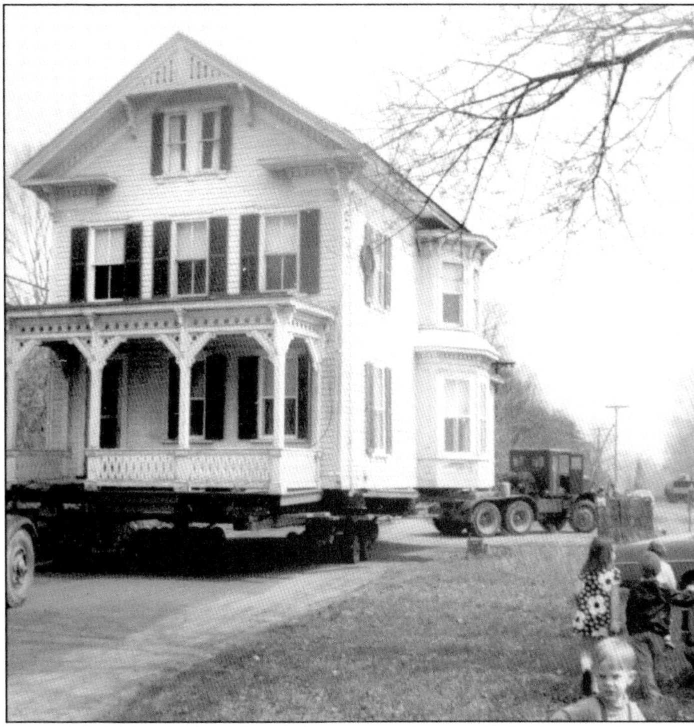

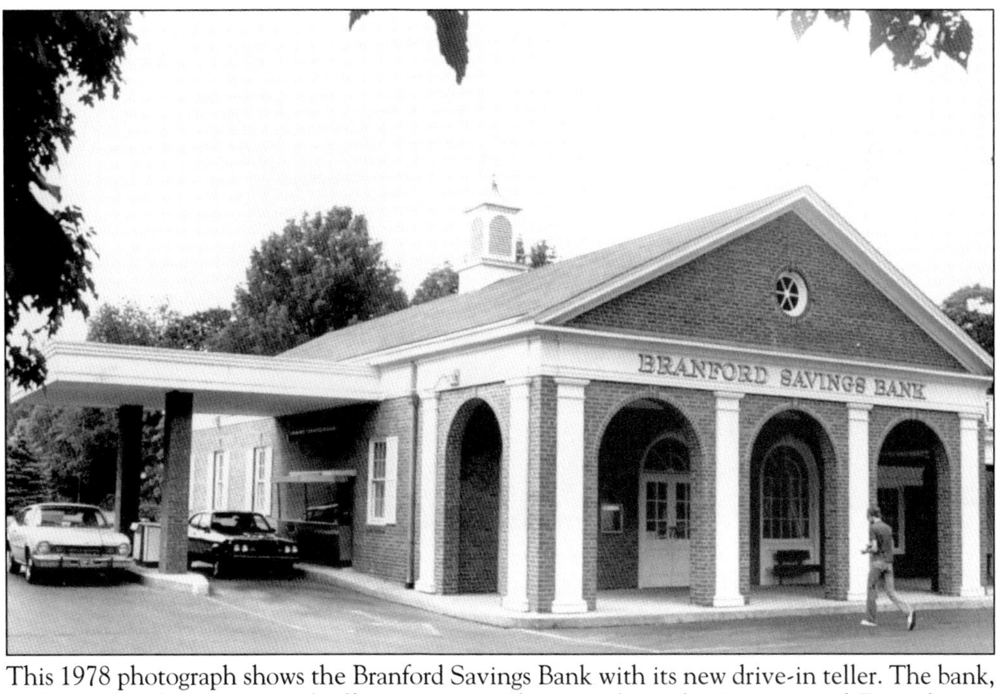

This 1978 photograph shows the Branford Savings Bank with its new drive-in teller. The bank, with its attendant stores and offices, occupies the site where the Stevens and Foote houses originally stood. The bank is now a branch of Citizens Bank. (Totoket Historical Society.)

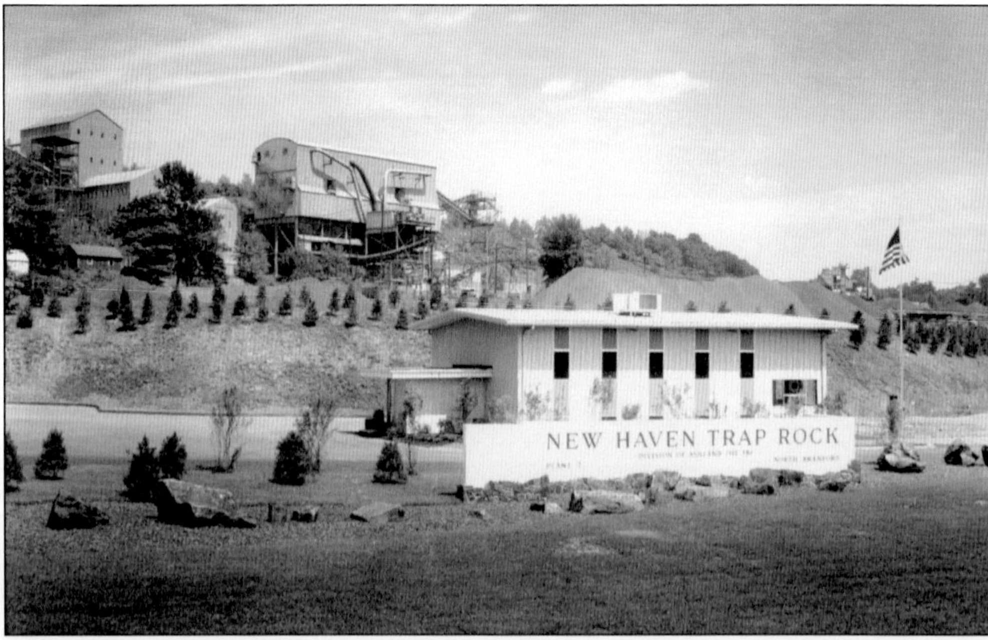

A fire destroyed the weighing scale and office building at the New Haven Trap Rock Quarry in 1968. The new office building, shown in this 1970 photograph, was built to replace it, and at the same time, a new interior road system, landscaping, and signage were designed by landscape architect James Skerrit. The quarry went through various ownerships during this period and is now owned by Tilcon. (Totoket Historical Society.)

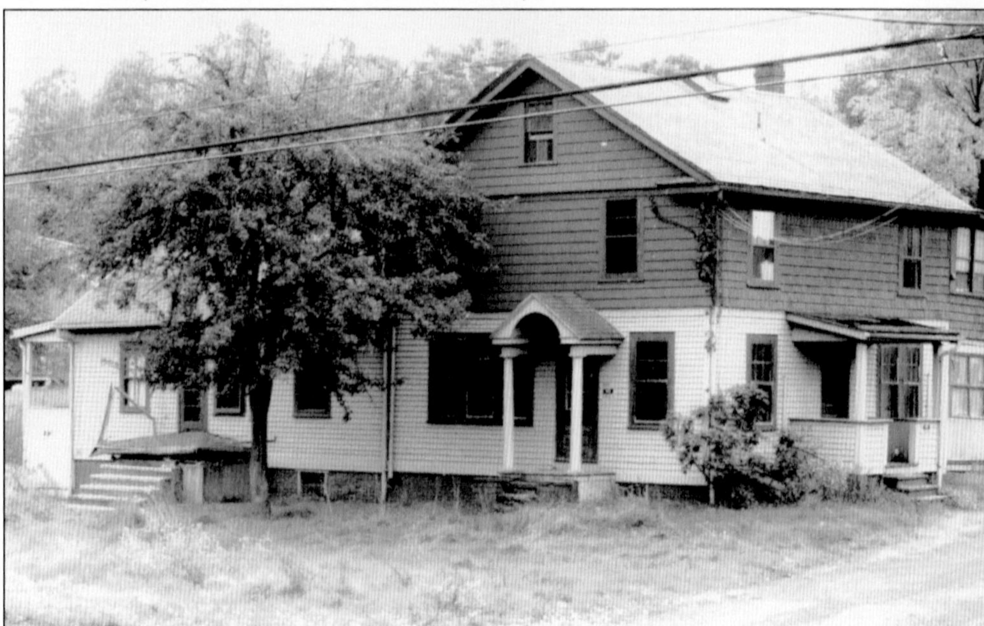

There were several houses on the corner of Route 80 and Twin Lakes Road across from the quarry. This 1989 photograph shows the C. Lanza house and was taken just prior to it being demolished. Twin Lakes Commons, an office and retail store complex, now occupies the site. (Totoket Historical Society.)

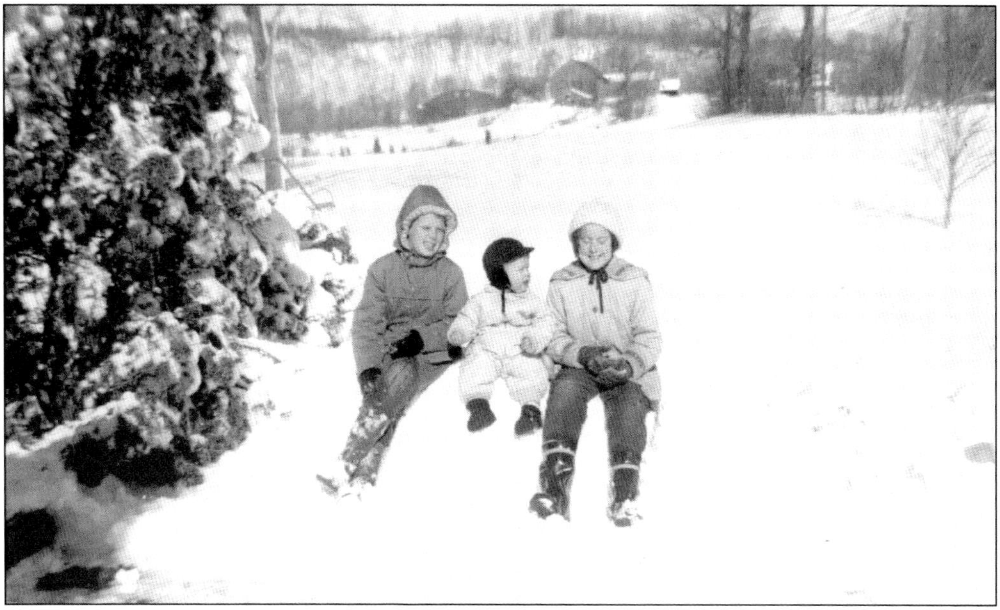

A snapshot taken in 1961 of Cynthia, Jason, and Robert Cole perched on a snow pile in front of their home shows the open fields along Branford Road (Route 139) behind them. The house and barns shown in the back belonged to the Bahsen farm. The property is now the site of several commercial and industrial buildings across from Harrison Road and the North Farms condominium entrance. (Shirley Cole.)

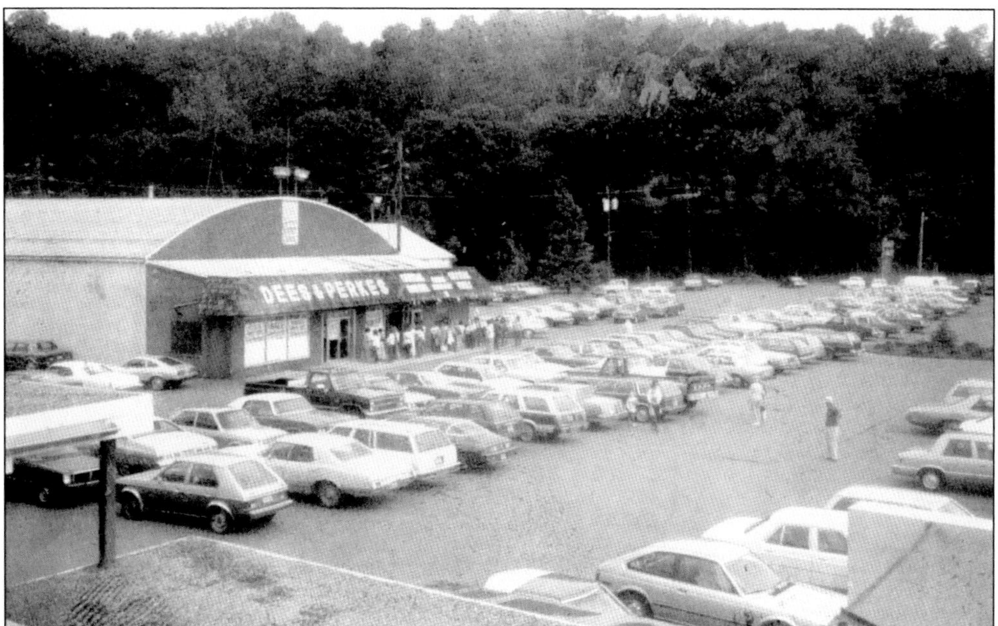

The Central Shopping Plaza was built at the intersection of Routes 80 and 139 in the early 1960s. This property has a long history. Originally, Jonathan Merrick, first minister of the Congregational church, owned the property. In 1920, the first Catholic Mass was celebrated in the house on the property, and in 1950, it was a lumberyard. Shown here is Dees & Perkes, a department store located in the old lumberyard. (Totoket Historical Society.)

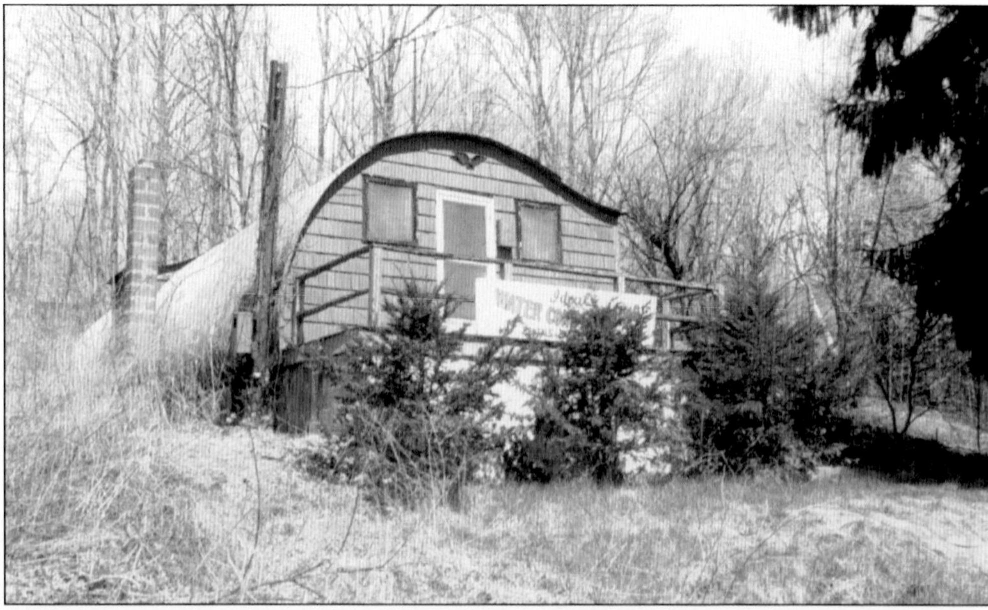

This Quonset hut sat on the hill across from Notch Hill Road on Route 80. It was brought here in 1946 from Yale University and used as a residence until 1970. In this 1980 photograph, it is an office for Ideal Water Conditioning. There were a couple of these c. 1943, World War II, prefabricated units in town. This one was later demolished, and a house was built on the site. (Totoket Historical Society.)

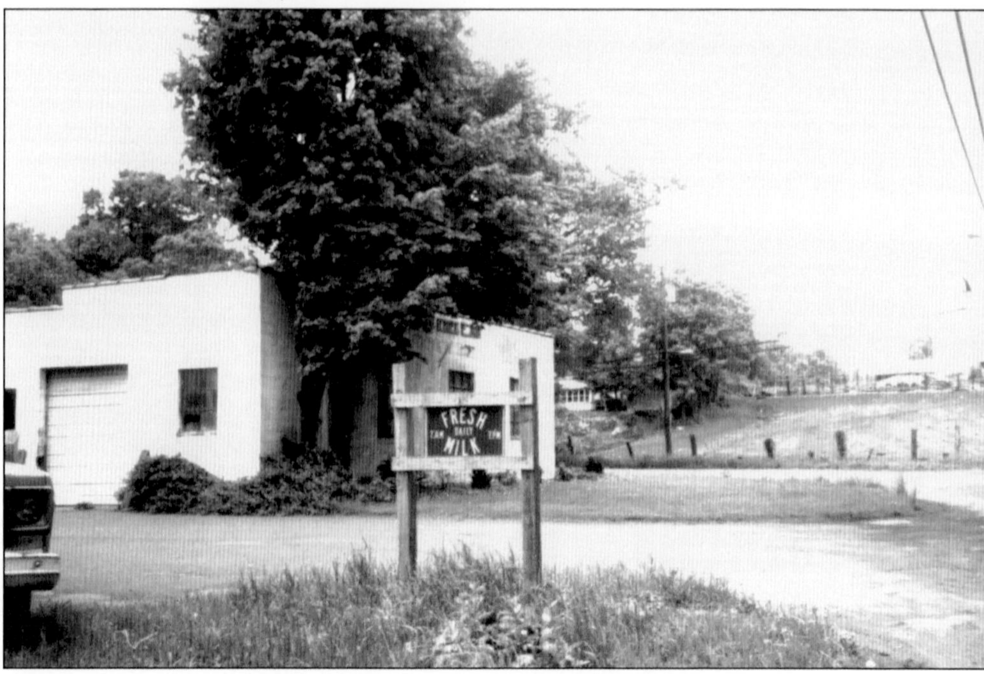

This retail dairy store was part of the Page farm on Totoket Road. Residents could purchase milk and dairy products at the Maple Tree Dairy using the honor system—take what you need and leave the money in the box. It closed down in 1986 and is rented out to a landscaping business. (Totoket Historical Society.)

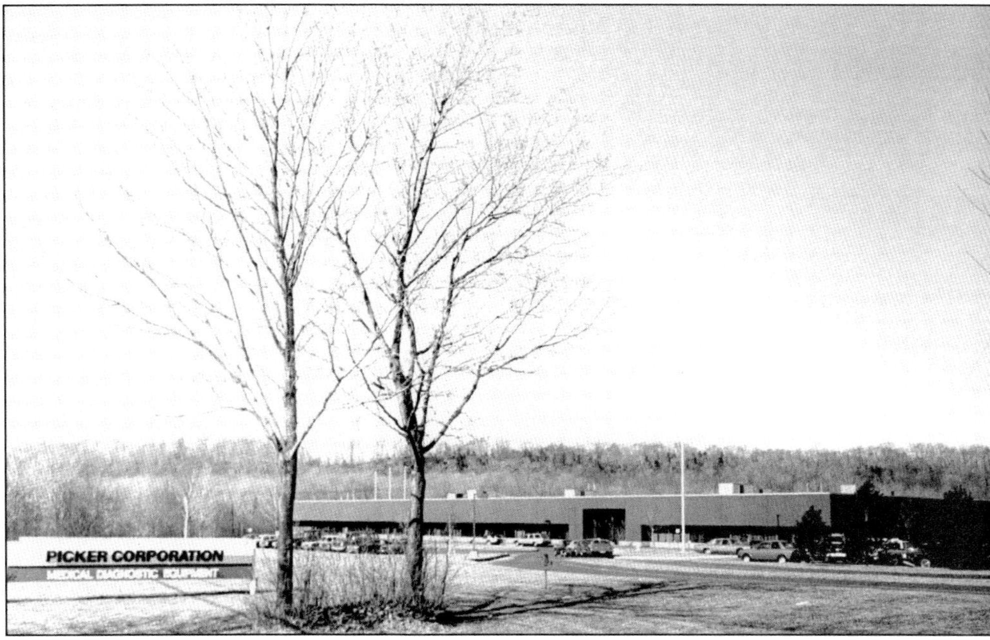

The Picker Corporation built a large facility on Clintonville Road in 1974 to manufacture medical diagnostic equipment. This was the first modern manufacturing plant to be built in the Northford section. The plant was sold to Firelite and now is a division of the Honeywell Corporation. (Totoket Historical Society.)

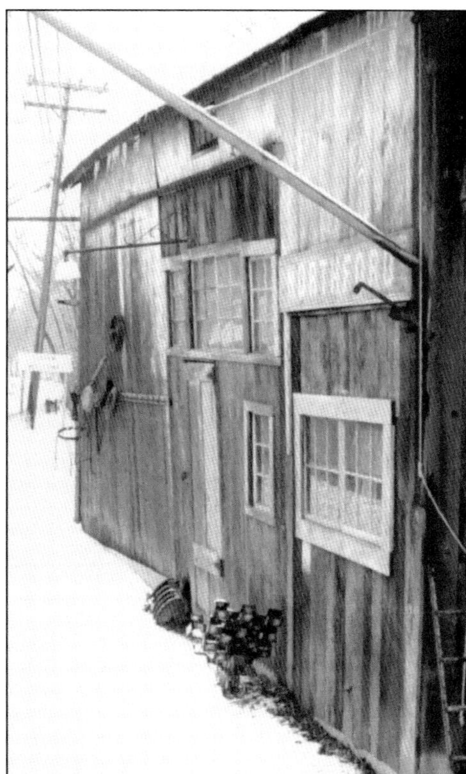

This old barn was located on Middletown Avenue just north of Northford Center on what is now the property of the Northford post office. According to oral tradition, Steven's Grocery and Produce Store was located here until *c.* 1910. The old barn, located almost on the highway, housed an antique business during this era and was eventually taken down *c.* 1975. (Jane Leschuk.)

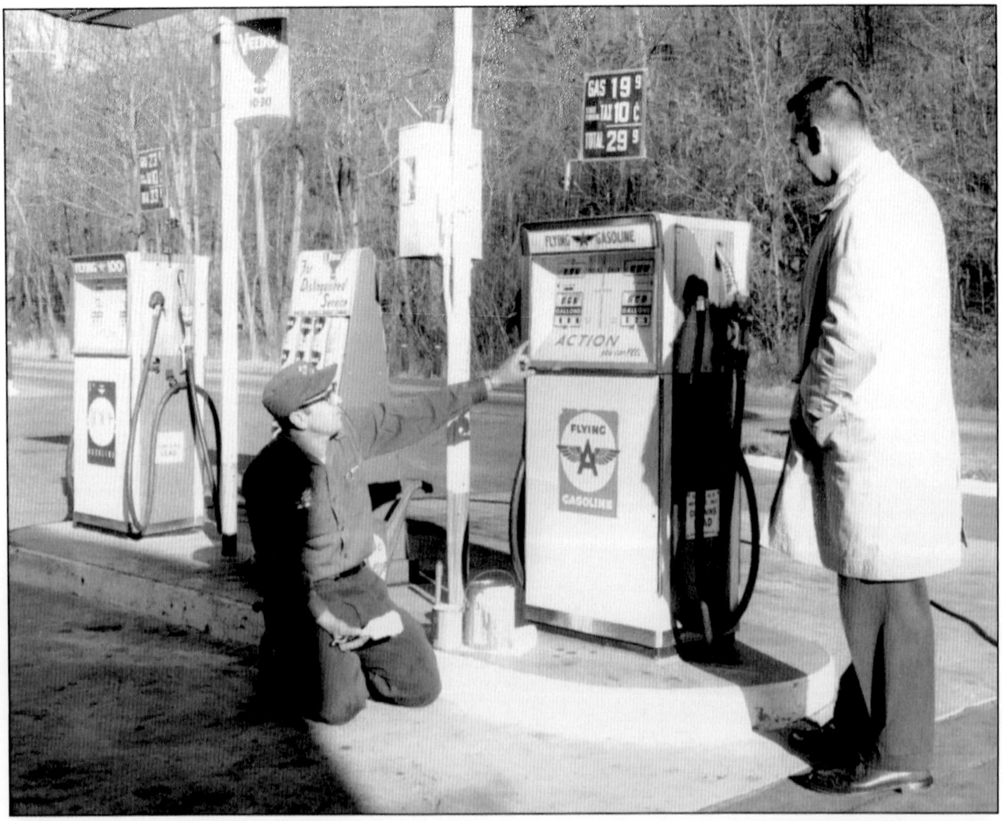

Michael Amatrudo relocated his gasoline station to a new location on Foxon Road (Route 80) in 1955. The Amatrudos owned one of the first gas stations in town. Here, Mike's son, Andy, chats with a sales representative from Flying A, Ed Johnson. The station is in operation on the same spot in 2003. (Barbara Amatrudo.)

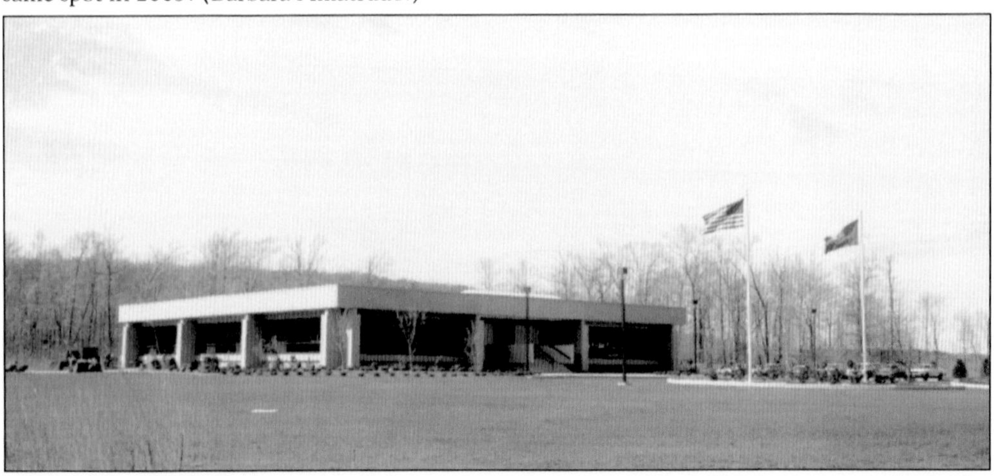

Tilcon-Tomasso, owner in 1978 of the original New Haven Trap Rock Company, built this corporate headquarters on marshlands across Route 80 from the quarry. The three-bay, one-story office building, designed by Kaestle and Boos Associates, was landscaped in a Japanese garden style by landscape architect John Wedda. Two more bays were added later, and in 2000, the building was sold to the town for use as a town hall. (Totoket Historical Society.)

Six

New Organizations and Recreational Activities Abound

It was not long before the newcomers who moved into North Branford went looking for opportunities to join together to meet new neighbors, serve their community, and provide recreational activities for themselves and their children. Since few wives worked outside the home during this era, there was a great interest in women's groups. By 1970, the town directory listed 18 different organizations for adults, most of them established after 1950. The list included two women's clubs, two garden clubs, the Jaycees, the Lions Club, the Rotary, the Library Associates, the historical society, the North Branford Land Conservation Trust, the Veterans of Foreign Wars, and the Urban League and Exchange Club. Some of the listings were founded prior to 1950, such as the Grange, the League of Women Voters, and Ladies Auxiliaries at two of the fire companies. A new town recreation department offered many programs for children and adults. A group of men started a Little League for both boys and girls, which continues to be active in 2003. There was also a Midget Football league for boys.

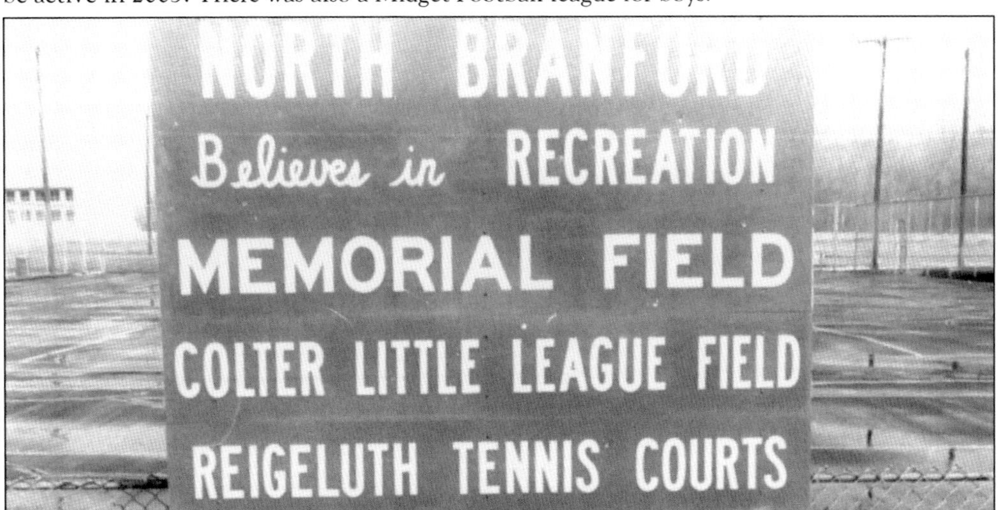

This sign, erected in February 1970 in front of the tennis courts and ball fields by the North Branford Intermediate School, says it all. (Totoket Historical Society.)

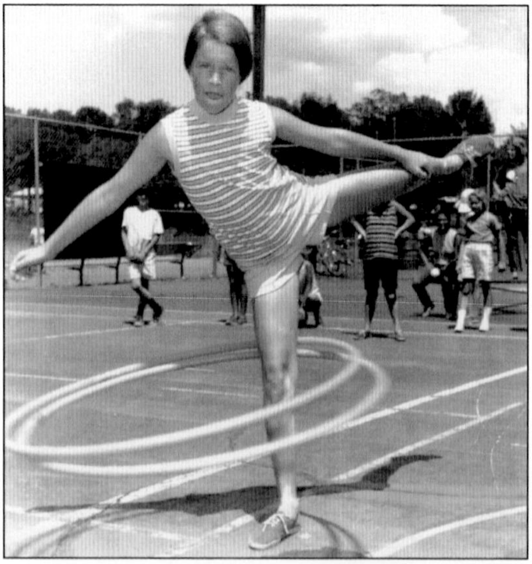

Diane Smith, daughter of Robert and Norma Jean Smith, was the 1971 Hula-Hoop champion. This activity was part of one of the park and recreation department programs. (North Branford Parks and Recreation Department.)

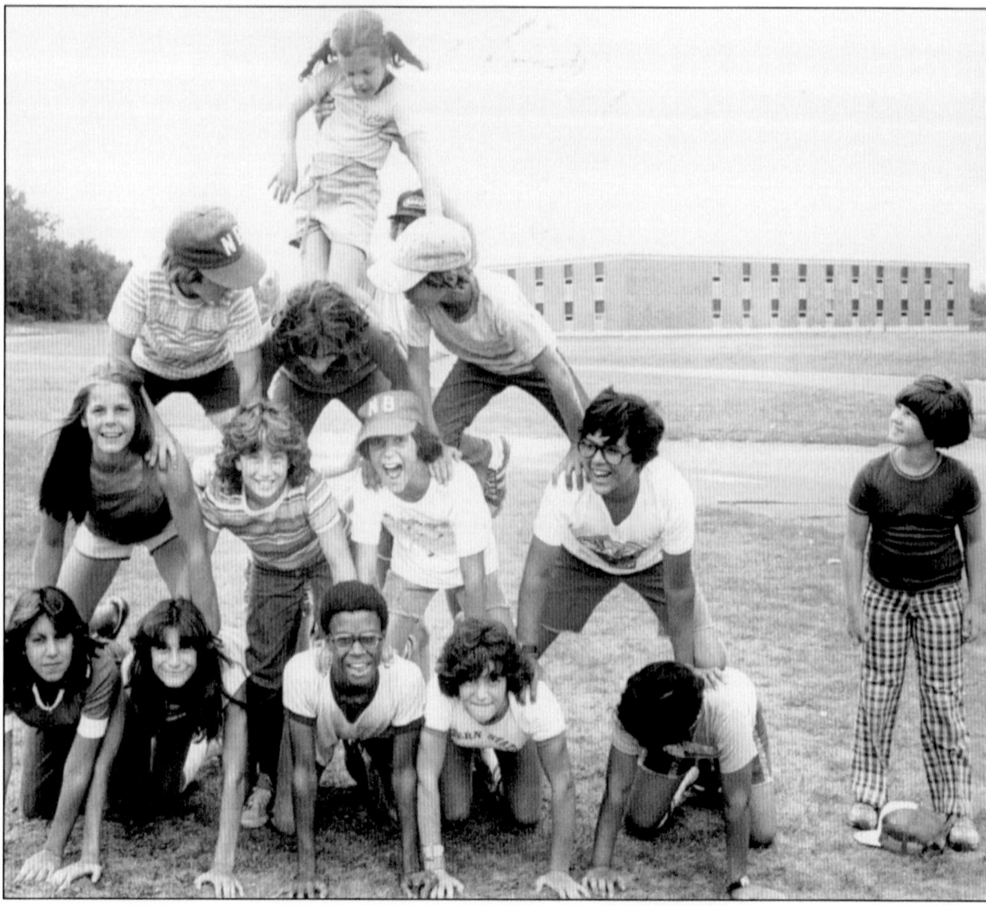

Children at the park and recreation department Summer Playground at North Branford Intermediate School have a good time forming a pyramid. Unfortunately, the participants were not identified. (North Branford Parks and Recreation Department.)

It was goat day at Stanley T. Williams Summer Playground. (North Branford Parks and Recreation Department.)

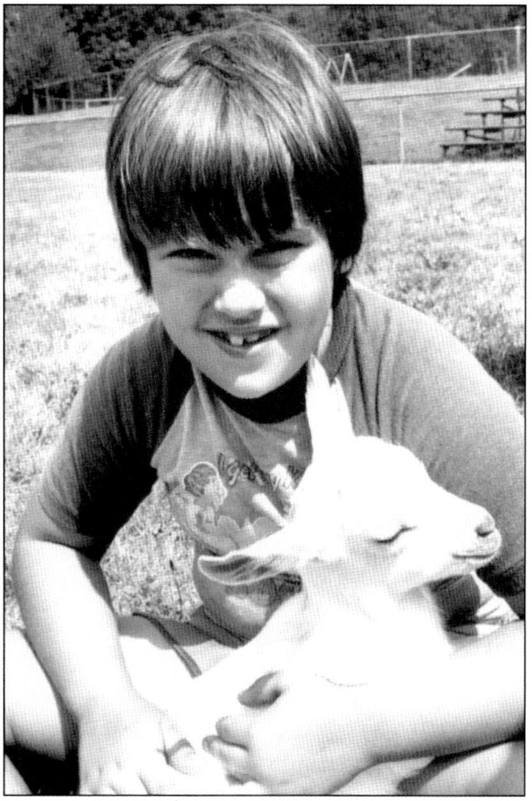

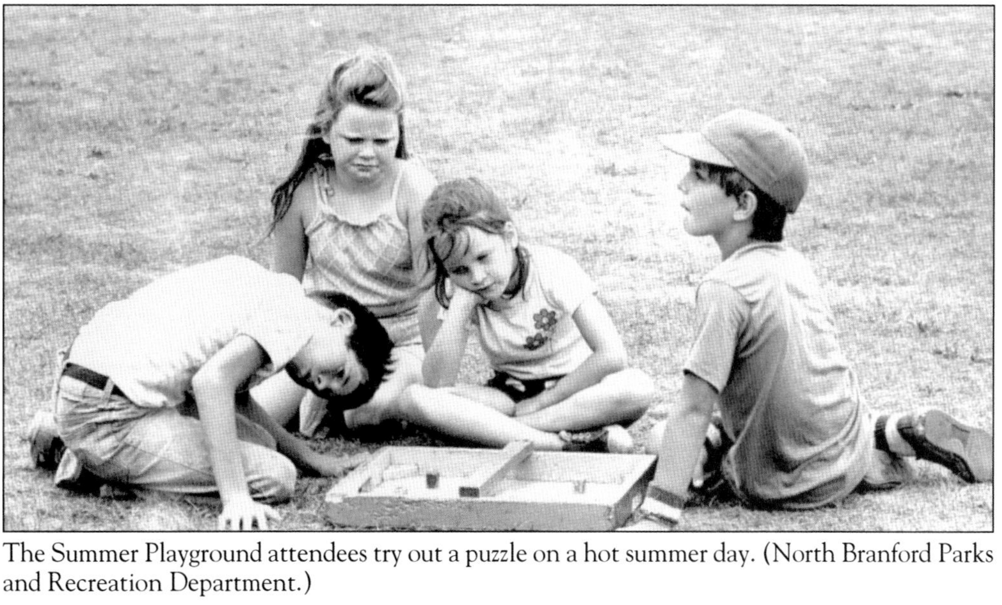

The Summer Playground attendees try out a puzzle on a hot summer day. (North Branford Parks and Recreation Department.)

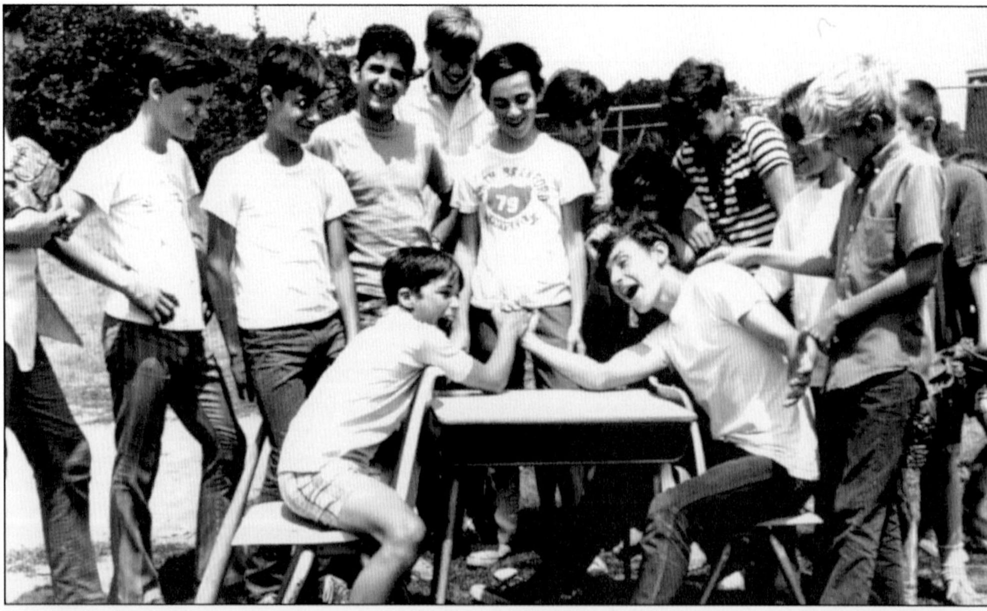

It is an Indian wrestling contest at the Stanley T. Williams School Summer Playground in July 1970. (North Branford Parks and Recreation Department.)

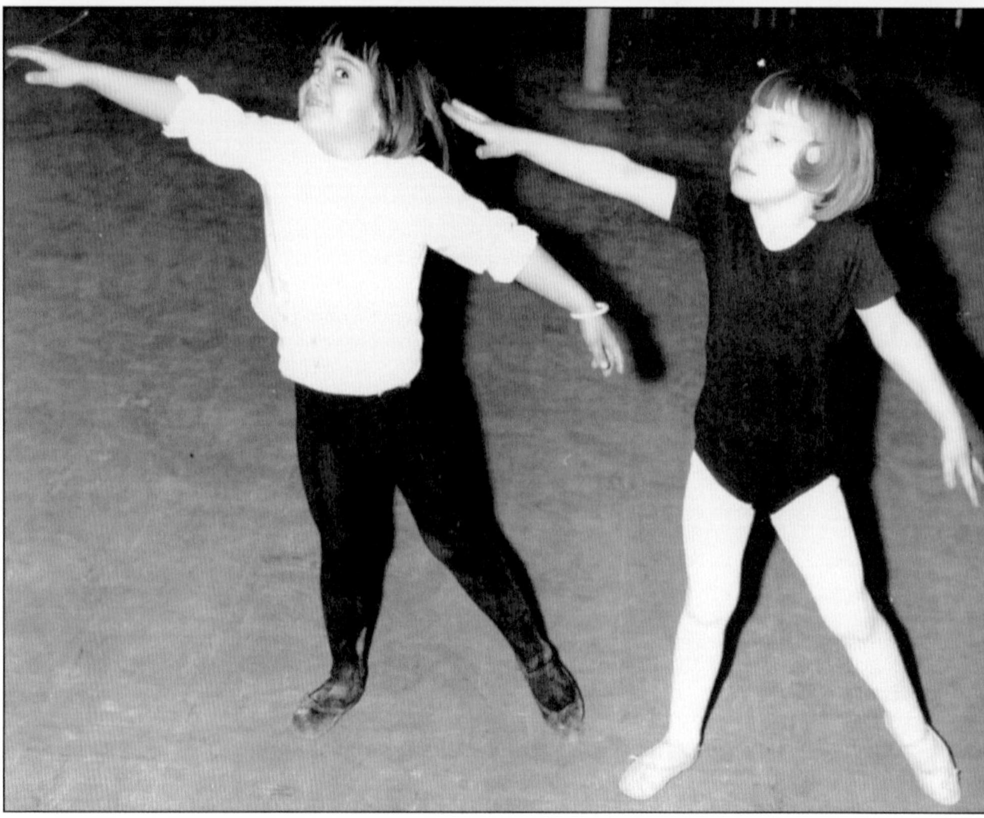

Another program offered by the park and recreation department was ballet lessons for beginners. (North Branford Parks and Recreation Department.)

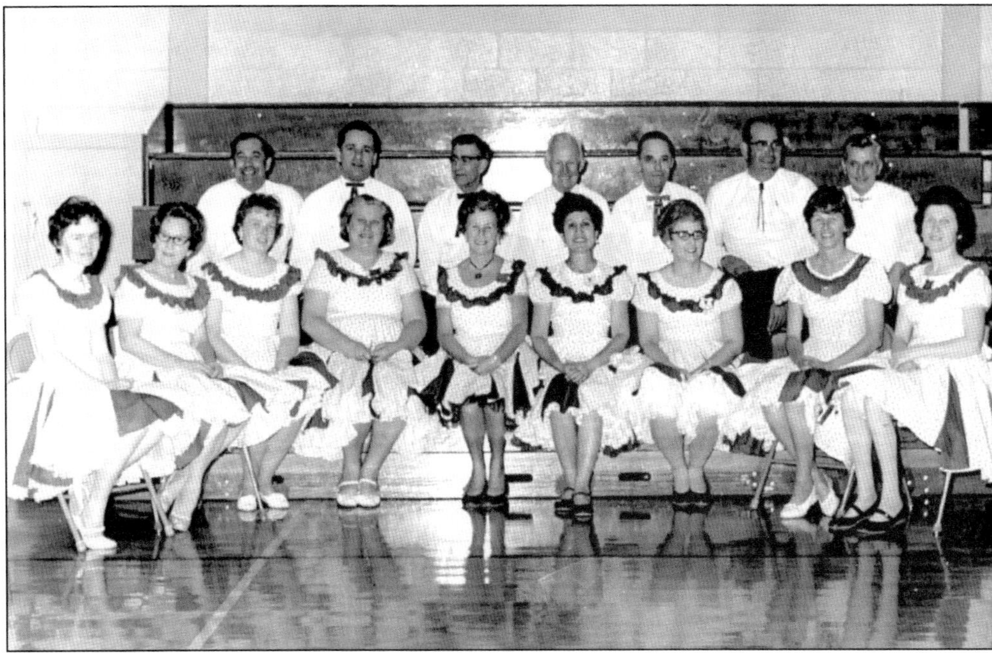

The Belles and Beaus Square Dance Club was sponsored by the park and recreation department. The dancers are not identified in this *c.* 1969 photograph. (North Branford Parks and Recreation Department.)

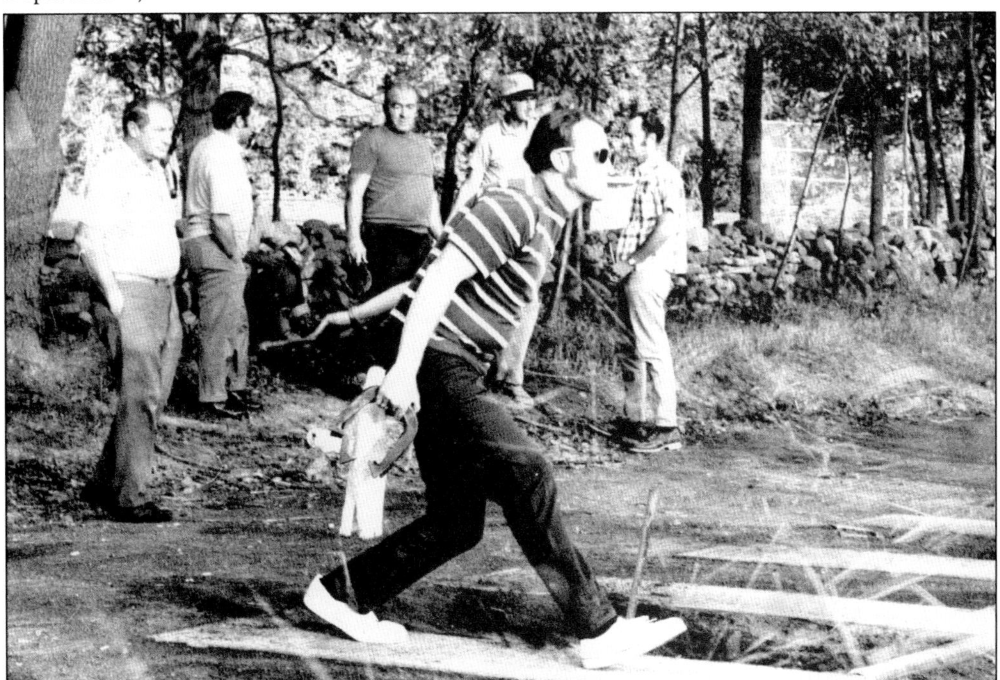

The park and recreation department sponsored a horseshoe league as another of their adult programs, but the players are not identified in this 1971 photograph. The horseshoe pits were located at the Northford Playground. (North Branford Parks and Recreation Department.)

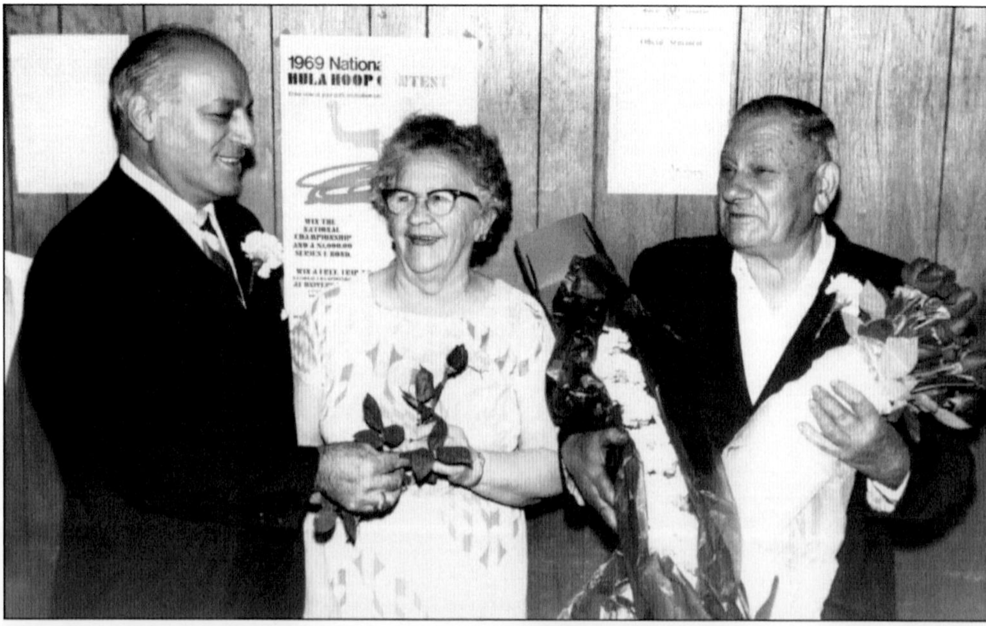

The Over 60 Drop-In Center was one of the earliest programs offered by the recreation department. In this May 1969 photograph, Stephen Lenzi of the Thompson and Lenzi Real Estate Company presents a rose to Katherine Miller, as Tony Marcucio holds the roses and carnations given to all the senior citizens at an anniversary celebration. Lenzi was chairman of the recreation commission. (North Branford Parks and Recreation Department.)

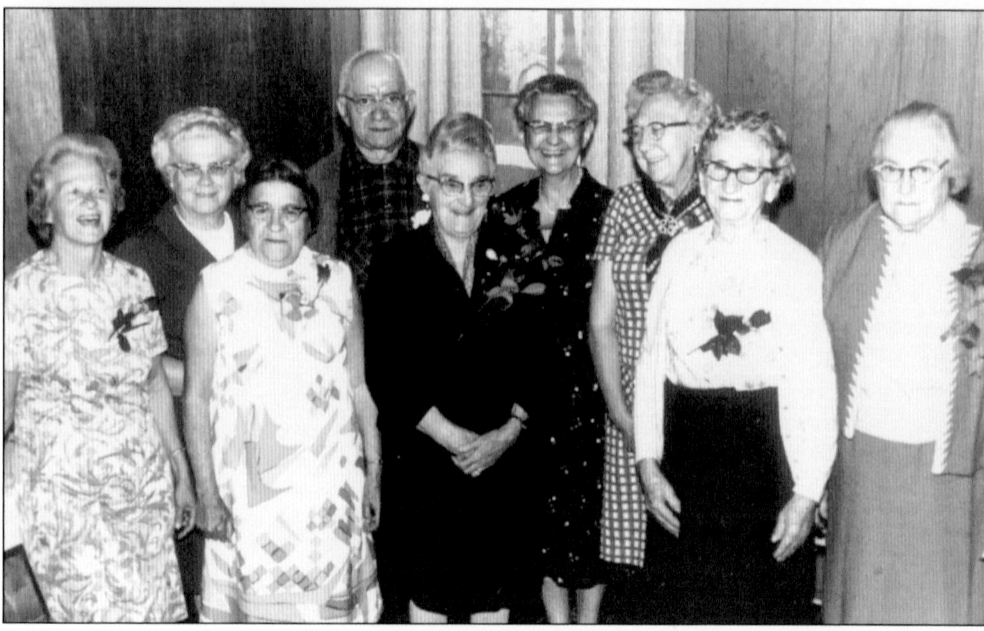

Senior citizens at the Over 60 Drop-In Center at North Branford Hall proudly display their roses and carnations. They are, from left to right as follows: (front row) Ann Fee, Mae Brockett, Minnie Miller, Anna Scholz, and Gertrude Abel; (second row) Irene Cox, John Hyland, Anna Campbell, and Sophie Maloney. The center, now commonly known as the senior center, is still very active today, in 2003. (North Branford Parks and Recreation Department.)

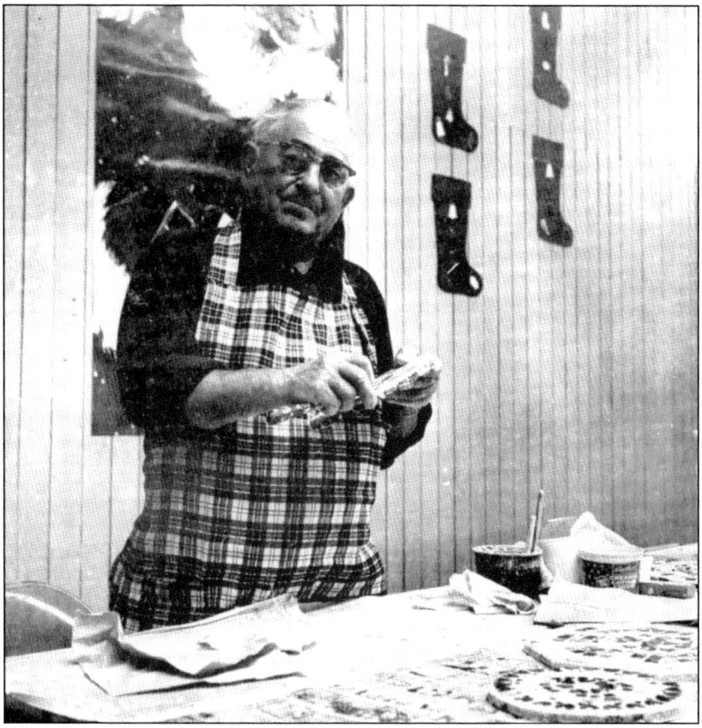

Fiore Rapone creates a mosaic trivet at the Over 60 Drop-In Center as shown in this December 1974 photograph. The senior citizens work throughout the year making items to sell at their fairs. The money realized is used to offset the center activities and other park and recreation department programs. (North Branford Parks and Recreation Department.)

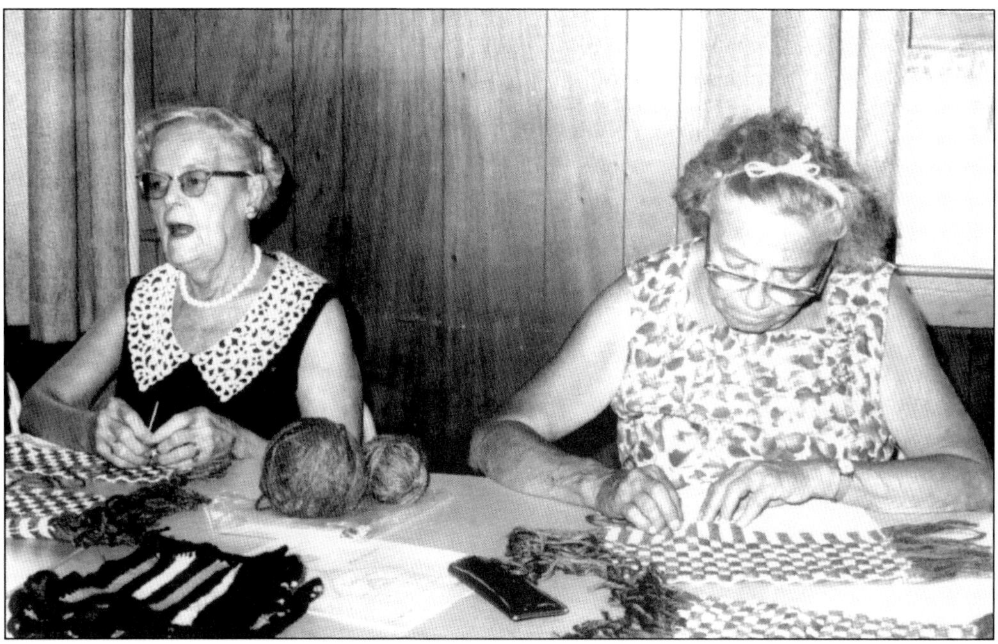

In this 1969 photograph, Julia Fowler and Gladys Patten make woven place mats to sell at the Christmas fair. Senior citizens are picked up at their homes and brought to the center in vans. They visit, play cards or board games, work on craft projects, and participate in exercise sessions and other activities. Several times a year, trips and tours to special destinations are scheduled. (North Branford Parks and Recreation Department.)

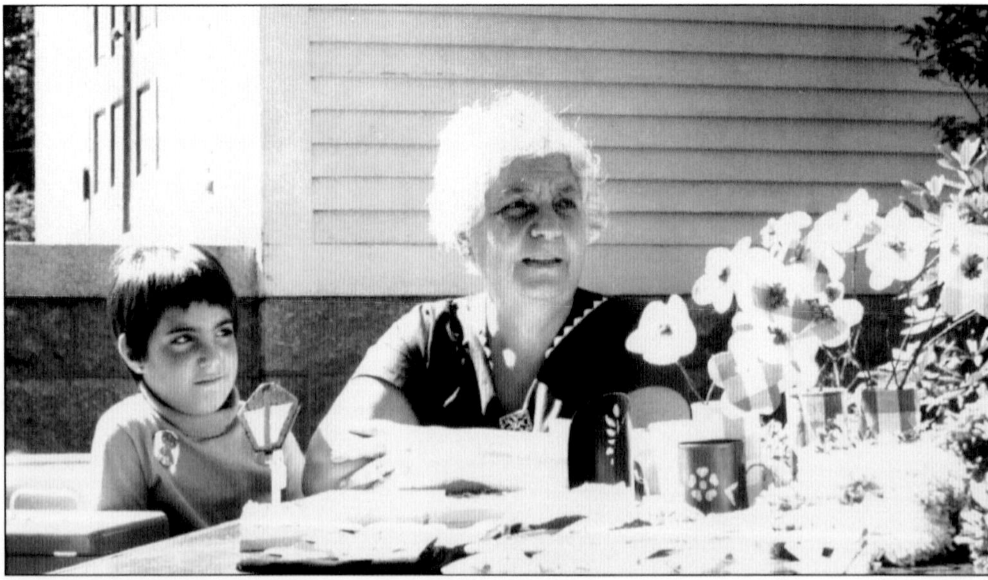

Senior citizen Mary Camarota and her granddaughter, Patricia Carofola, oversee one of the booths at the arts and crafts fair sponsored by the North Branford Parks and Recreation Department and the North Branford Women's Club in September 1970. (North Branford Parks and Recreation Department.)

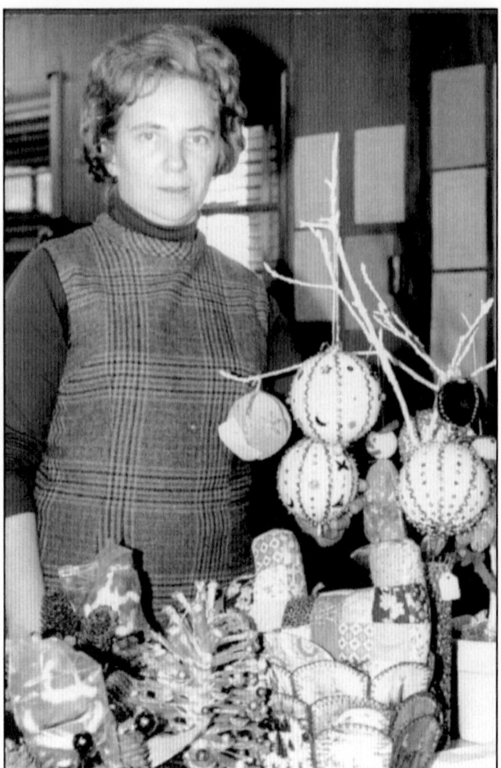

Anna Mae Doody, one of the assistants at the senior center, shows off some of the items to be sold at the November 1970 Christmas fair. Members of both the town's women's clubs assisted at the senior center, and later some became paid part-time employees. (North Branford Parks and Recreation Department.)

Judith Lundberg and Eva Williams dress up for the 1969 Halloween party at the Over 60 Drop-In Center. (North Branford Parks and Recreation Department.)

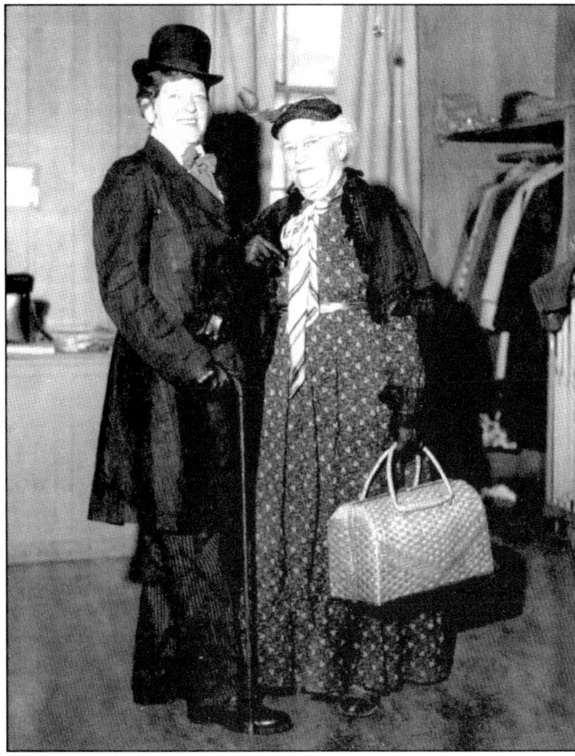

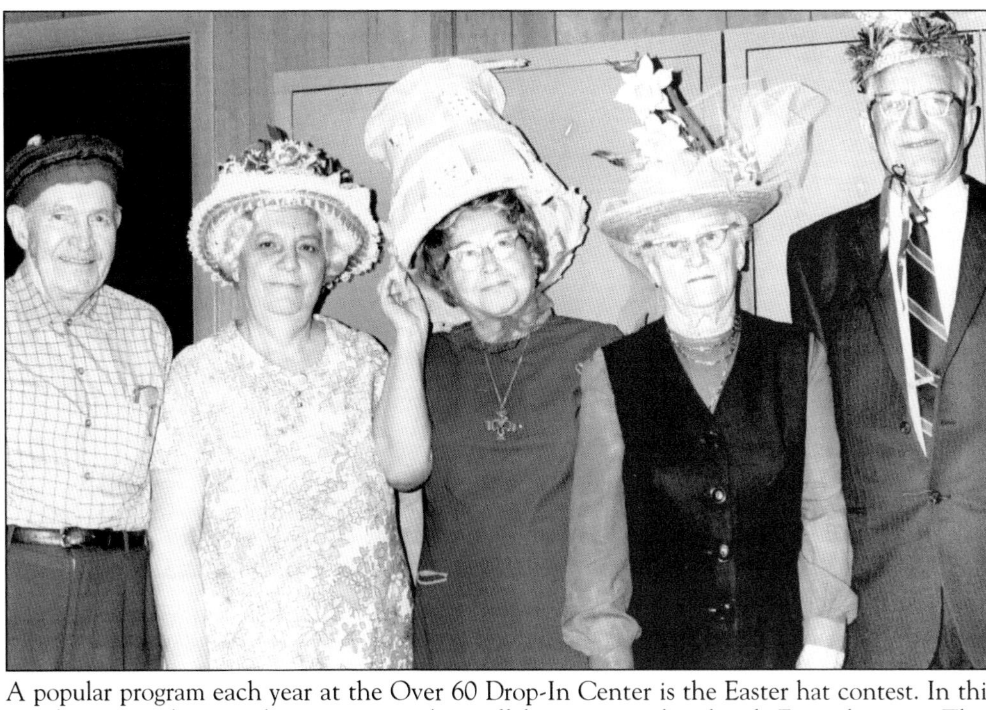

A popular program each year at the Over 60 Drop-In Center is the Easter hat contest. In this April 8, 1971, photograph, participants show off their creative handmade Easter bonnets. They are, from left to right, Willgot Wahlstrom, Mary Camarota, May Traub, Eva Williams, and Ward Marsh. (North Branford Parks and Recreation Department.)

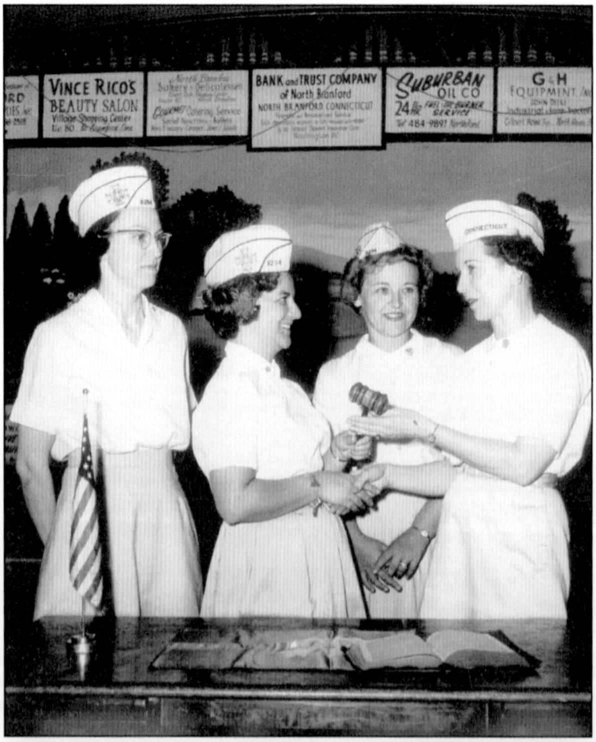

At the May 18, 1965, installation of officers of the Ladies Auxiliary of the Veterans of Foreign Wars, the gavel is handed to the new president. The women shown in this photograph, which was taken in the old North Branford Hall, are, from left to right, Katherine Scalise, Marie Wysocki, Barbara DaCunto, and Eleanor Lloyd. Both the Veterans of Foreign Wars and its Ladies Auxiliary were founded in 1954. (Linda Bunnell.)

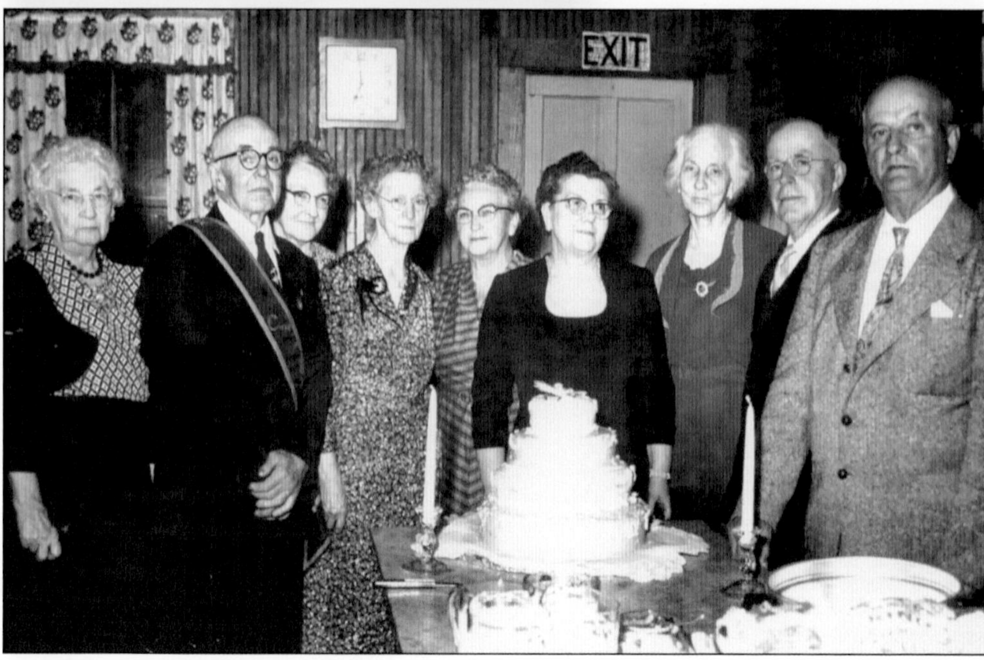

The oldest members of the Totoket Grange No. 83 pose for this photograph at its 50th anniversary celebration in 1956. Pictured from left to right, with the dates they joined the Grange, are Mae Merrick (1881), Charles Linsley (1906), Mrs. C. Oscar Nordberg (1907), Alice Carey (1906), Mrs. Harold Shaw (1910), Lucretia Baily (1906), Mable Bartholomew (1907), George H. Doebrick (1910), and Frank Snow (1906).

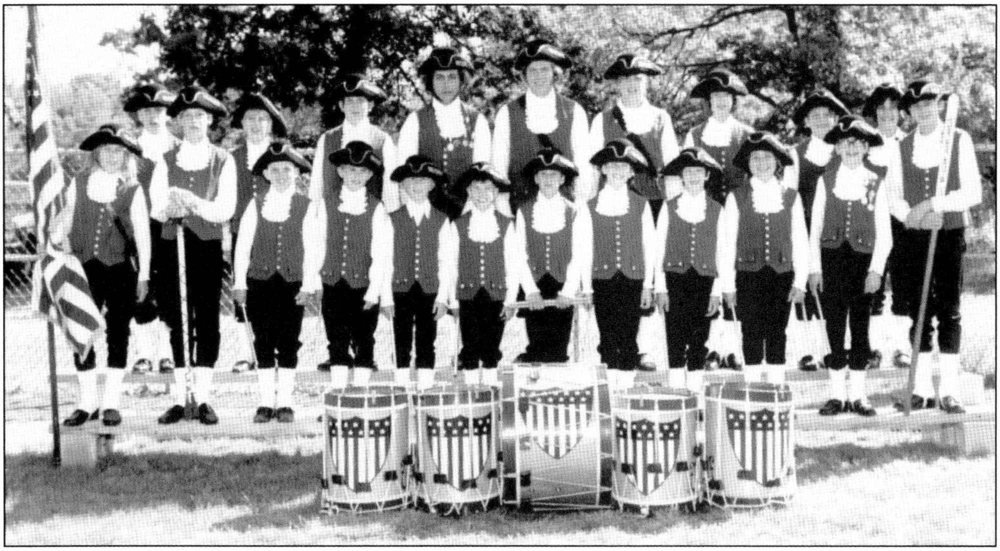

The North Branford Minutemen, a fife-and-drum corps, was organized in 1966 through the efforts of David Hall. Pictured in this June 1972 photograph taken at the Old Saybrook Muster are, from left to right, the following: (front row), Todd Thorpe, Phil Mason, Stanley Sheades, Greg Bucher, Mike Halloran, Ronny Mason, John Carafeno, Gary Mason, Jeff Bauer, John Calamita, Chris Bauer, and Mark Carafeno; (back row) John Cudgma. Eric Lucas, Greg Price, Doug Daddio, Mike Severino, Doug Lehr, Bruce Taylor, Steve Cudgma, and Scott Taylor. (Louise Mason.)

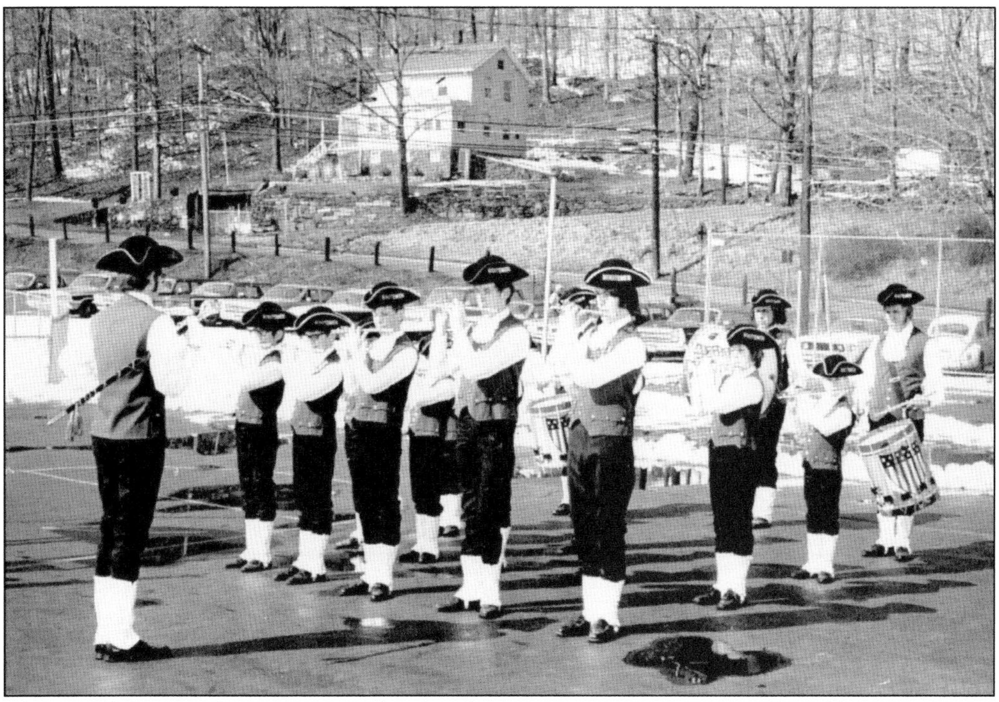

The North Branford Minutemen play for the opening ceremonies for the All-America City celebration on the basketball courts in front of the administration building in 1971. The town hall was built on this site in 1979. (Totoket Historical Society.)

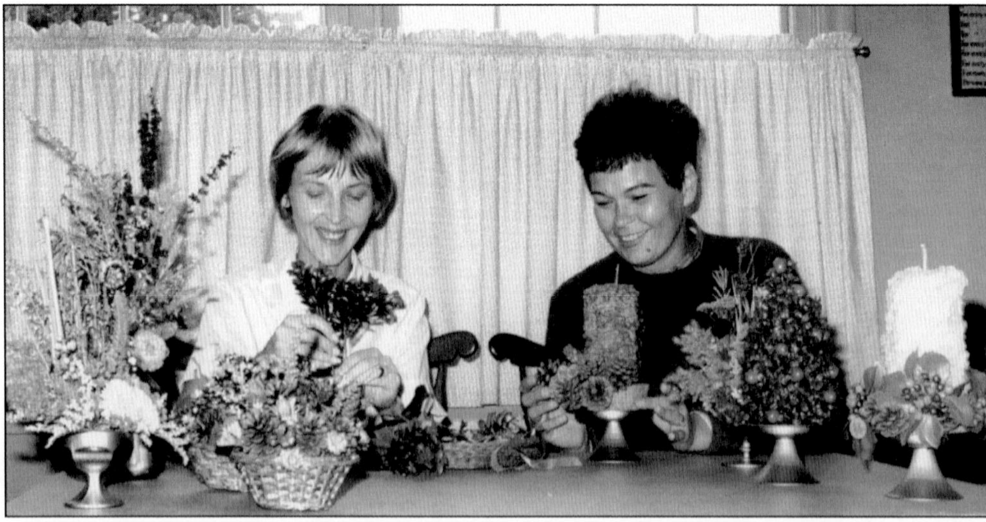

The North Branford Garden Club was organized in 1965. In this 1969 photograph, Mrs. Michael Tarantino (left) and Mrs. James McNamara (right) work on dried flower arrangements to sell at their Christmas craft fair. (Totoket Historical Society.)

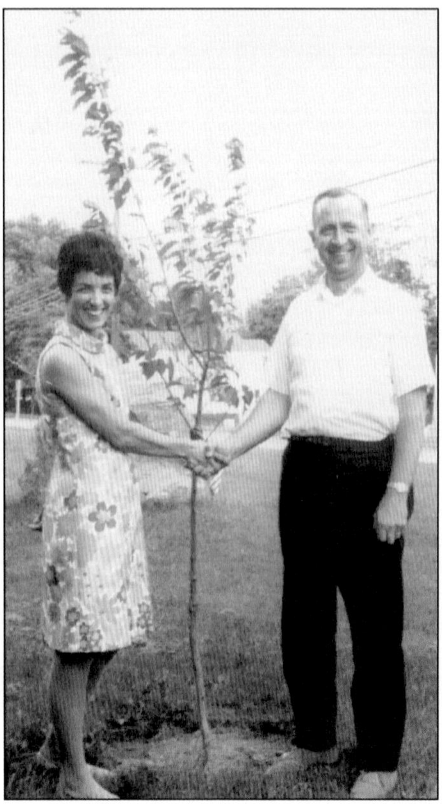

Sally Grogan of the North Branford Garden Club and Patrick Miller of the North Branford Congregational Church show off the cherry trees newly planted on the green in July 1968. The beautification of the town green was a joint effort of the two organizations; they followed a landscape plan by landscape architect Rudy Favretti. (Totoket Historical Society.)

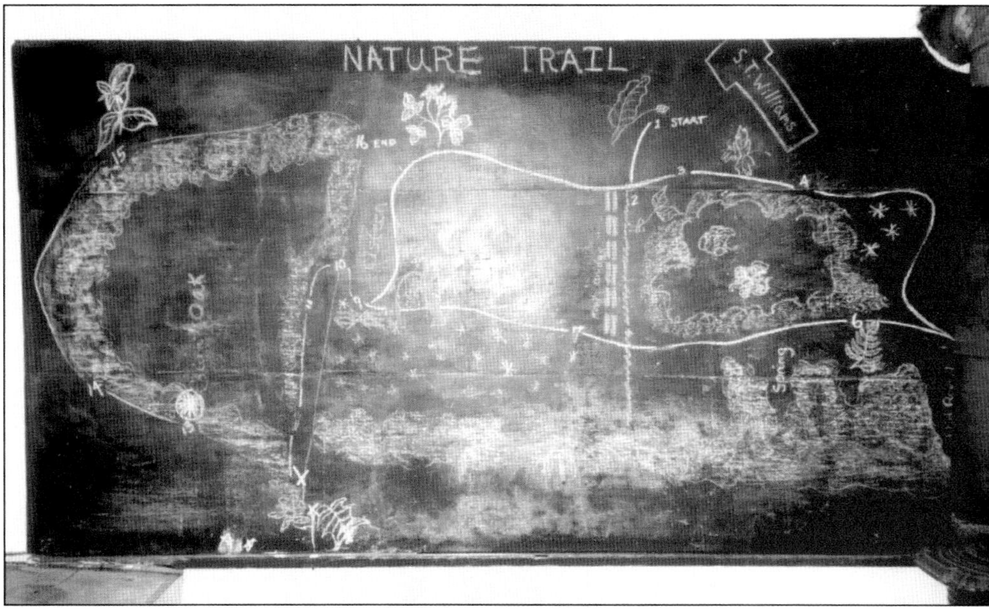

As one of their projects, the Northford Garden Club created a nature trail behind the Stanley T. Williams School. School students and youth and adult groups were invited to visit its various nature stations. The plan was sketched on the Little Red School House's blackboard as a backdrop for a flower show and remained there until the club disbanded in the 1990s. The club was founded in 1961 with 26 members. (Totoket Historical Society.)

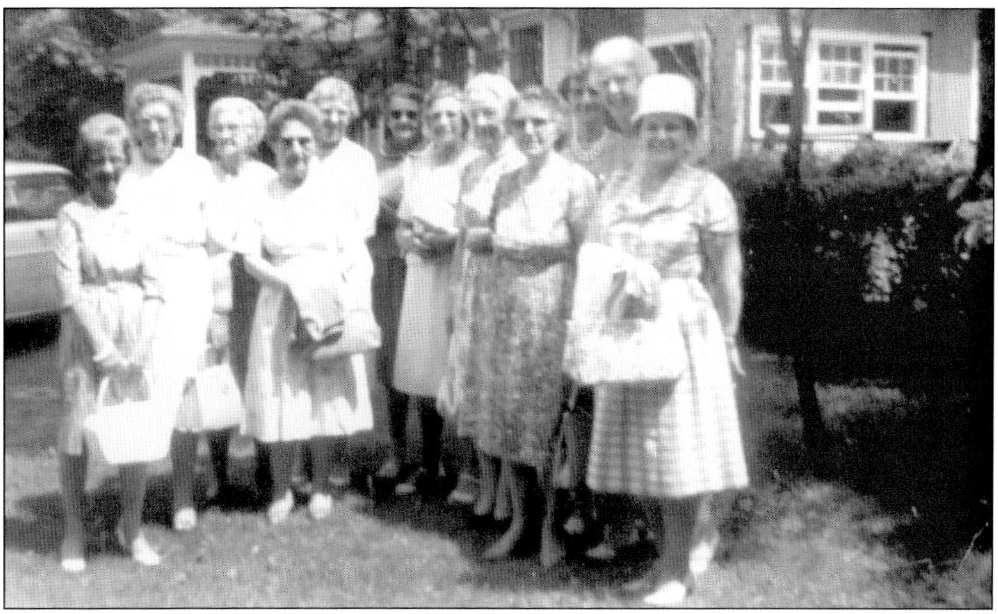

The North Branford Congregational Church Ladies Sewing Society is the town's oldest women's organization, established in 1877. Here, the ladies gather at the Johnny Cake Inn in Ivoryton for their annual dinner outing. Included in the photograph are Edie Barker, Hazel Hill, Carrie Holabird, Emma Griswold, Eloise Smith, Nettie Chipman, Mae Goodwin, Marion Rose, Edith Harrison, and Beatrice Cook. The 1966 photograph was taken by Lucy Holabird Snow. (North Branford Congregational Church.)

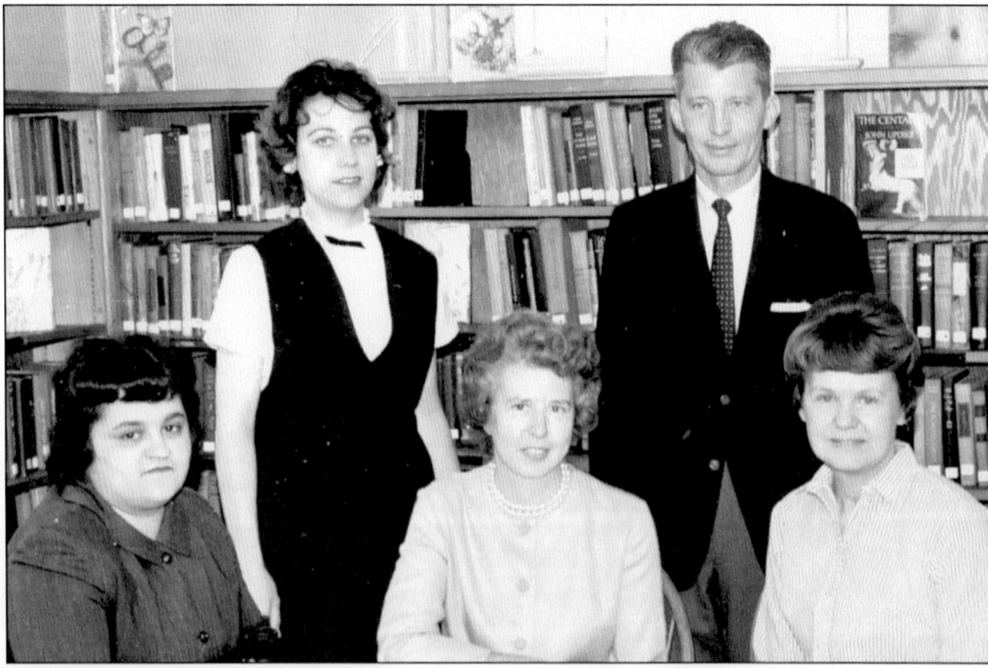

The North Branford Women's Club was instrumental in the formation of the North Branford Scholarship Association in 1962. It was incorporated the following year and has raised thousands of dollars and given scholarships to hundreds of high school graduates. The scholarship association officers shown in this *c.* 1965 photograph are, from left to right, Lillian Deno, Frances Beaumont, Dorothy Roberts, Charles Benson, and Maryann Ryder. (Totoket Historical Society.)

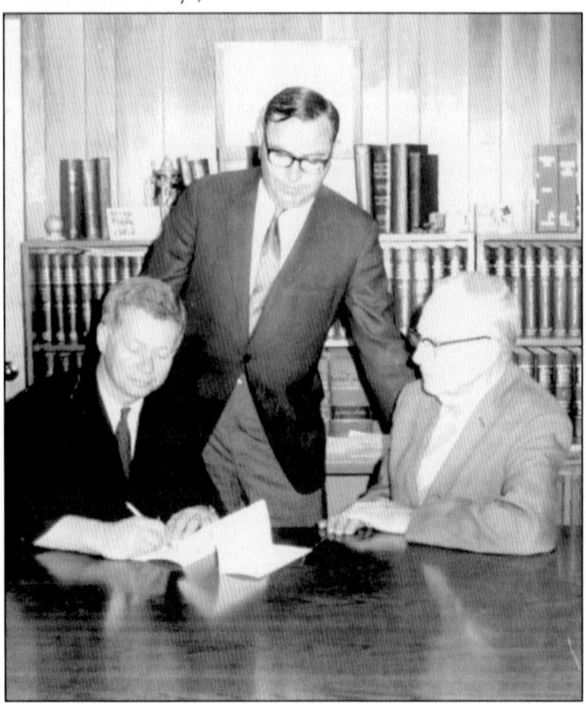

The North Branford Land Conservation Trust was created in 1968 at the instigation of the conservation commission as a way to preserve land in its natural state forever. In this photograph, developer Harvey C. Anderson (left) donates to the trust its first parcel of land located off Echo Circle in the Whispering Hills subdivision. Accepting the deed are treasurer John Calcagni (center) and president Herbert Lunt. (Totoket Historical Society.)

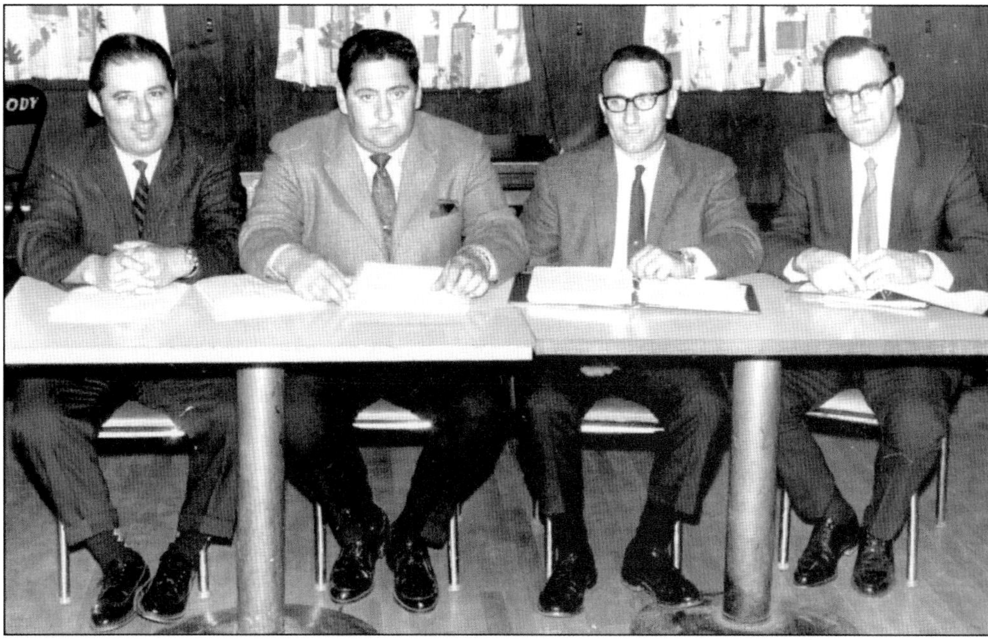

Another organization still functioning in 2003 is the North Branford Slow Pitch League, which was formed in the early 1960s. The officers of the league in May 1969 were, from left to right, treasurer Angelo Frione, vice president Anthony Farino, president Leo Tancreti, and secretary Thomas Slater. (Totoket Historical Society.)

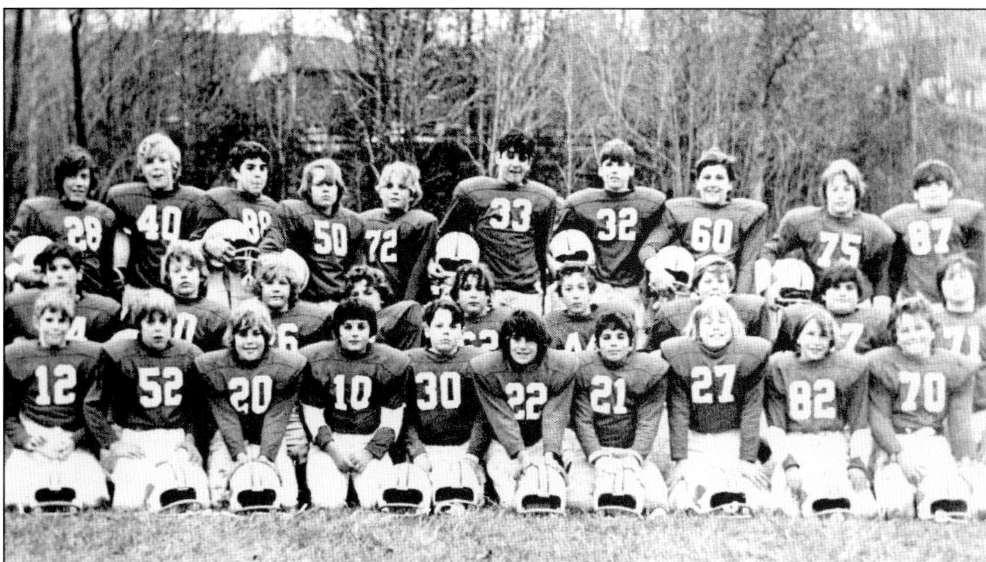

Midget Football players pose for this 1972 photograph. They are, from left to right, as follows: (front row) Jeff Barton, Tommy Fair, Mike DePaul, Arnie Cestari, Billy Jacques, Mike Esposito, Dino Esposito, J.R. Fiondella, Tommy Morris, and Bruce Johnson; (middle row) Bob Beech, Kenny Zemke, unidentified, Mike Torniero, Bob Cotter, Steve Burdick, John Grumbeck, Donnie Marx, and Bob Beattie; (back row) Mike Doman, Danny Grunbeck, Jim Kenny, Scott Sherban, David Grumbeck, Jimmy Gleason, Kevin Dempsey, Tommy Jones, Jack Cotter, and Billy Beattie. (Grace Marx.)

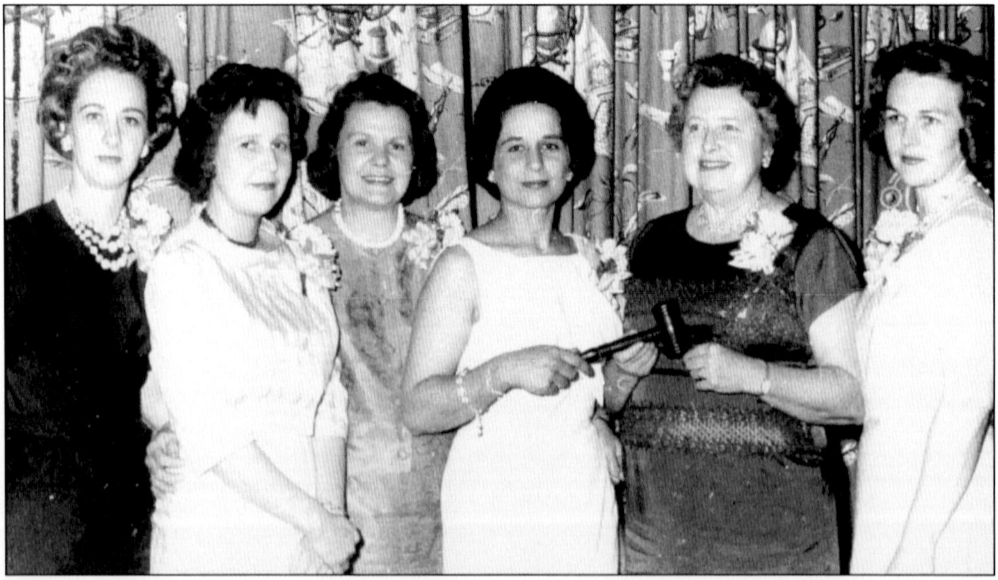

The North Branford Women's Club was organized in 1961 as an outgrowth of the Welcome Wagon. The club is committed to community service, and over the years, it has helped and supported schools, libraries, recreational programs, hospitals, beautification and conservation efforts, and much more. These officers, from left to right, were installed in May 1964: Joanne Jeppesen, Rosemarie Priestly, Betty Ryder, Jean Bright as president, Mary Gately of the Federation of Women's Clubs, and Edith Matson. (North Branford Women's Club.)

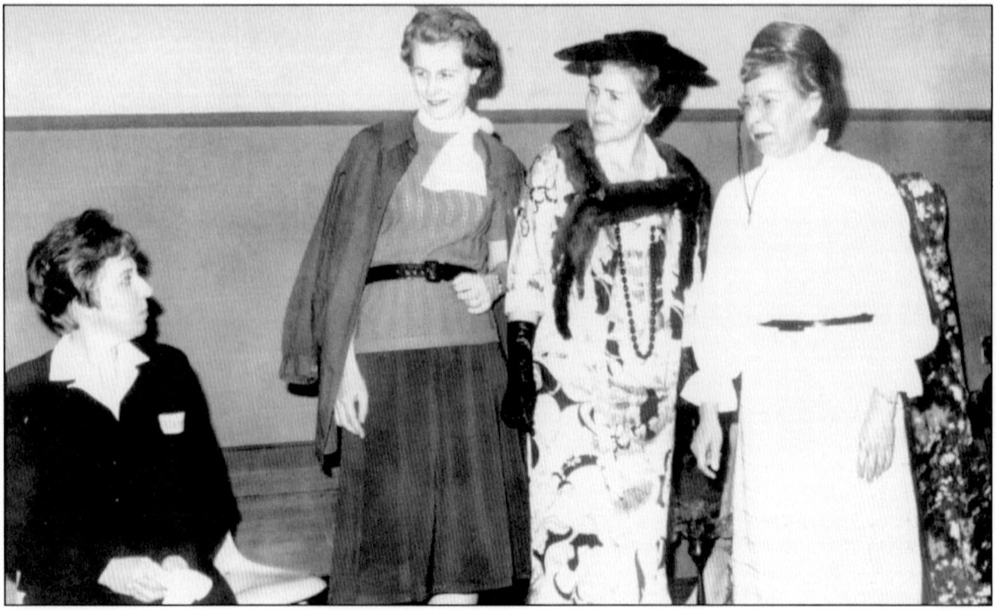

The North Branford Women's Club, still in existence, holds monthly meetings with interesting programs for the 10 winter months of the year. During the early years, women rarely worked outside the home and had more time to spend in volunteer activities. Some of those early activities were a chorale group and a drama group. In 1968, members of the club participated in a play, "Little Prison." The actresses portrayed here, from left to right, are Betty Moore, Marilyn O'Connor, Joyce St. John, and Sonny Dayton. (North Branford Women's Club.)

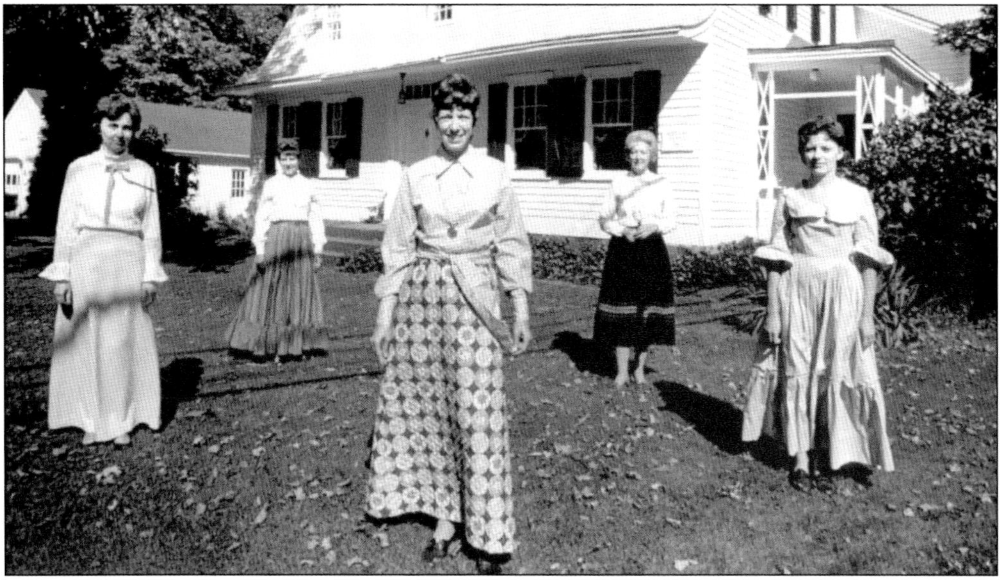

Many special events were held to raise money for various charities and community projects. In October 1971, the North Branford Women's Club sponsored a house tour, featuring several old houses in town. Club members pose in front of the Ruth Beers Arnold house (now the Reynolds-Beers House museum) for a publicity photograph. They are, from left to right, June Strawson, Marilyn Janeway, Ursula Spath, Irene Talburtt, and Sheila Juniver. (North Branford Women's Club.)

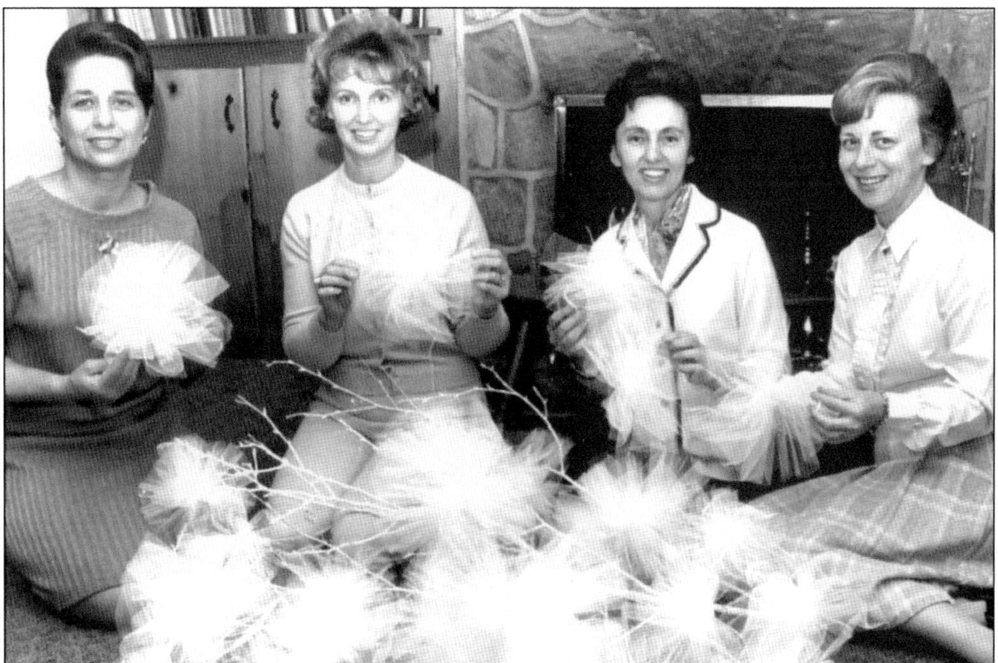

The social committee of the North Branford Women's Club prepares decorations for the December 15, 1967, Sno-Ball at Jean Bright's house. Seen here are, from left to right, Jean Bright, Charlotte Tietjen, June Strawson, and Janet Xeller. (North Branford Women's Club.)

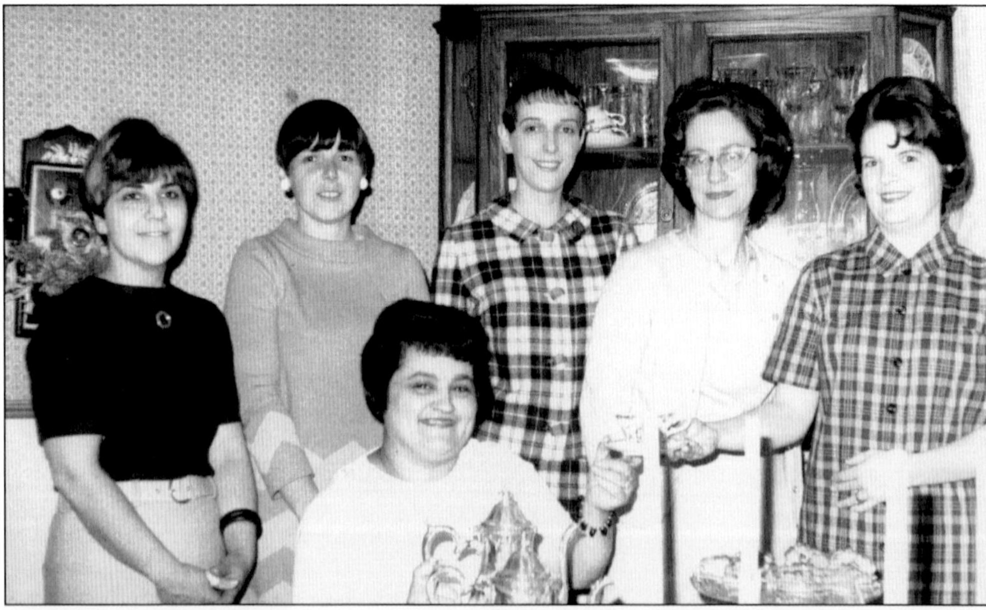

The Northford Women's Club was organized April 18, 1963, with a membership of 58 women. This club is dedicated to community service. The officers installed in June 1967 are pictured here. Standing from left to right are Rosalie Lowenbaum as first vice president, Rose Marie Sullivan as corresponding secretary, Jane Haskell as treasurer, and Marilyn Johnston as secretary. Seated is Lillian Deno as president. (Northford Women's Club.)

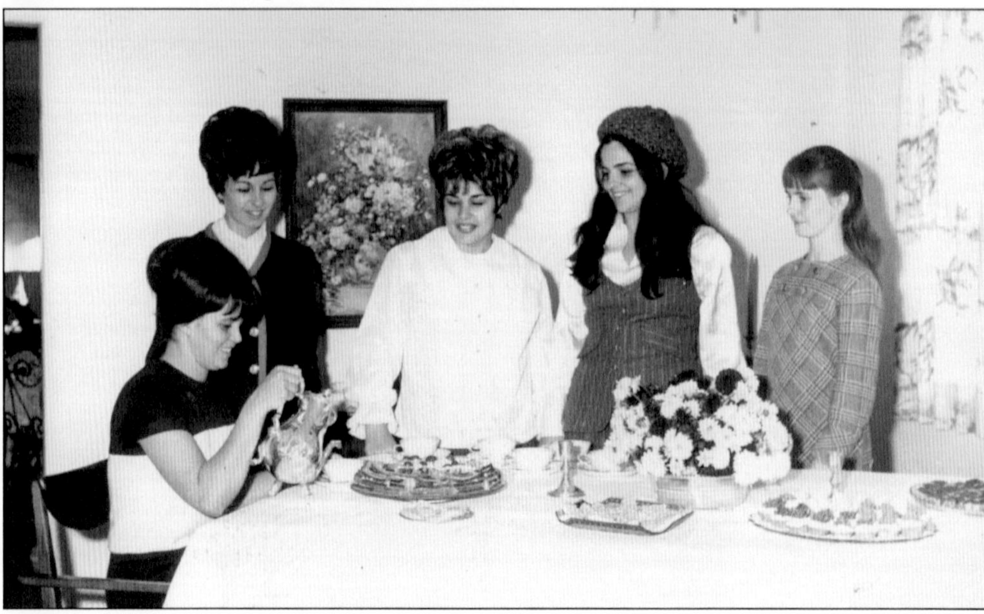

Three new members of the Northford Women's Club were welcomed at a tea in October 1969. Shown here standing from left to right are Mary Beth Buckoff and new members Terry Cappello, Bonnie Sulkowski, and Mary Tamulevich. Pat Owens is pouring the tea. The club has supported many community programs, such as Girl Scouts, Little League, vision screening, library programs, scholarship association, public park beautification, and the Youth and the Law Program. (Northford Women's Club.)

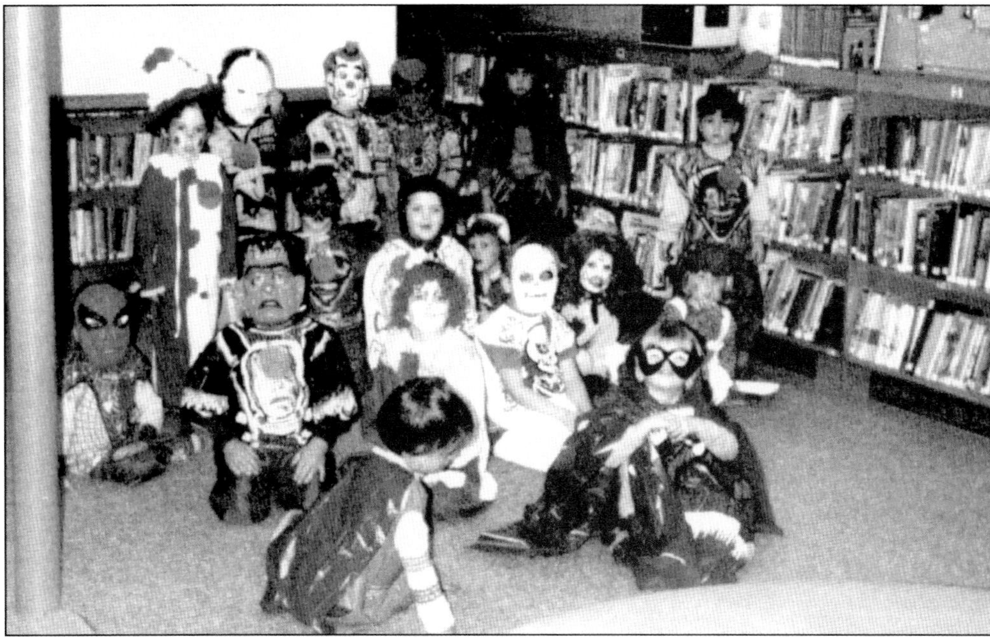

The women's clubs at both ends of town have conducted a story hour for preschoolers at the libraries. In this photograph, the Northford Women's Club provides a Halloween party for the story hour children at the Edward Smith Memorial Library in October 1979. (Northford Women's Club.)

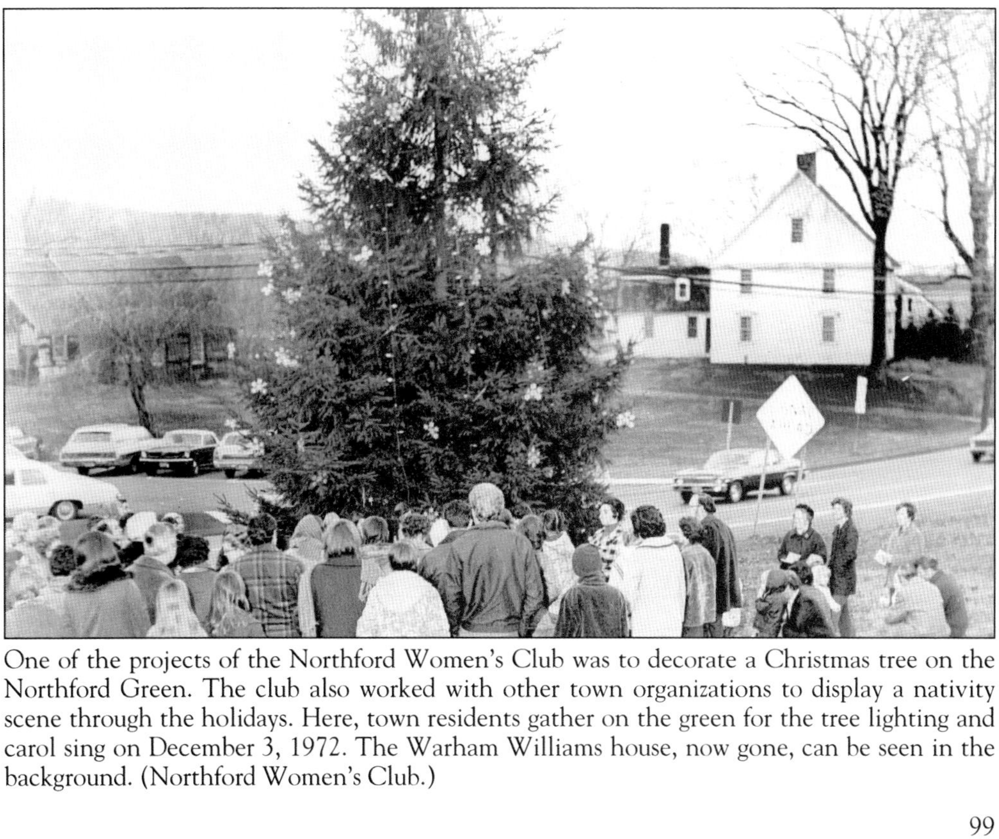

One of the projects of the Northford Women's Club was to decorate a Christmas tree on the Northford Green. The club also worked with other town organizations to display a nativity scene through the holidays. Here, town residents gather on the green for the tree lighting and carol sing on December 3, 1972. The Warham Williams house, now gone, can be seen in the background. (Northford Women's Club.)

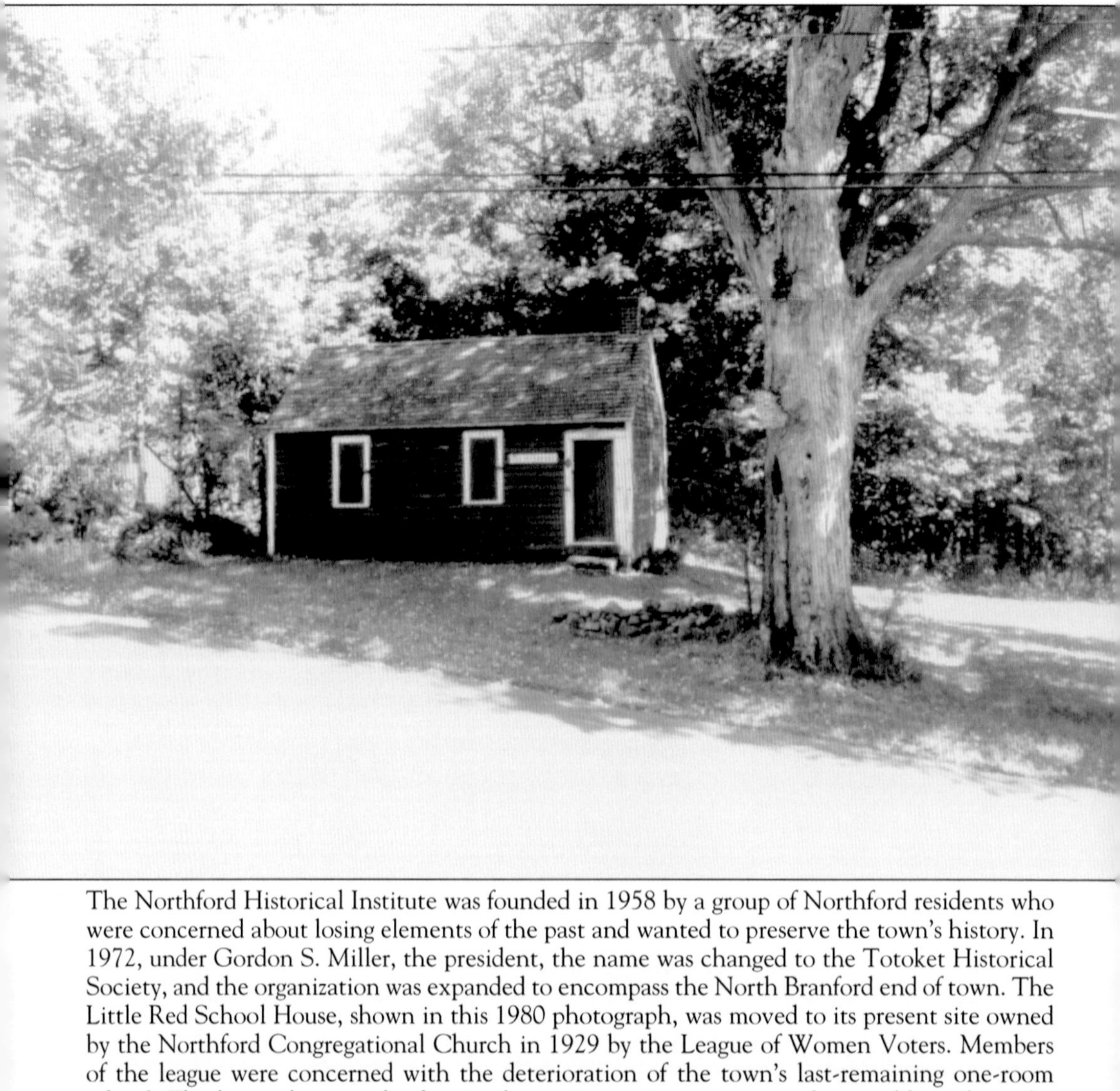

The Northford Historical Institute was founded in 1958 by a group of Northford residents who were concerned about losing elements of the past and wanted to preserve the town's history. In 1972, under Gordon S. Miller, the president, the name was changed to the Totoket Historical Society, and the organization was expanded to encompass the North Branford end of town. The Little Red School House, shown in this 1980 photograph, was moved to its present site owned by the Northford Congregational Church in 1929 by the League of Women Voters. Members of the league were concerned with the deterioration of the town's last-remaining one-room school. The league became the first in the nation to incorporate so they could purchase the old building. It was used as a library from 1932 to 1957, when the Edward Smith Memorial Library was built, and the old school reverted to the ownership of the church. In 1966, the church leased the building to the historical society, which maintains it as a museum. (Totoket Historical Society.)

One of the Totoket Historical Society's early goals was to publish a written history of the town. Society members researched local history, and in 1978, persuaded Dr. Herbert Miller to incorporate all the information into a comprehensive town history. The society raised money through auctions and antique shows to underwrite the publication. Here, Esther Smith and Lydia Davis look over some items donated for the 1968 auction. (Totoket Historical Society.)

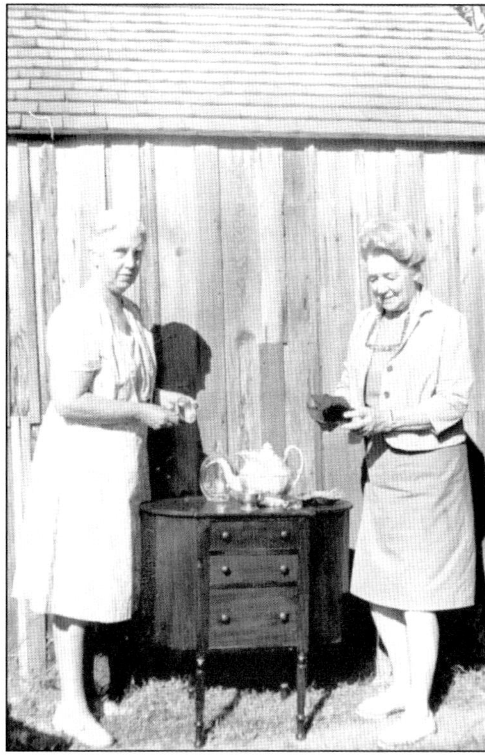

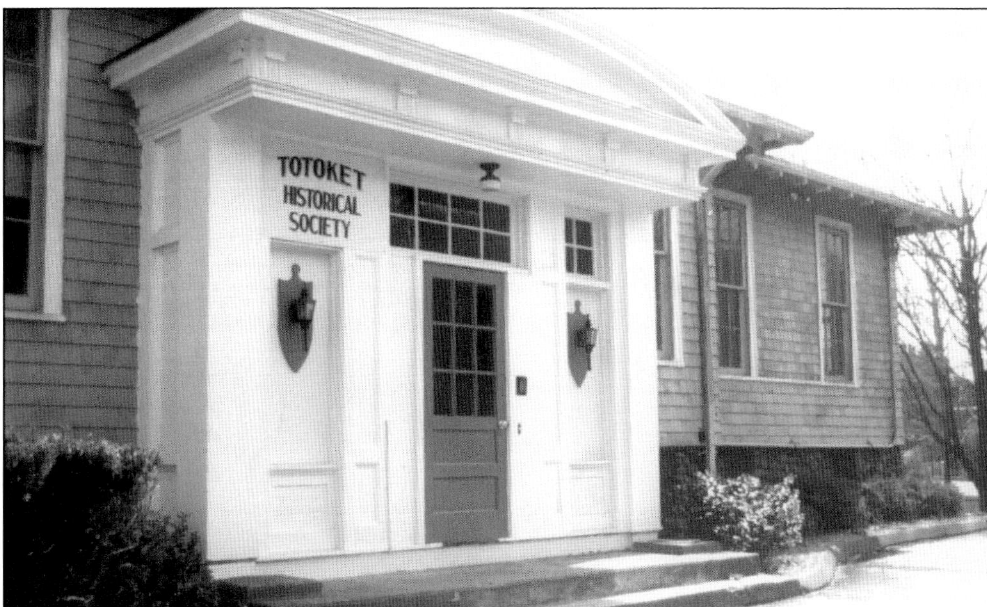

When the new town hall was occupied in 1979, the Totoket Historical Society leased the old administration building to store and display their collection. For the first time, the society had a home. The society maintained the building for several years, roofing and painting it. In 1997, the historical society moved into the town-owned Reynolds-Beers House on Library Place. (Totoket Historical Society.)

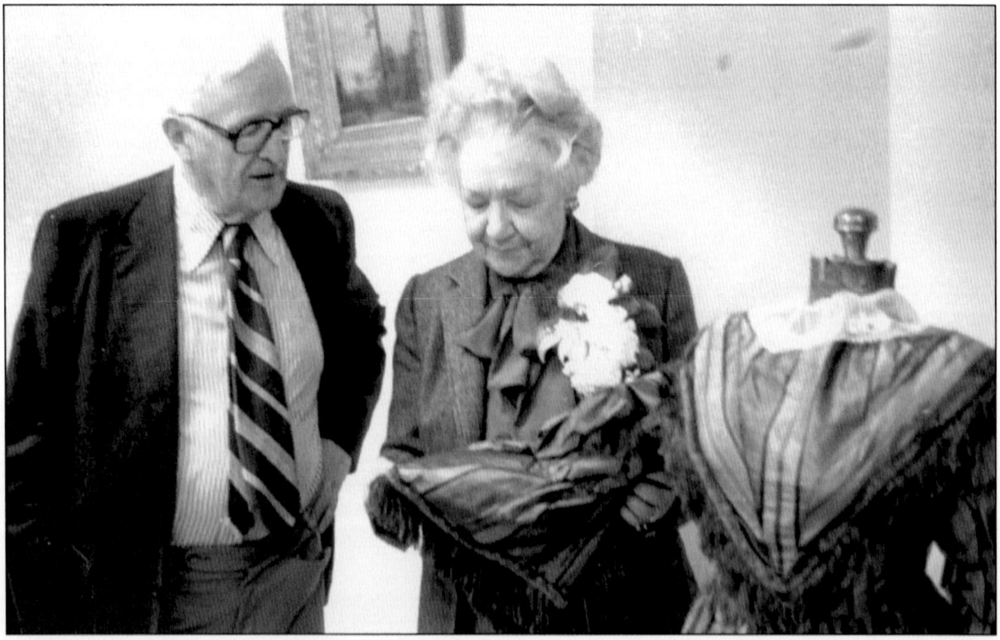

In this 1981 photograph, Lydia Davis, a charter member of the Totoket Historical Society, shows a dress from the Civil War period to Dr. Herbert C. Miller, president of the society. Davis donated this costume and a large amount of textiles and other items to the society. Dr. Miller is the author of *The History of North Branford and Northford*. (Totoket Historical Society.)

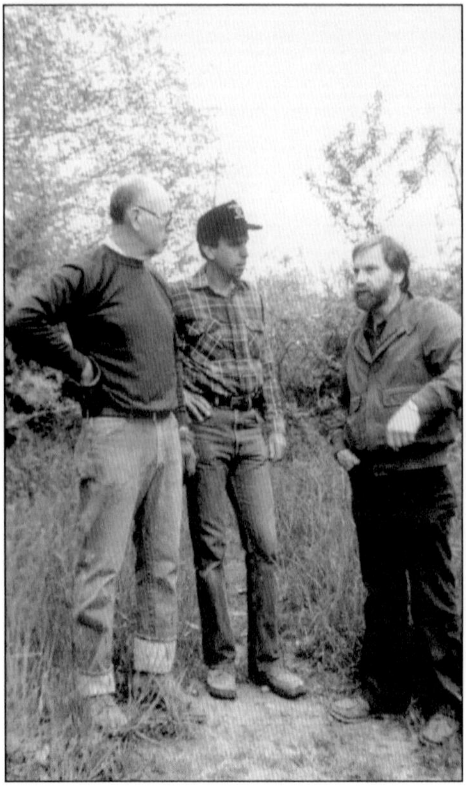

Gordon McGuire and Steve Zehrlinger, members of the North Branford Rotary Club, meet with Bob Gregan, former chairman of the conservation commission, to discuss making the 77-acre Branford River property—purchased in 1974 from the New Haven Water Company—into a bicentennial park. Gregan, a landscape architect, drew up a plan for the property that later became North Farms Park. The rotary club built a pavilion there in 1988. (E. Robert Gregan.)

Seven

Celebrations and Uncommon Events

In the years between 1950 and 1981, several celebrations on a national, state, and local level occurred. In 1976, the nation celebrated 200 years of independence. North Branford rejoiced at being named an All-America City in 1971. Local churches and civic organizations celebrated special anniversaries. During this time period, there were some events that stand out in the memories of those who witnessed them. A few of these special events and celebrations have already been mentioned in this book; the following photographs portray some of the others.

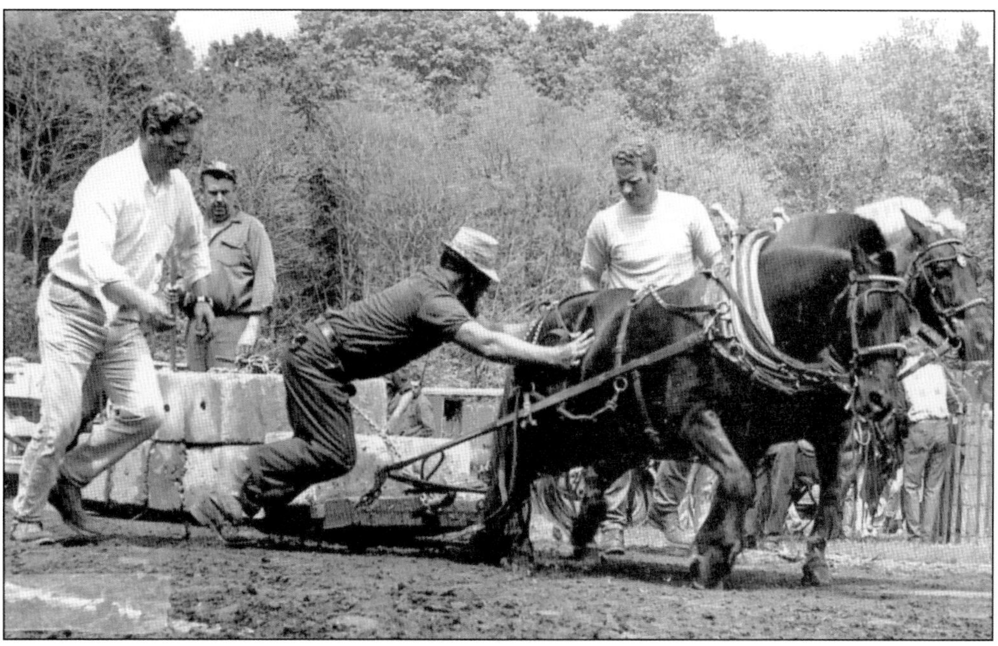

The Troiano brothers sponsored a pony pull at Worthen Field, an athletic field located on Forest Road (Route 22) below the trap rock quarry, to benefit the recreation department. The field is now a drainage pond for Tilcon. In this May 22, 1972, photograph, Ed Wall Jr., Sammy Troiano, and Jerry Wall urge their pony team to pull the weighted sled to victory as Owen Cole watches in the background. (North Branford Parks and Recreation Department.)

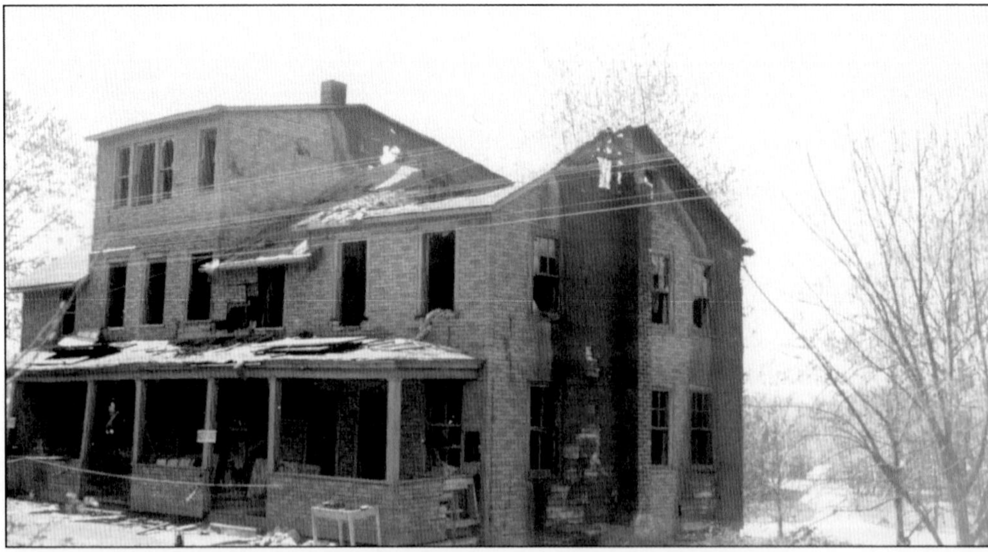

Three small children died in the fire that occurred here on May 5, 1950. It started in the basement apartment of a six-family tenement house when the family retired, leaving burners on the kitchen stove burning low. At about 6:15 a.m. Raymond D'Amico awoke to smoke, and shortly thereafter, flames burst through the roof. The fireproof shingling and all-out efforts of the volunteer firemen prevented the Quarry Road structure from burning to the ground. (Barbara Amatrudo.)

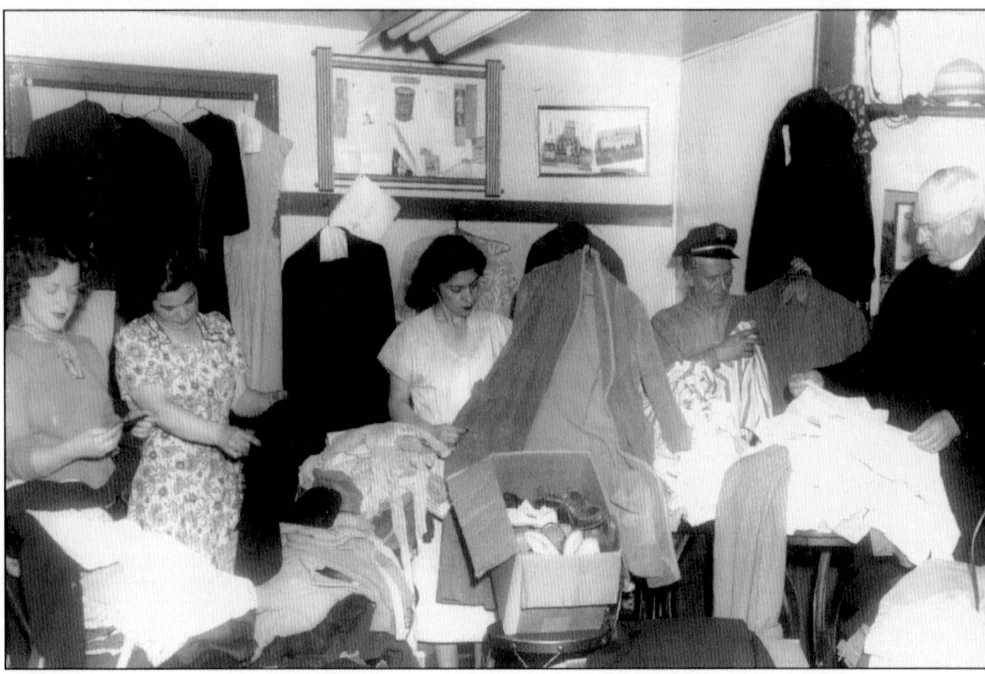

Donations for the victims of the Quarry Road apartment house fire were collected at Amatrudo's Service Station on Route 80. The tenement house that burnt was located between Quarry Road (now an interior road at Tilcon) and Route 80. Pictured here, from left to right, are an unidentified woman, Angelena Amatrudo, Rose Lanzo, Michael Amatrudo, and Rev. Francis Smith. (Barbara Amatrudo.)

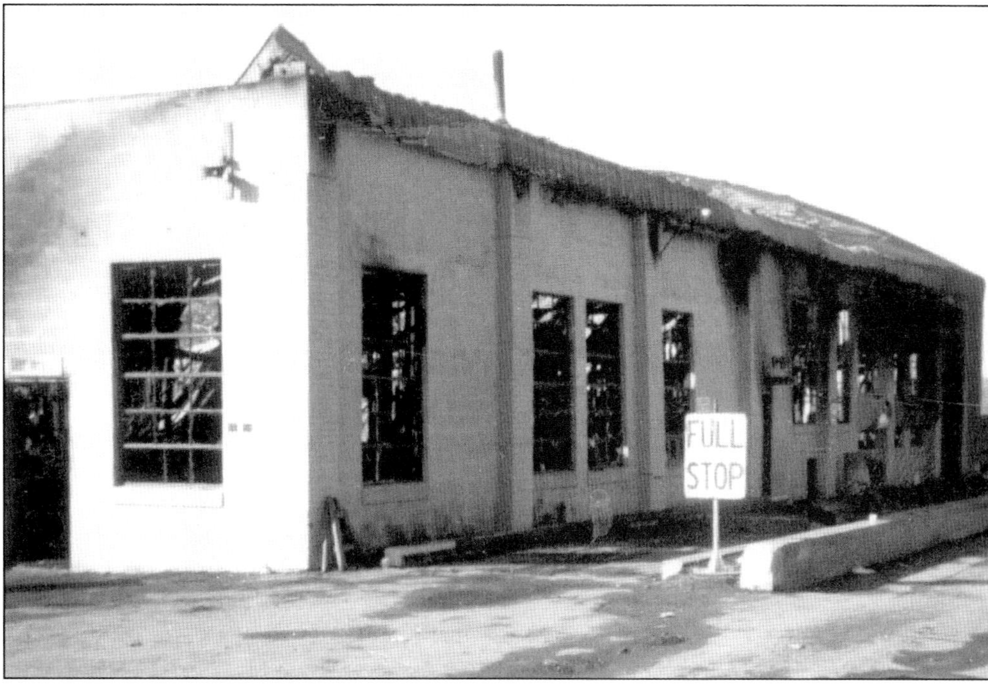

Another disastrous fire occurred at the New Haven Trap Rock Company on November 30, 1968, during which the office building and weigh scale were destroyed. This building was replaced with the new building pictured on page 76. (Barbara Amatrudo.)

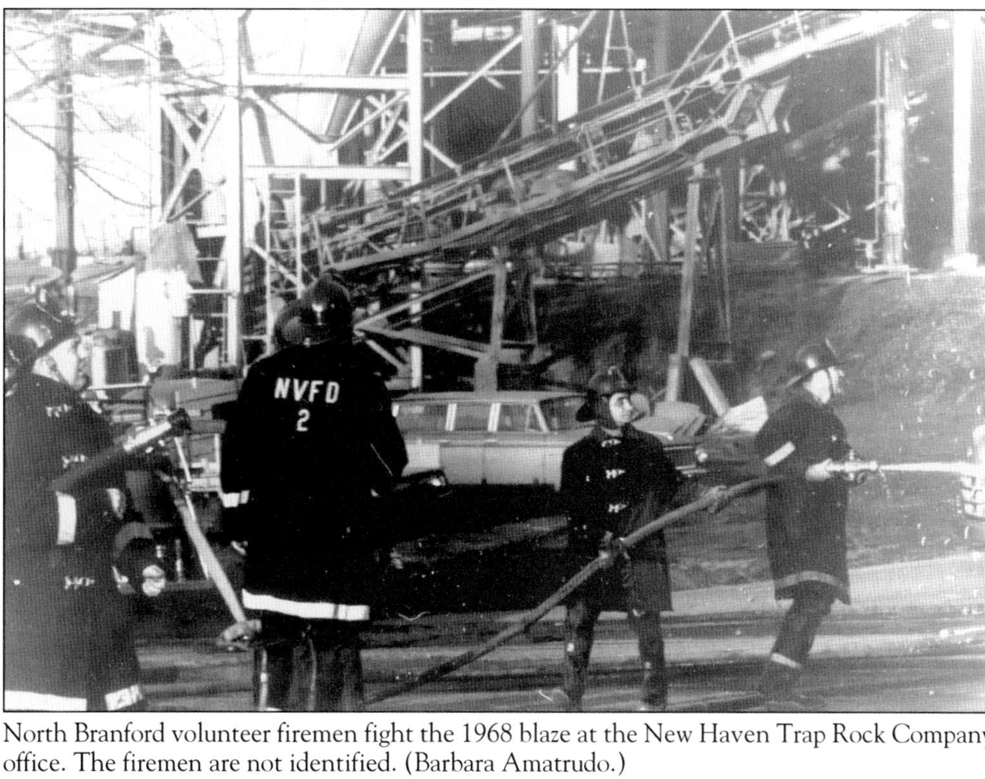

North Branford volunteer firemen fight the 1968 blaze at the New Haven Trap Rock Company office. The firemen are not identified. (Barbara Amatrudo.)

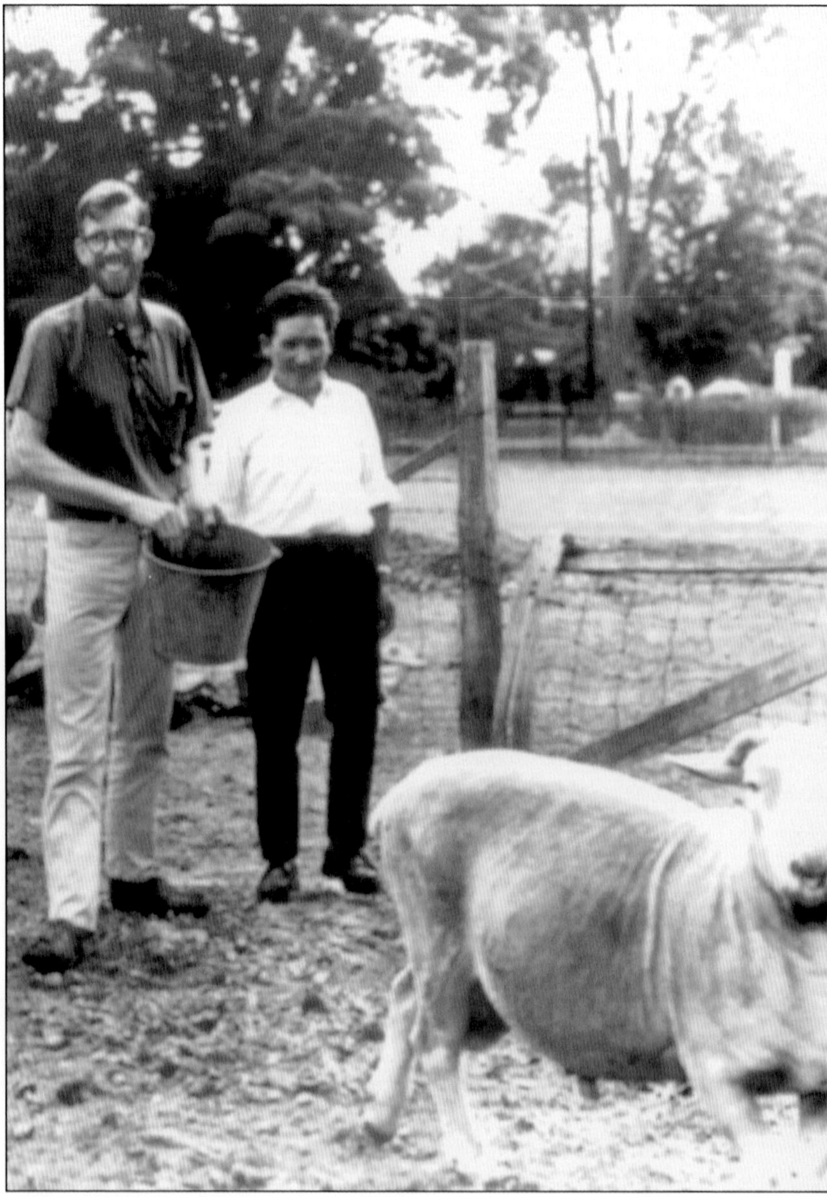

Daniel E. Doody, son of Carrie and Daniel M. Doody, is pictured in the barnyard of the family's Route 80 farm. With him is one of the Sherpas who, with Doody, was a member of the successful 1963 American Mount Everest Expedition. A few days earlier, they traveled to Washington, D.C., where expedition members received the Hubbard medal from Pres. John F. Kennedy. During that expedition, two two-man teams reached the top of Everest, and a third was the first to climb the West Ridge and traverse the mountain. Doody was the expedition's official photographer. Doody was also a member of the first team to climb the north face of Mount Edith Cavell in Canada. In 1964, he was leader of an expedition to the Peruvian Andes that successfully climbed five peaks, one of which was Mount Chacraju, where they were the first team to climb the north ridge. On March 14, 1965, Dan and his climbing partner, Craig Merrihue, were killed in a fall in Mount Washington's Huntington Ravine in New Hampshire. The exact cause of the fall was never determined. (Marion Doody Bradley.)

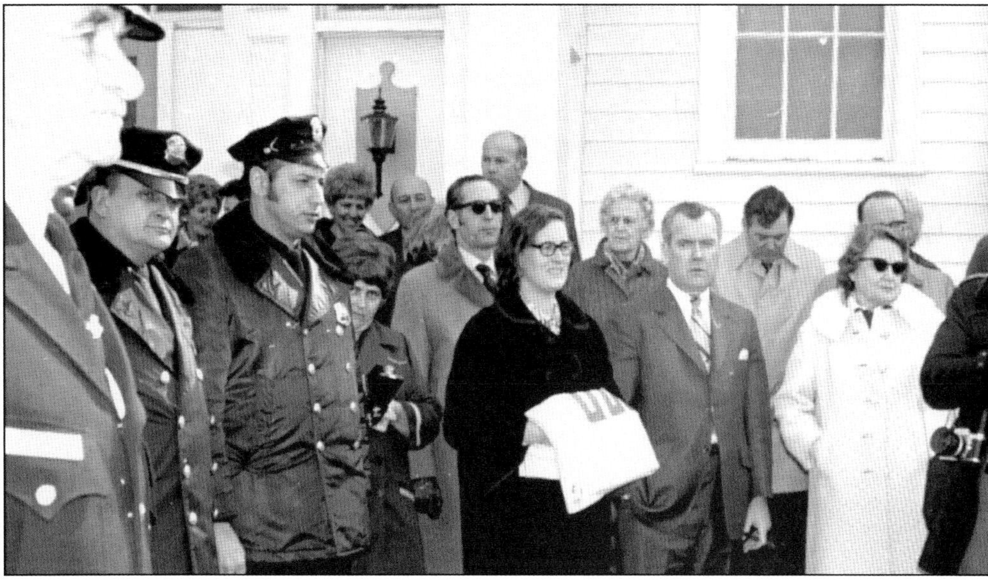

In 1971, North Branford was named an All-America community by the National Municipal League. Here, town officials attend the flag raising at the opening ceremony in March. Pictured from left to right are Fire Chief John Hartigan, Sergeant Robert Smith, Patrolman Robert Onofrio, *Branford Review* reporter Joanne Wentworth (behind policeman), Councilwoman Joan Farrissey (holding flag), Mayor Timothy Ryan, and Councilwoman Phyllis Newberry. (Totoket Historical Society.)

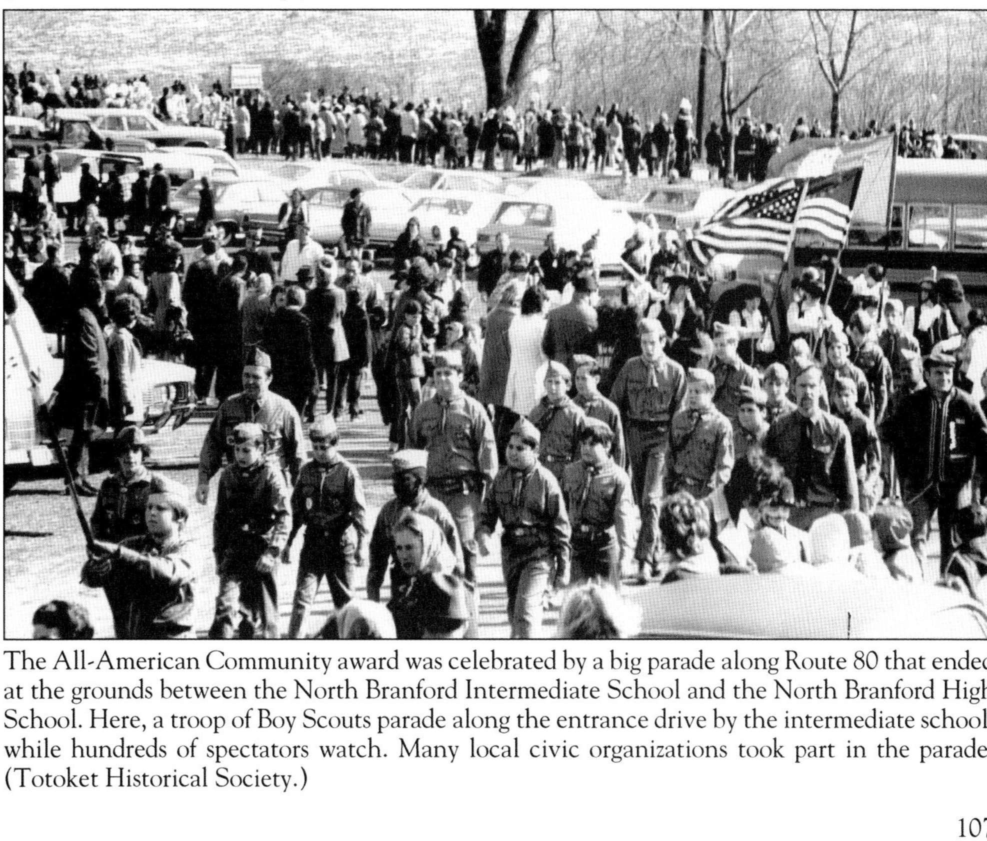

The All-American Community award was celebrated by a big parade along Route 80 that ended at the grounds between the North Branford Intermediate School and the North Branford High School. Here, a troop of Boy Scouts parade along the entrance drive by the intermediate school, while hundreds of spectators watch. Many local civic organizations took part in the parade. (Totoket Historical Society.)

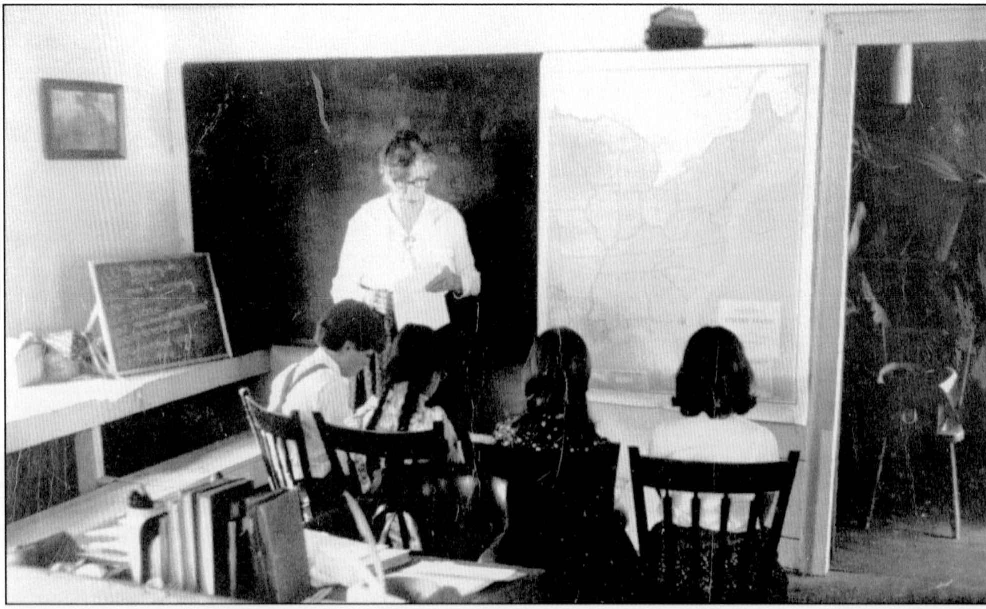

The bicentennial of the United States was celebrated by a number of local events that included an Old-Timer's Day, an exhibition of old-time crafts and antique items at the North Branford Green, Congregational Church, and Hall. Another event was a day at the Little Red School House, where selected students spent a school day learning their lessons. In this photograph, teacher Carrie Doody instructs the students in geography. (Totoket Historical Society.)

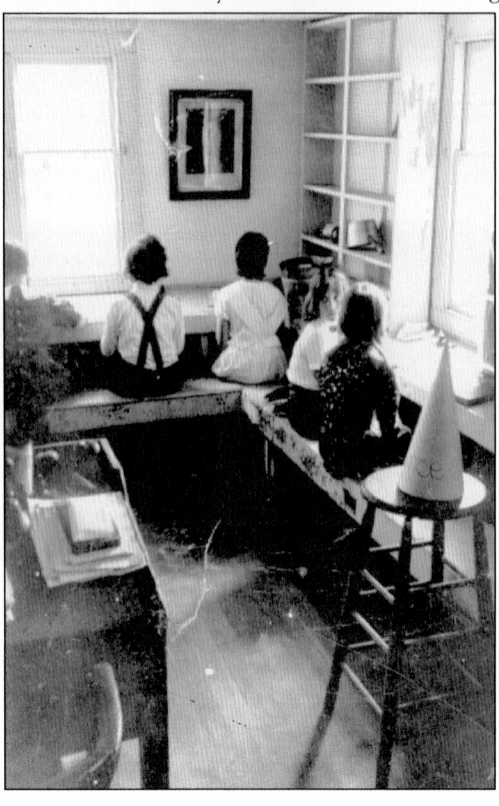

Students in grades four through eight study their assignments at their desks in the Little Red School House. The bicentennial year was a major theme in all the town schools, emphasizing American history. Activities included plays, assemblies, arts and crafts, trips, speakers, poem writing, tree plantings, flag displays, choral presentations, and much more. The North Branford Intermediate School put on a band concert of American music. (Totoket Historical Society.)

In this photograph, students at the Little Red School House play a game during recess as teacher Carrie Doody looks on. Churches and civic organizations scheduled special events throughout the bicentennial year. An ecumenical church service was held at St. Monica's, and the recreation department scheduled a special bicentennial program with children's activities, many of them modeled after children's play 200 years ago. (Totoket Historical Society.)

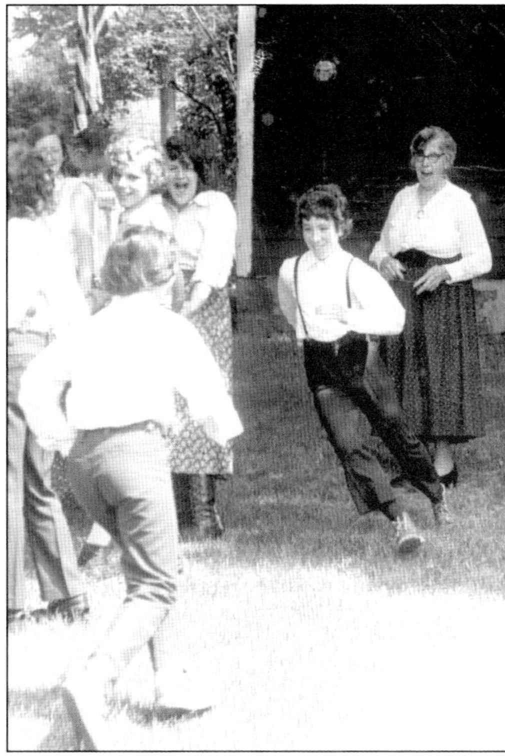

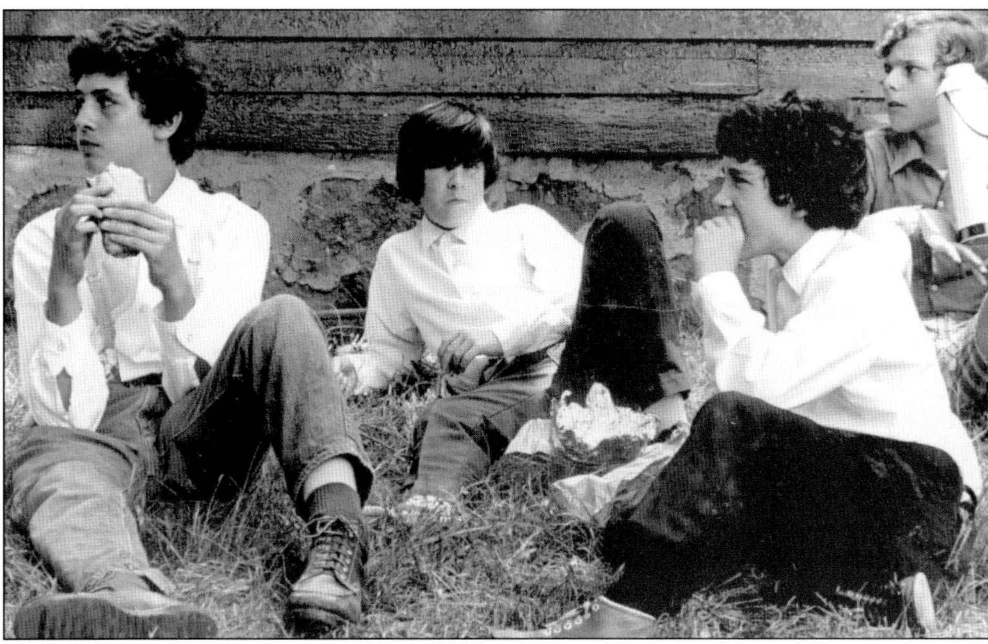

Boys participating in the Little Red School House day eat their lunch outside, as was done 200 years before. As part of the bicentennial activities, the Totoket Historical Society identified all houses and buildings in town built prior to 1876; plaques were made by high school students and presented to house owners at a special ceremony. Also, tours of the quarry, Lake Gaillard dam, and the Pickers factory were conducted. (Totoket Historical Society.)

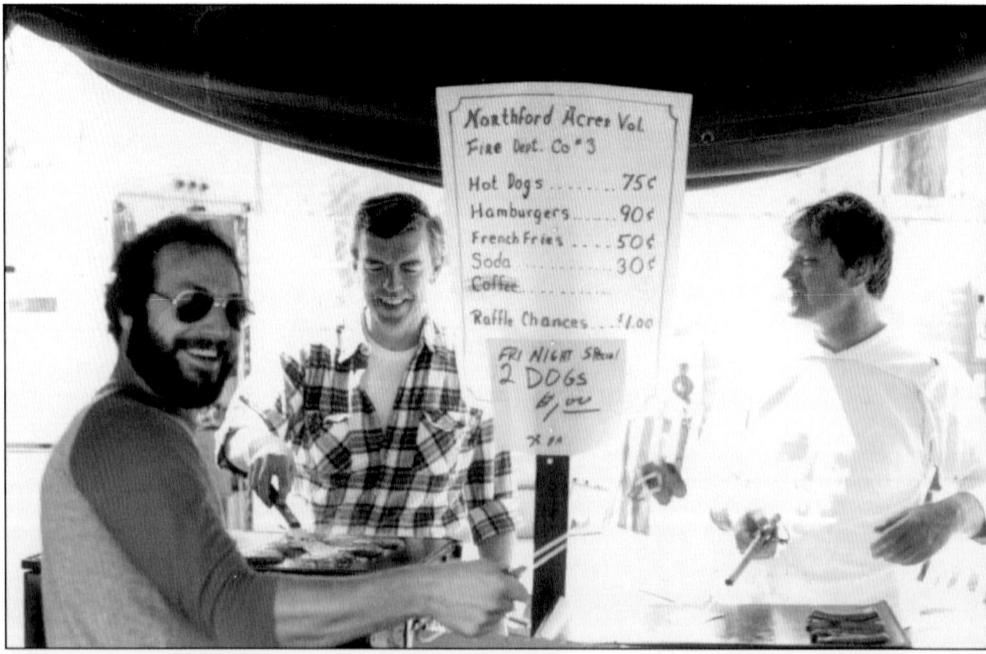

The volunteer firemen sponsored a carnival every year to raise funds for building fire stations and purchasing fire apparatus and equipment. In this 1981 photograph, firemen of the Northford Acres Volunteer Fire Department, Company No. 3, sell hotdogs, hamburgers, French fries, and soda at their booth at the sesquicentennial carnival. They are, from left to right, an unidentified man, Jim Carr, and Dennis Owens. (Company No. 3.)

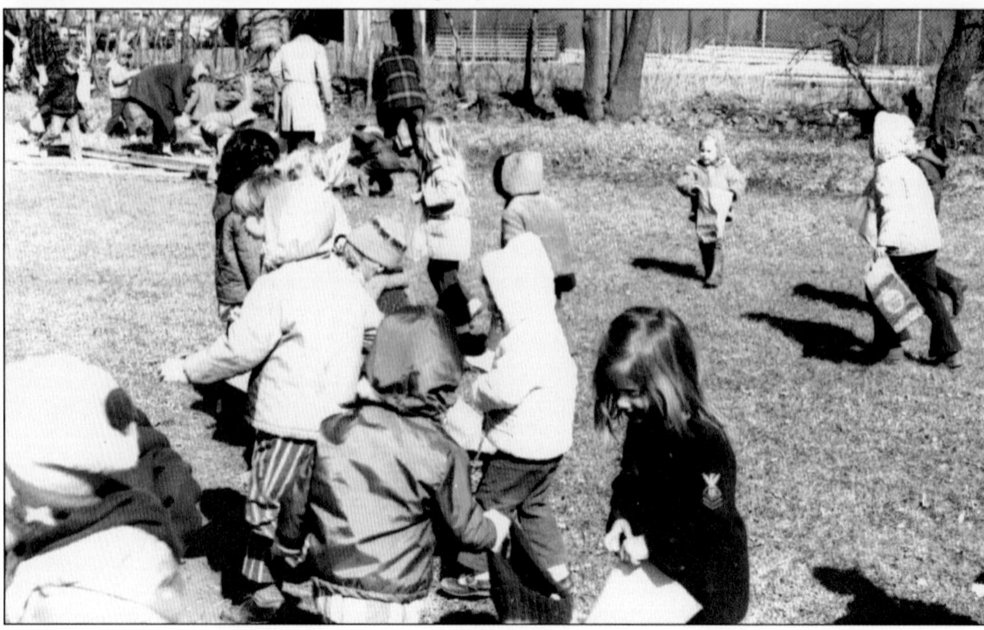

Volunteer fire companies and later civic organizations began sponsoring Easter egg hunts during this era. In this 1972 photograph, little children scurry around the Northford Playground hunting for candy eggs during an Easter egg hunt put on by the Northford Acres Volunteer Fire Department, Company No. 3. (Company No. 3.)

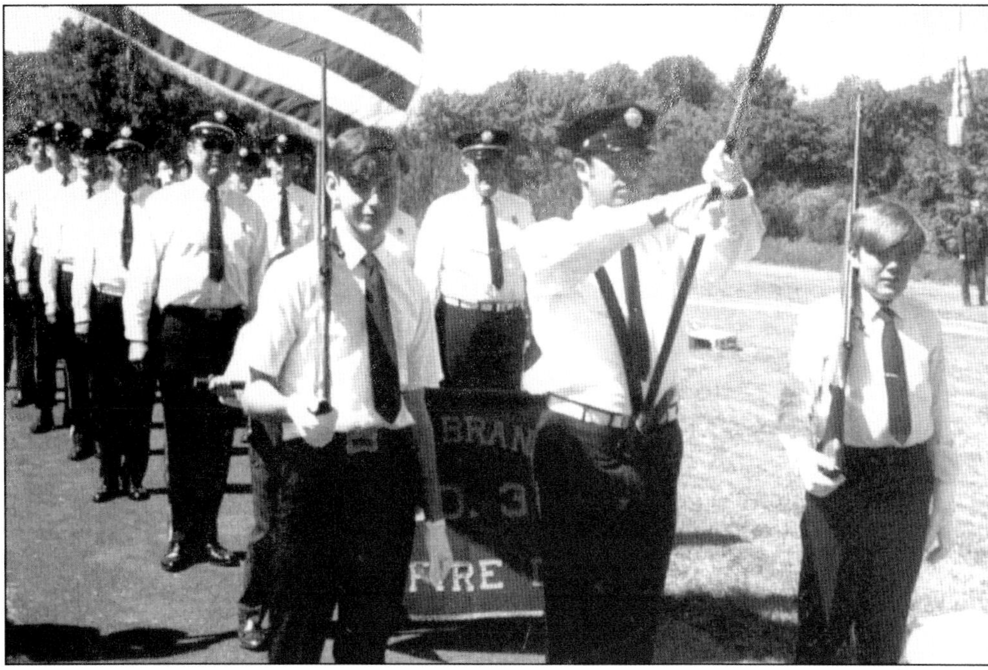

Memorial Day has been celebrated in North Branford since the 1920s. The town's fire companies have participated in the Memorial Day parades since 1938. At first, two parades were held, one at each end of town. In the mid-1960s, it was decided to alternate the parade location each year, a tradition that continues today. In this 1970 photograph, the volunteer firemen of Company No. 3 march in the parade. (Company No. 3.)

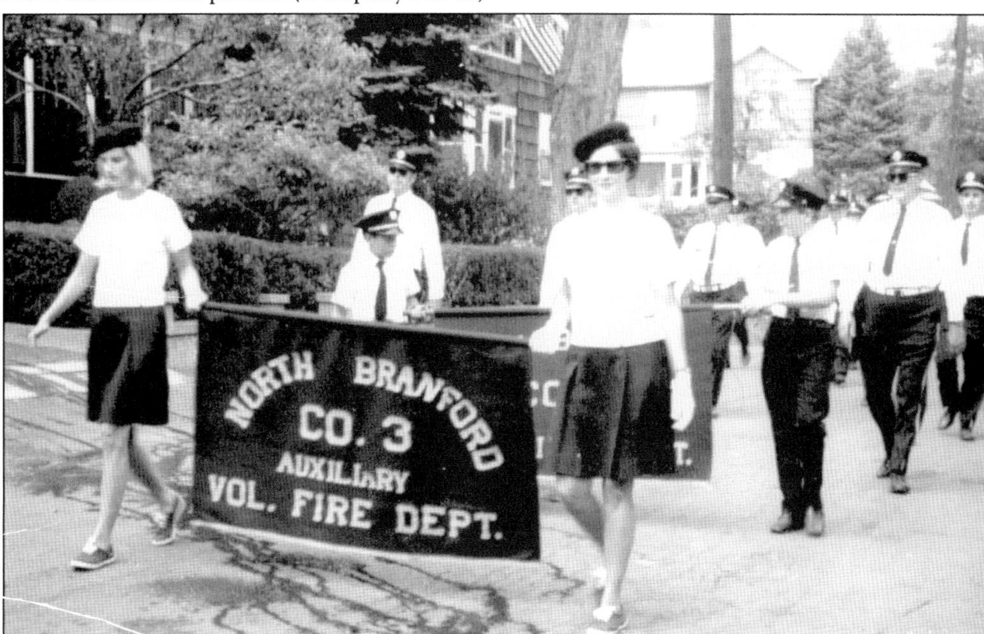

Ladies auxiliaries were part of the three volunteer fire companies in town soon after each company was founded. This 1970 photograph shows a couple of members from the Company No. 3 Ladies Auxiliary marching in a parade in front of the firemen. (Company No. 3.)

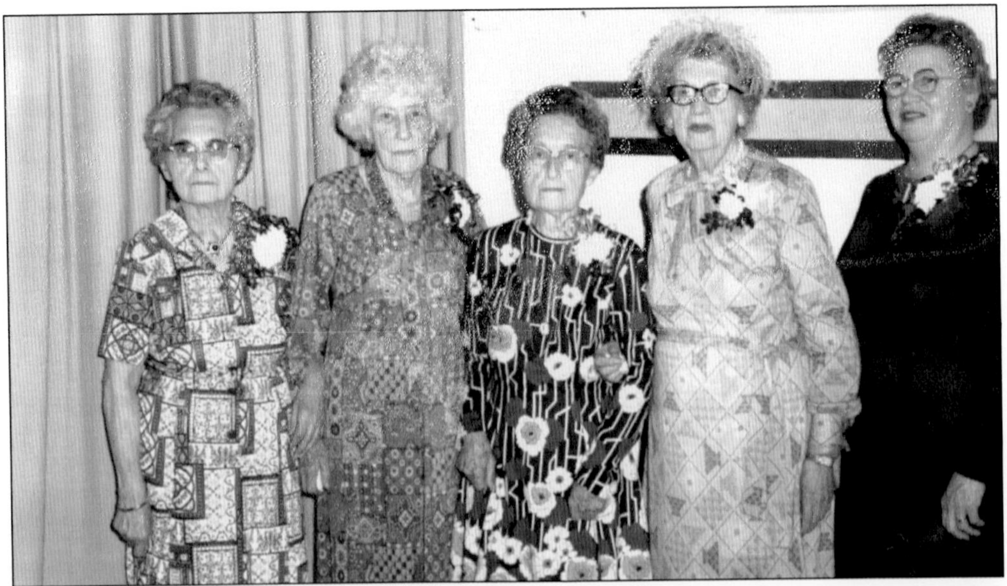

In 1977, the North Branford Congregational Church celebrated its 250th anniversary with a variety of events scheduled throughout the year. A birthday party was held in January with a cake, party games, and presents for the church. The oldest church members were recognized and honored at the party. Seen here, they are, from left to right, Marion Harrison Rose, May Holabird, Emma Harrison Griswold, Hazel Hill, and Florence Linsley Juniver. (North Branford Congregational Church.)

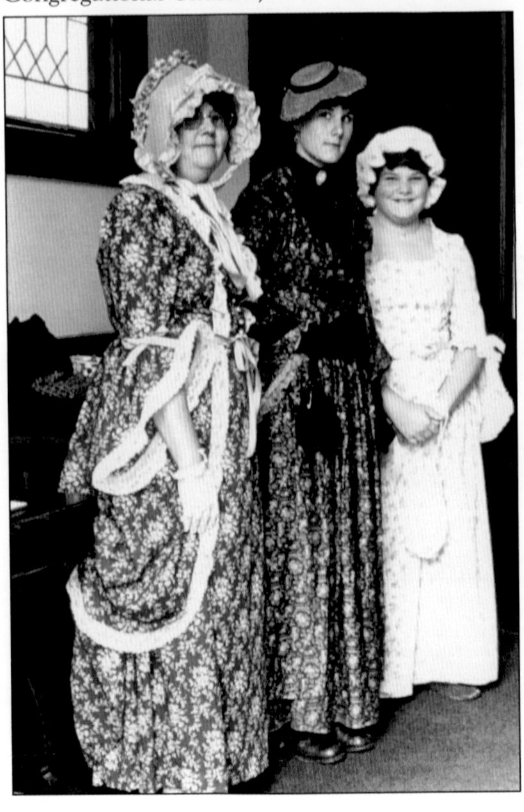

The church was rededicated in May at a special worship service followed by a dinner for former pastors. Later, there was a reception for town officials and residents where historical items were displayed. In October, the celebration continued with a reenactment of a Colonial Sunday. In this photograph, Janet S. Gregan (the church historian) with her daughters, Darianne and Christyn, poses for a picture in the church narthex. (North Branford Congregational Church.)

The Reverend James Ameling reads a 1777 sermon written by the church's second minister, Samuel Eells. Sabbath in the first meetinghouse lasted all day with a two-hour morning meeting, a break for the midday meal, and a two-hour meeting in the afternoon. The 275th anniversary Colonial Sunday lasted all day with a worship service, a potluck luncheon, and a performance of an original play written by Jeffrey Matson. (North Branford Congregational Church.)

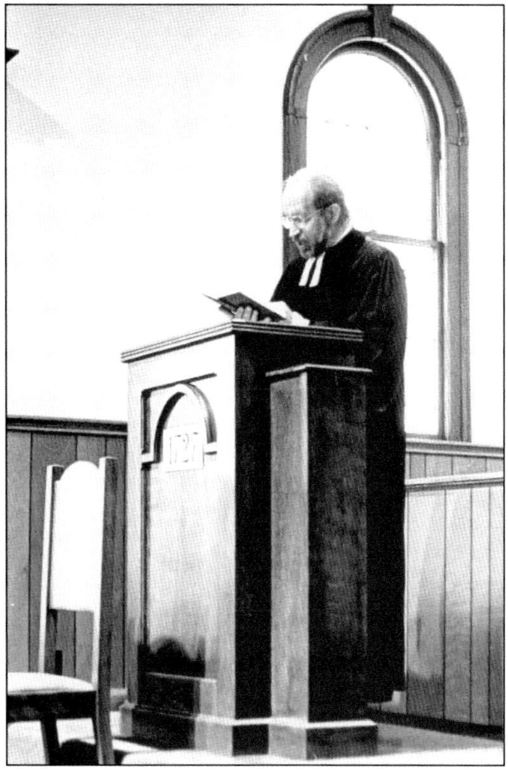

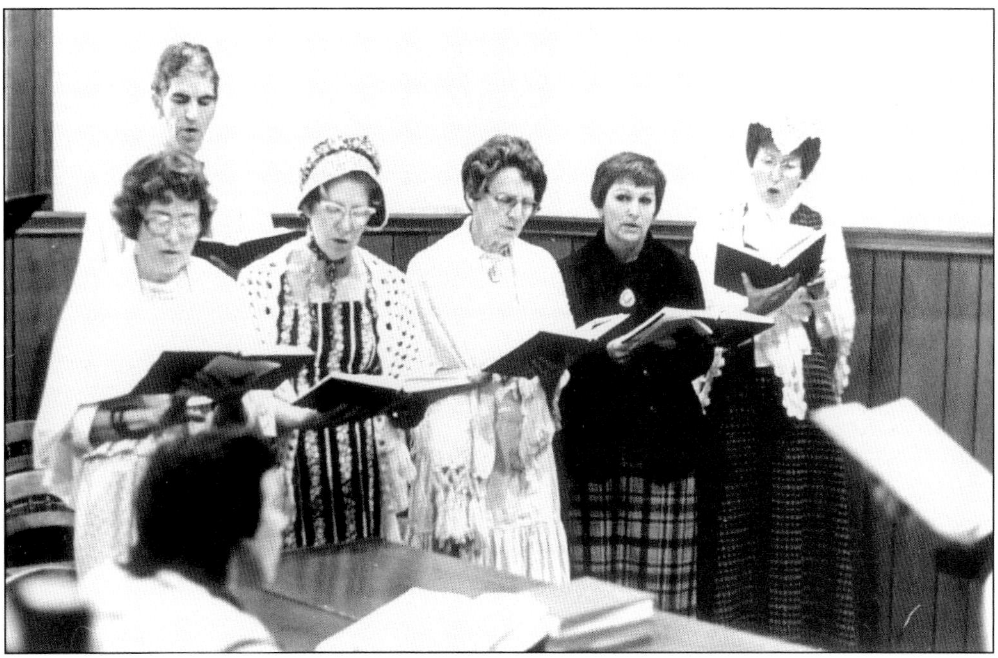

The choir, appropriately dressed for the North Branford Congregational Church's 275th anniversary celebration, sings during the Colonial Sunday worship service. From left to right are Marie Vincent, Richard Harrison, Evelyn Mautte, Jeanette Linsley, Judith Bauer, and Katherine Whitney Scalise. (North Branford Congregational Church.)

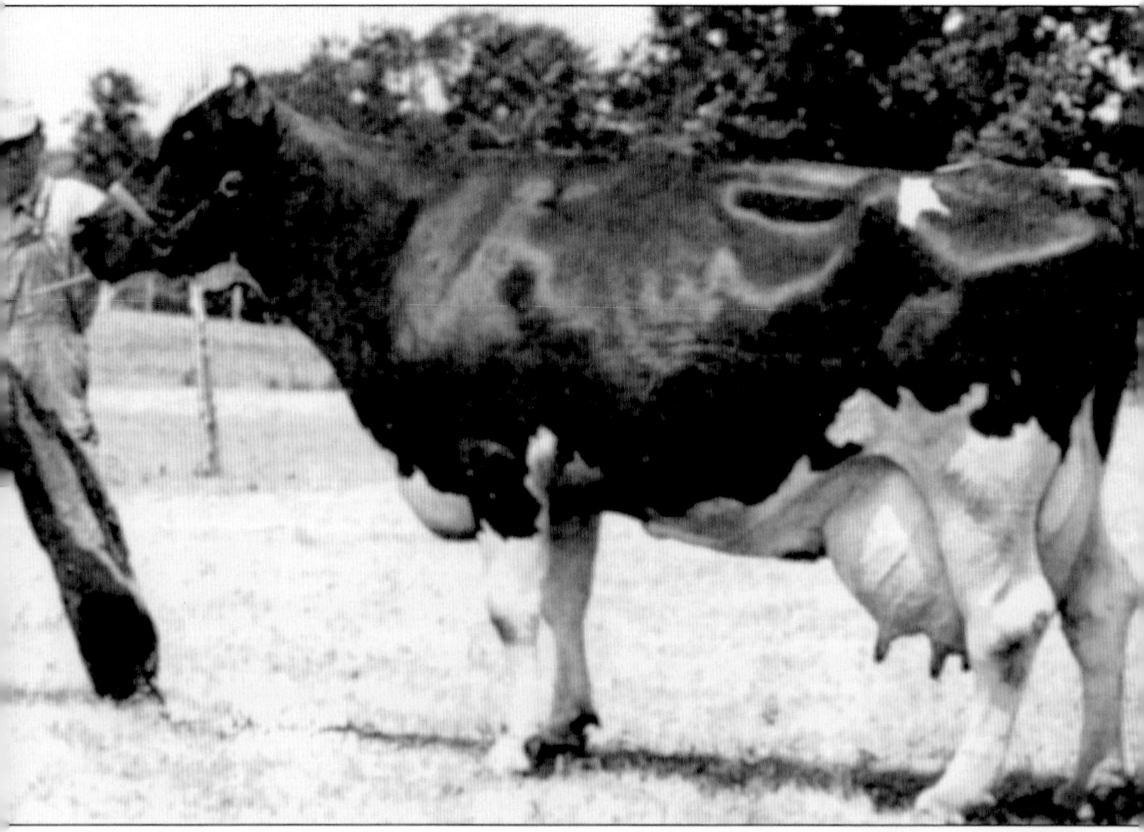

Donald Augur sold his 72-animal dairy herd, the highest-producing Holstein herd on the continent of both milk and butterfat, at a December 1966 auction for a "whopping $627,750" that smashed all previous sales records. The average price paid per head was $8,719, more than double a national sale of $3,236 per head set earlier in the year. Two Augur bulls, Mothermartha's Promise and Mothermartha's Pride, were the highest-priced Holstein animals sold in North America at $108,000 each. Augur's herd, which he began 16 years earlier, was dispersed to buyers from the United States, Canada, and South America. The animals earned world prominence by maintaining the top 12-year production average in the United States and setting 35 records in 1966 and a series of records throughout the previous 12 years. In this photograph, Don Augur shows off 16-year-old Amity Dauntless Martha, called "Unmatched Martha," the foundation and key cow in the development of his herd. Martha and 10 other head of cattle were not sold that day. The Augur farm was located on Forest Road next to the police station. (Totoket Historical Society.)

Eight

North Branford Celebrates Its Sesquicentennial

In 1981, the town of North Branford had been in existence for 150 years. In 1831, on the first Monday in May, the General Assembly of Connecticut resolved "that all that part of the old town of Branford, which is not comprehended within the limits of the first School Society . . . be and the same is hereby incorporated into a new and distinct town by the name of North Branford." These words created a new town that included the village of Northford within its boundaries. As the anniversary date approached, the town council under Mayor Timothy Ryan appointed a committee of interested residents to plan a gala celebration. It took place during the week of June 20 through 27, 1981, with the theme "Enjoyment, Fun, Participation and Memories." The sesquicentennial celebration was a huge success full of special events that drew thousands of people to town. It will be long remembered.

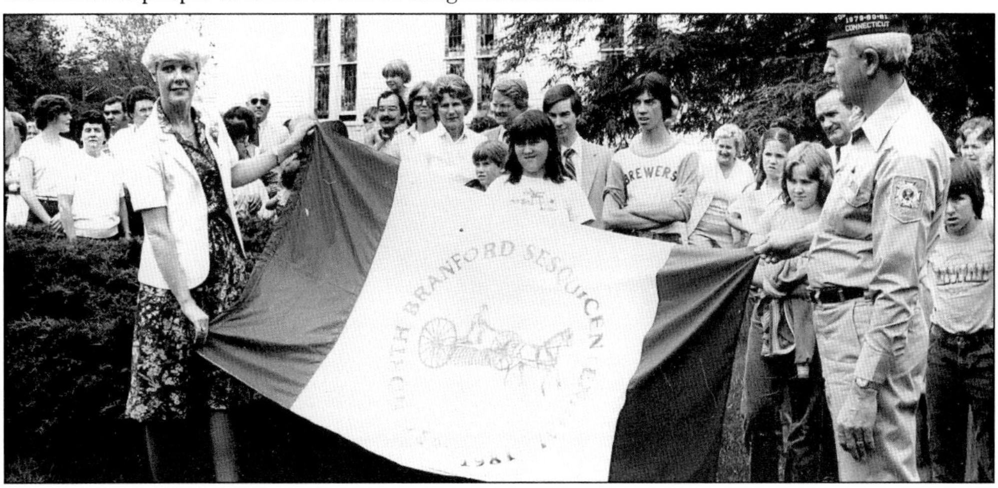

North Branford Sesquicentennial Week opened with a ceremony at the North Branford Congregational Church on Saturday held inside because of rain. In this photograph, Eileen Donadio, secretary of the committee, and Al Anderson, representing the Veterans of Foreign Wars, display the sesquicentennial flag, specially designed for the occasion. Many spectators watched as the flag was raised on the Memorial Flagpole on the North Branford Green. (Totoket Historical Society.)

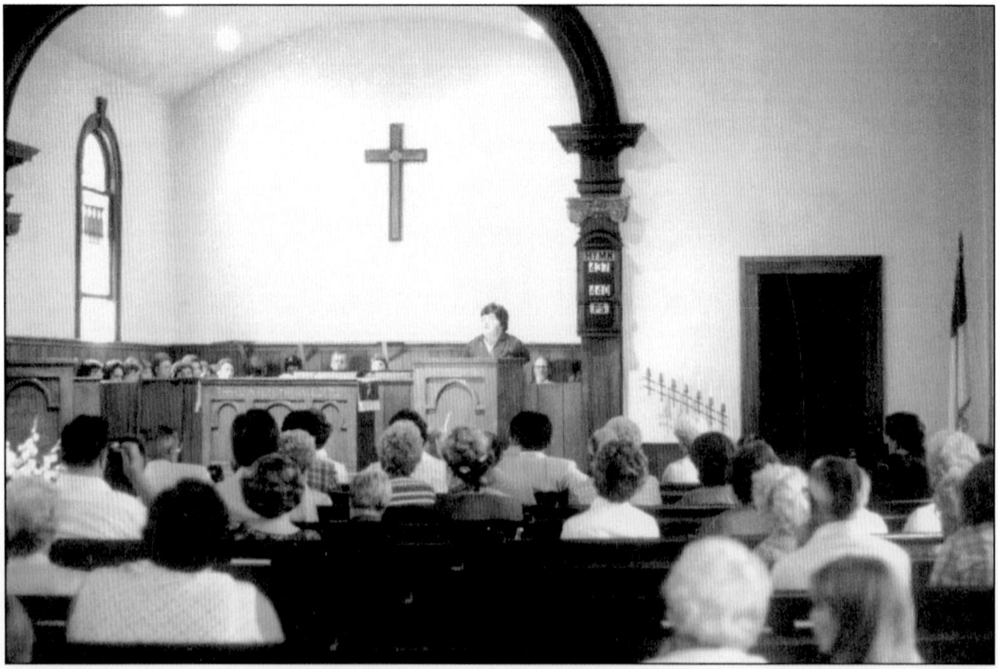

President of the Totoket Historical Society, Janet S. Gregan, gives a historical overview of the town during the opening ceremonies. The community chorus, conducted by Chris Briendel, is seated behind the speaker in the choir area. (Totoket Historical Society.)

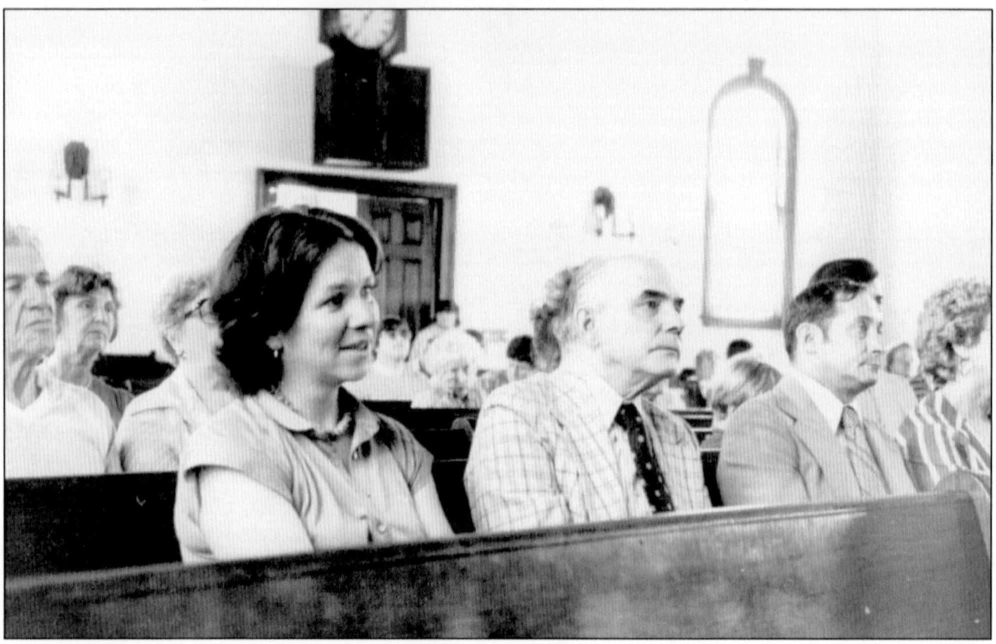

Town council members Nancy Miller, William Gardner, Reginald Corey, and Barbara Bisacky are seated in one of the church pews, listening to the speakers and music of the opening ceremony. Mayor Timothy Ryan spoke, opera singer Randy Simpson sang a song of the 19th century, Yvonne Bartemy, the town clerk, read an original poem she had written for the occasion, and the Community Chorus sang two songs. (Totoket Historical Society.)

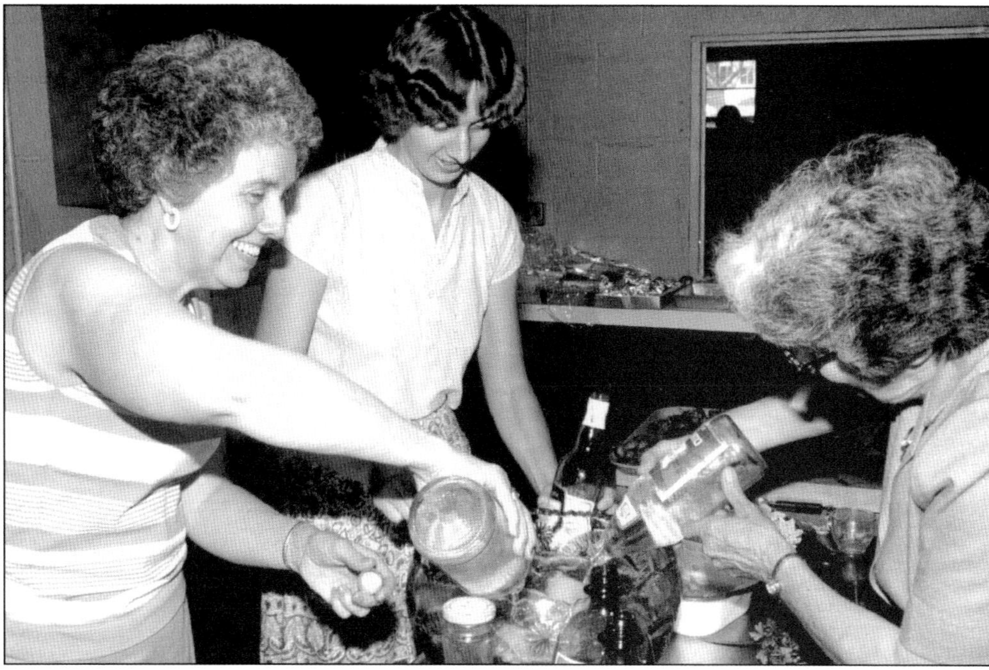

A reception was held in the North Branford Congregational Church Fellowship Hall after the opening ceremony. In this photograph, Louise Roberts (left) and Amy Montelius (center) make a punch. The other woman is not identified. (Totoket Historical Society.)

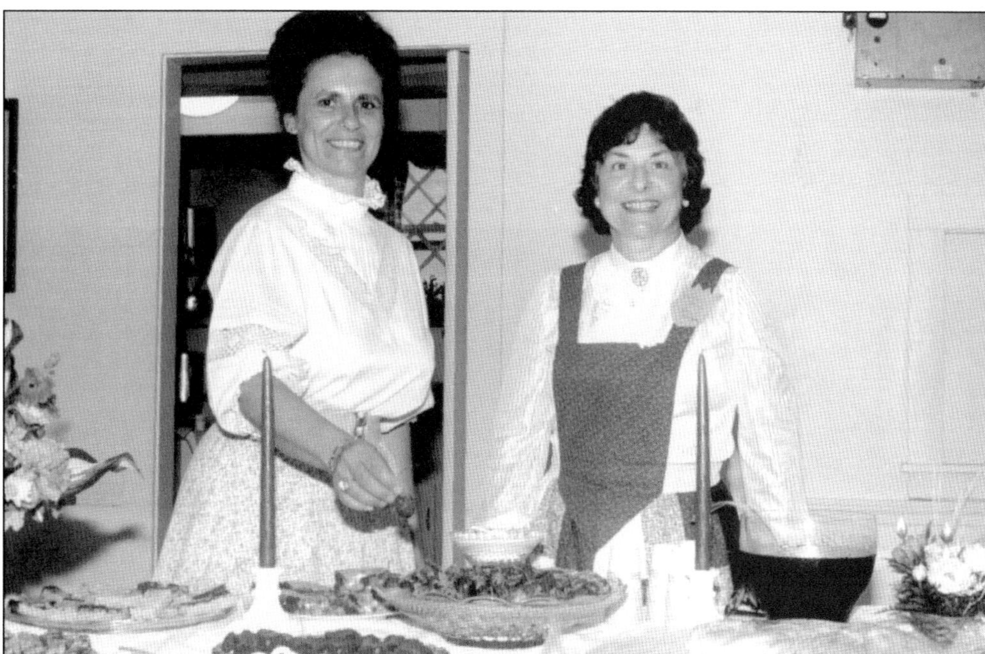

Alma LaCourciere and Alice Murphy preside over the well-stocked table at the opening ceremony reception. (Totoket Historical Society.)

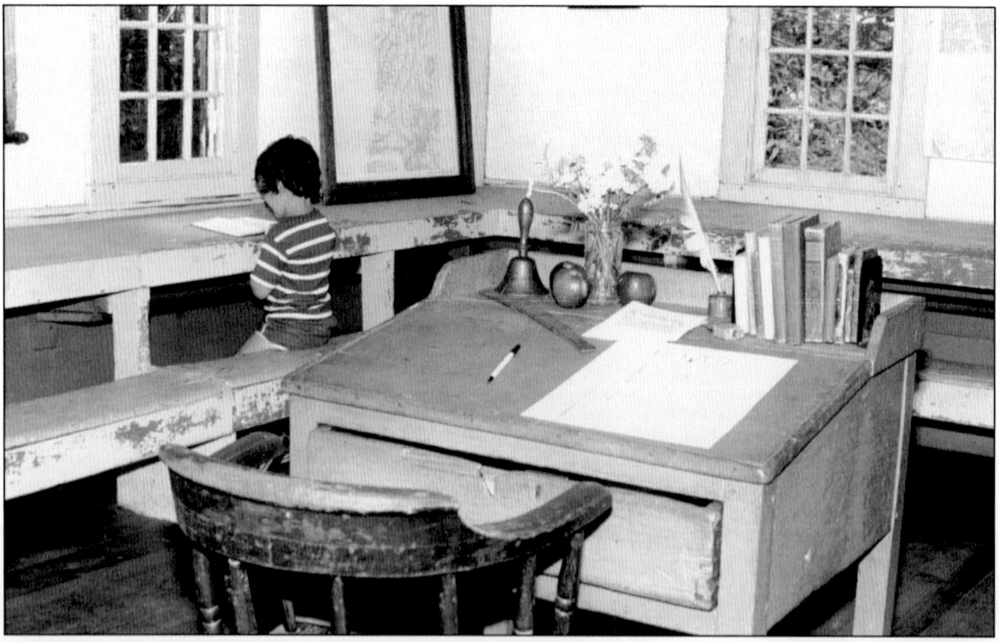

A historical building and garden tour was one of the activities on the first Saturday of Sesquicentennial Week. Three churches, three homes, two gardens, and the Little Red School House were opened to the public from 12:00 p.m. to 4:00 p.m. In this photograph, a young visitor checks out an old school book at the schoolhouse, maintained as a museum by the Totoket Historical Society. (Totoket Historical Society.)

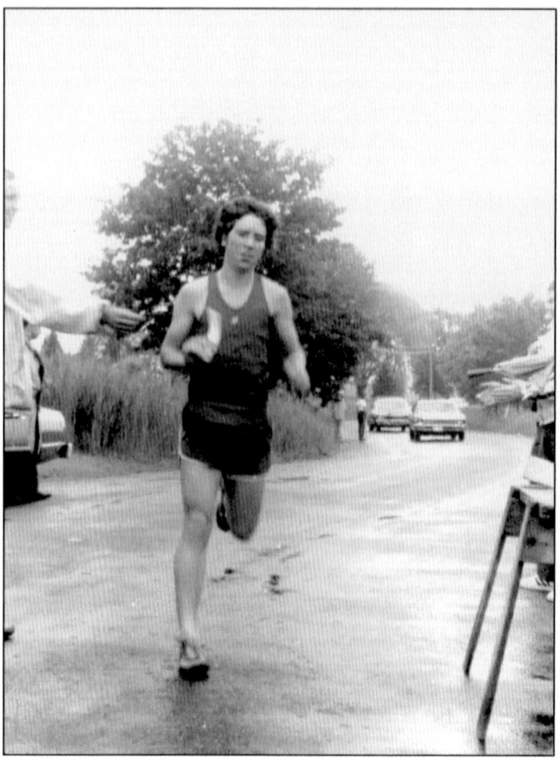

An unidentified runner picks up the pace in the road race that took place on the first Saturday of the sesquicentennial. Many men, women, and children ran the five-mile course over town roads. Also, the Regional Water Authority opened up the North Street gates for the Sesquicentennial Week so visitors could view the Lake Gaillard dam and historic valley where some of the north farmers originally settled. (Totoket Historical Society.)

A well-attended sesquicentennial ball was held on Saturday, June 20, at St. Augustine's Catholic Church Hall. Costumed couples and groups took time out from their dancing to pose for photographs. Here, Bob and Ginny Montelius show off their Revolutionary War–era costumes. (Totoket Historical Society.)

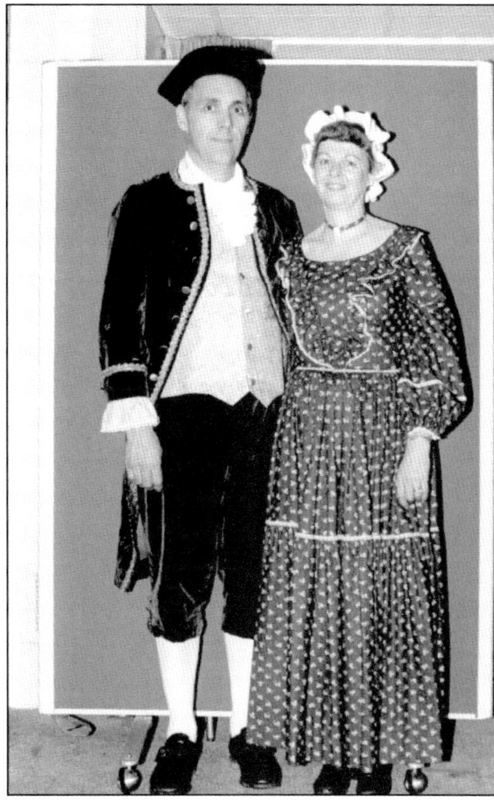

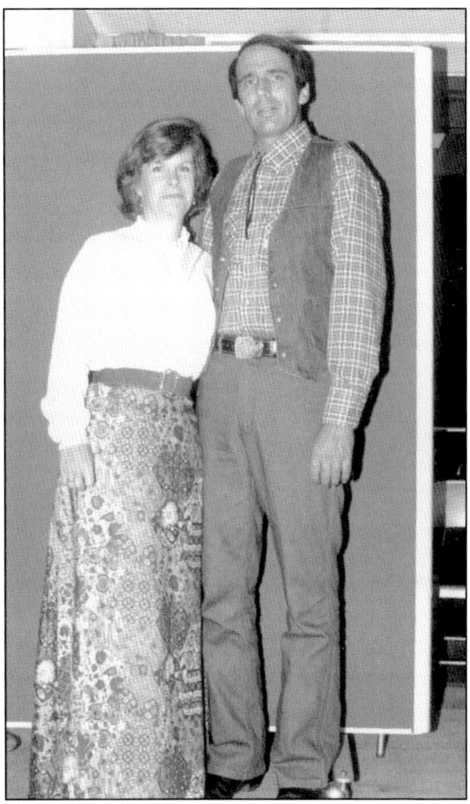

In this photograph, taken at the sesquicentennial ball, Joan and Bob Fitch pose in their American frontier-style costumes. Joan was very active in town affairs, serving on the planning and zoning commission for many years and is now, in 2003, a member of the town council. (Totoket Historical Society.)

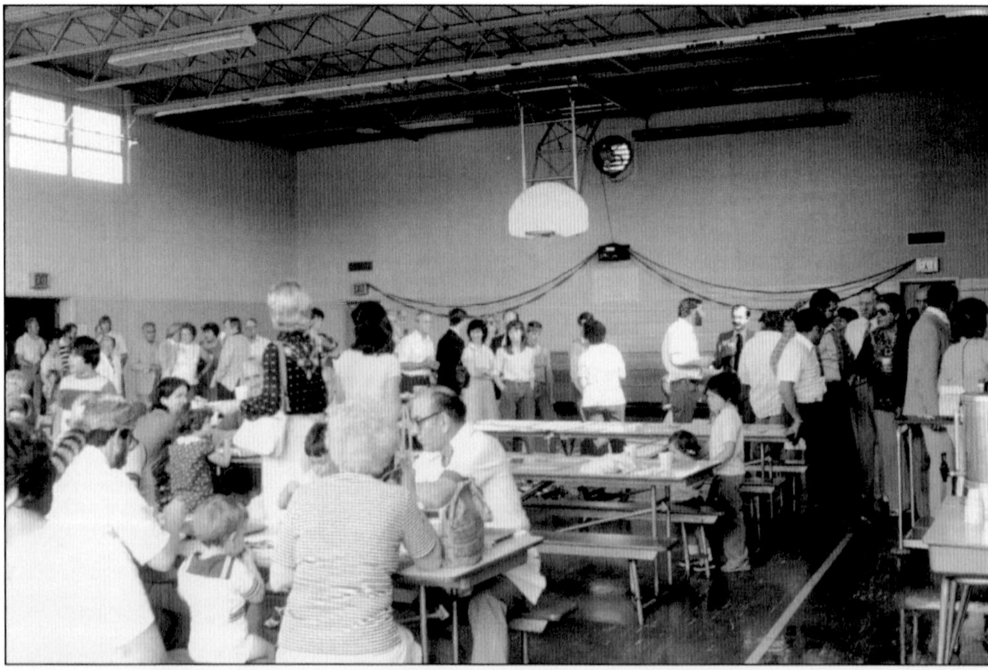

On Sunday morning during Sesquicentennial Week, a pancake breakfast was held at Stanley T. Williams School after an interfaith church service there. The photograph shows that many townspeople attended this popular event. (Totoket Historical Society.)

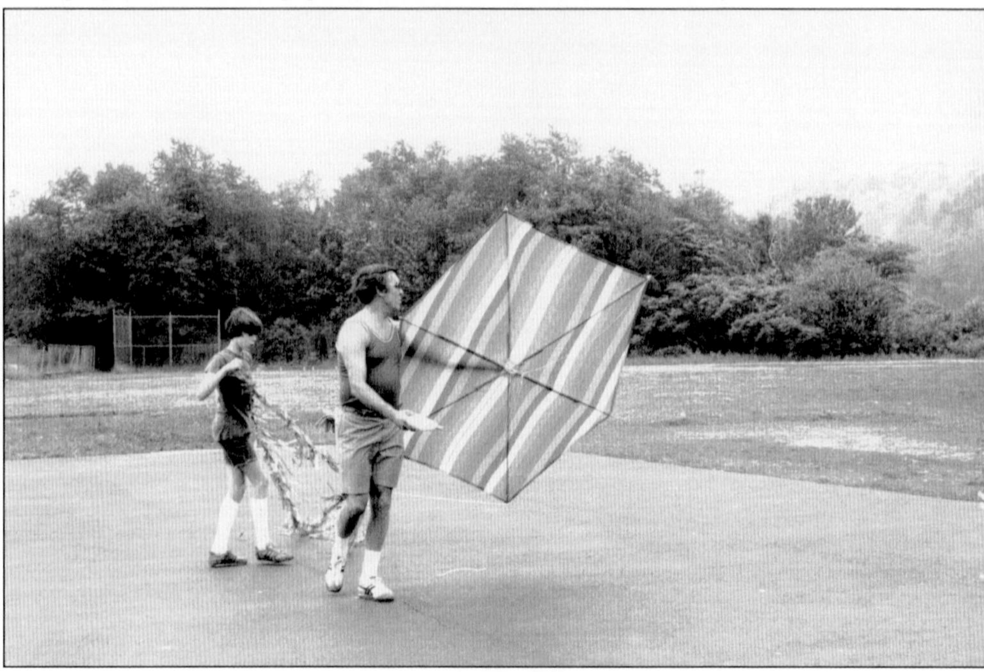

A kite flying event was held at the North Branford High School soccer field on Sunday afternoon. The event was free, and prizes were given for the largest, smallest, and best-flying kite in all age categories. A couple of unidentified kite flyers ready their large kite in this photograph. (Totoket Historical Society.)

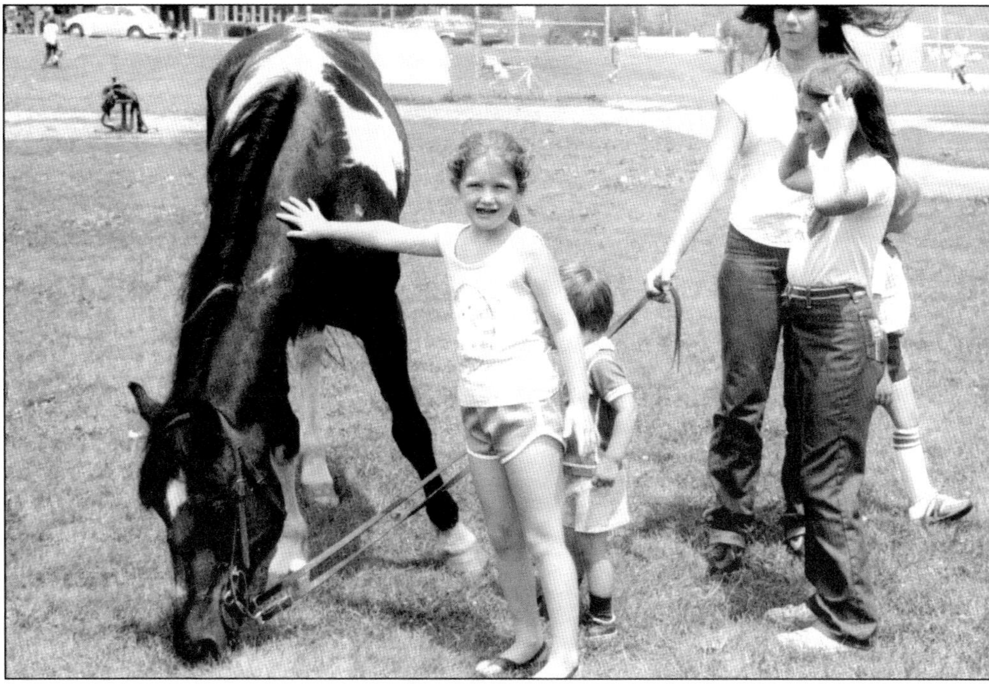

Monday was Children's Day at Stanley T. Williams School, where there were old-fashioned games, a clothesline art show, pony rides, a bicycle decoration contest, and other activities. In this photograph, some unidentified children pet a horse. (Totoket Historical Society.)

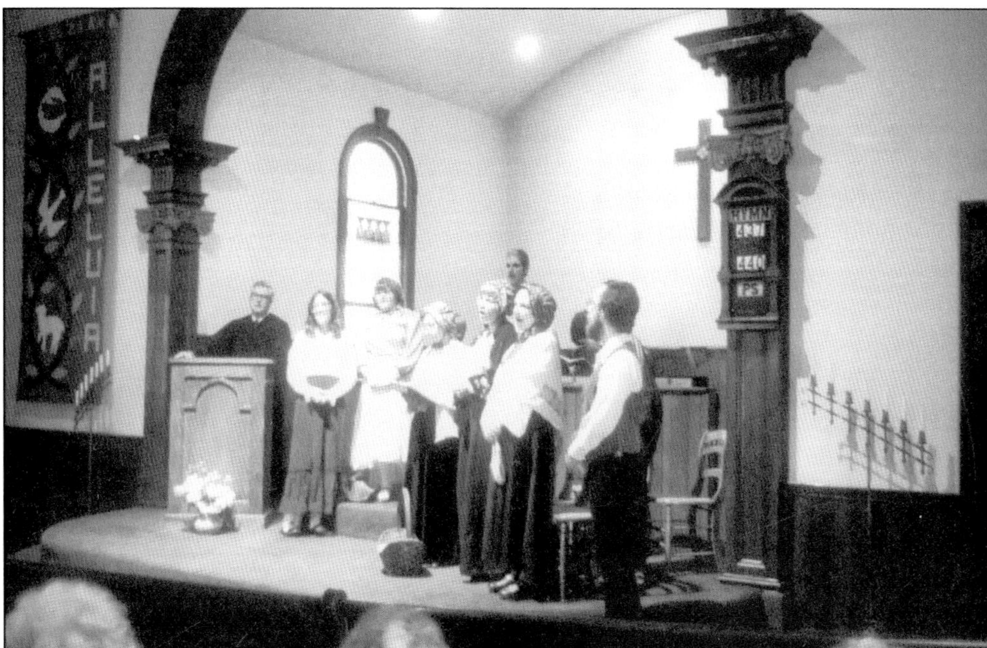

The members of the North Branford Congregational Church put on an old-fashioned church supper and historical play as part of the sesquicentennial celebration. The actors were not identified in this photograph. (Totoket Historical Society.)

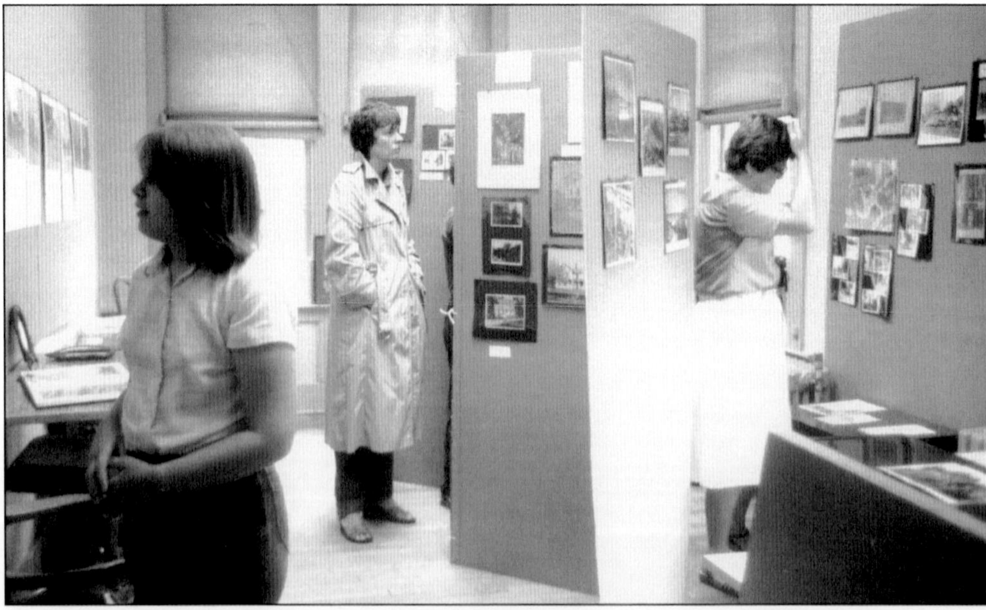

On the Thursday of Sesquicentennial Week, there was an exhibition of historic items at the Totoket Historical Society center. The society had just leased the administration building, formerly Center School, and displays of its collection in all the rooms were set up. In this photograph, Diane Ozols (left), Jane Richmond (center), and Dorothy Ozols look over the photographs displayed in the room that was the tax collector's office. (Totoket Historical Society.)

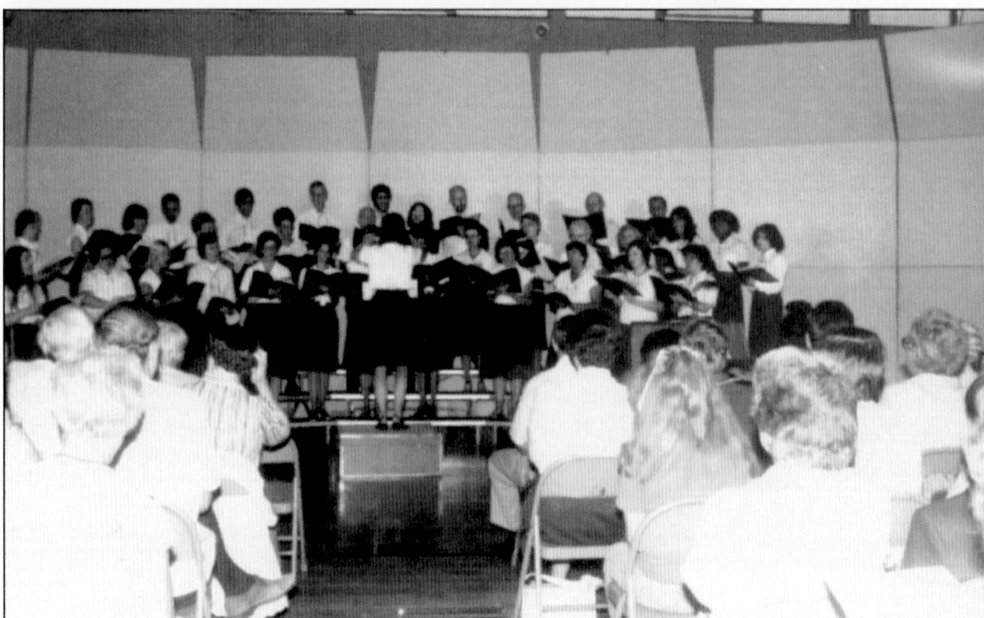

The Community Chorus, assembled especially for the sesquicentennial, gave a concert in the North Branford High School gymnasium on Wednesday and Thursday evenings. Chris Briendel conducted the chorus. The audience was delighted with the concert and "couldn't believe that the chorus could have accomplished such a high level of expertise in such a short time," according to the 1981 annual town report. (Totoket Historical Society.)

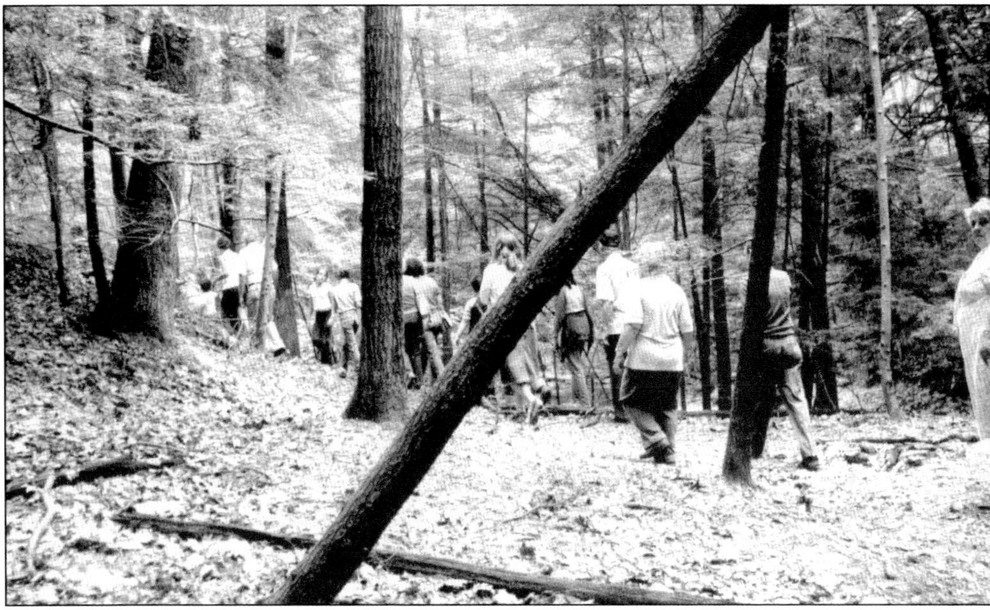

A historical nature walk took place at North Farms Park on Friday afternoon. Led by Andrew Black, walkers hiked the rugged terrain along the Branford River to view remains of the dams built for 18th- and 19th-century mills. Later, a pedestrian bridge was built across the river, and Boy Scouts marked a walking trail. A soccer field is now located in the front portion of the park. (Totoket Historical Society.)

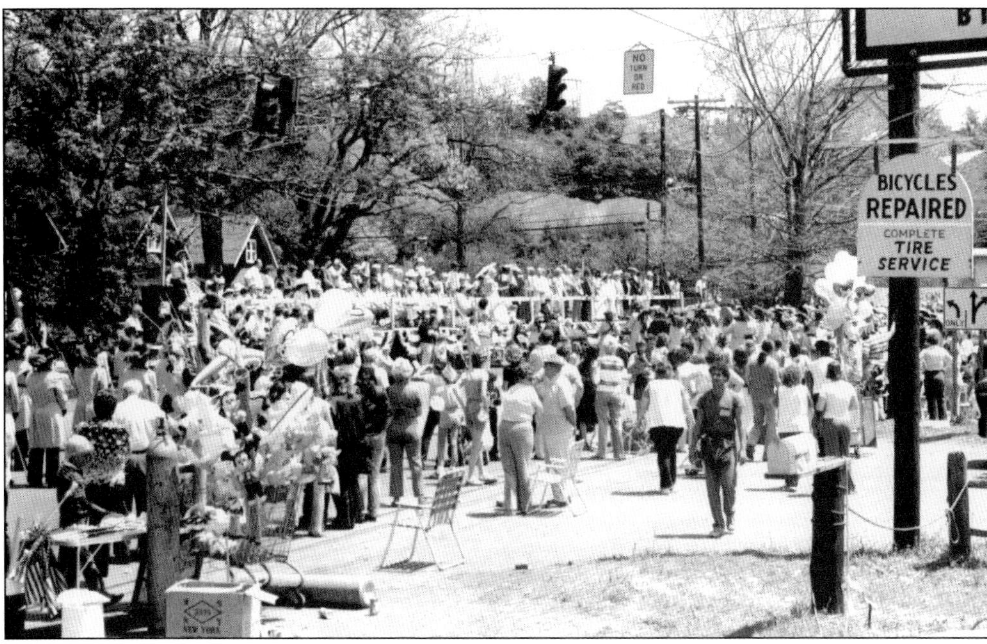

Saturday, June 27, was the climax of Sesquicentennial Week. A huge parade marched down Route 80 from Commerce Drive to the North Branford Intermediate School. Many bands, the fife-and-drum corps, floats, and other marching units paraded in front of the viewing stand located in front of the three houses on Quarry Road near the intersection of Forest Road. (Totoket Historical Society.)

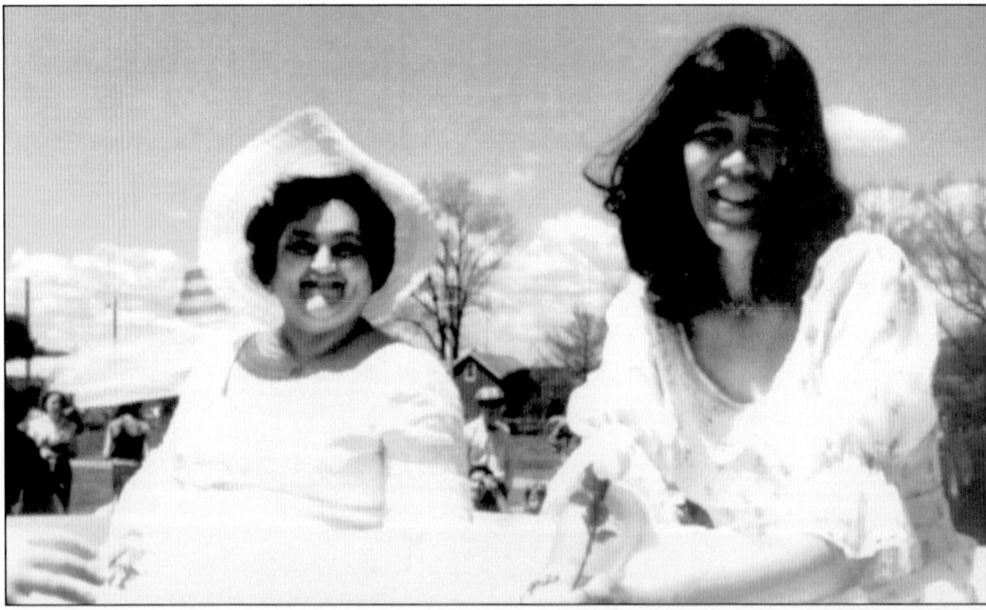

Two members of the sesquicentennial committee, Lillian Deno and Mary Bigelow, ride on the committee float to the viewing stand where they disembarked and watched the parade. (Totoket Historical Society.)

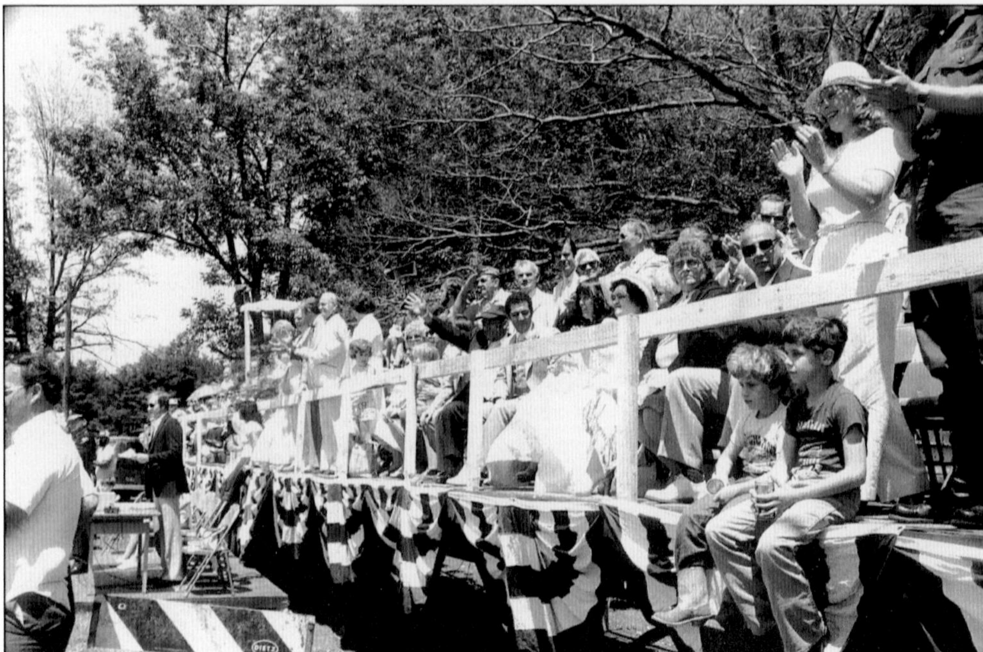

Town dignitaries are seated in the viewing stand, listening to Master of Ceremonies Pat Sheehan, a news commentator from Channel 3 WTIC, who is standing at the microphone. On the stand on the right are Mayor Timothy Ryan and Eileen Donadio (with a parasol). Town Manager Thomas Wontorek is the tall man in the back row. Beginning with the sixth person from right, from left to right are Mary Bigelow, Lillian Deno, Joanne Wentworth, and the Reverend James Ameling. (Totoket Historical Society.)

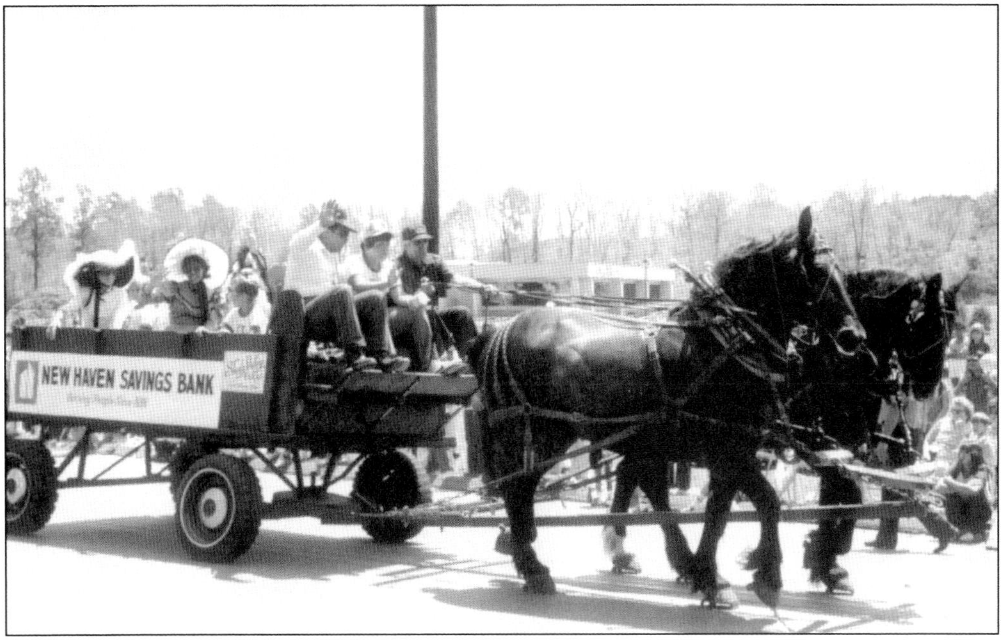

A float, sponsored by the New Haven Savings Bank, passes by the viewing stand. The riders on the float were the employees who worked in the North Branford branch of the bank, located on Route 80 near the Guilford line. The Tilcon office building can be seen in the background. It is now, in 2003, the town hall. (Totoket Historical Society.)

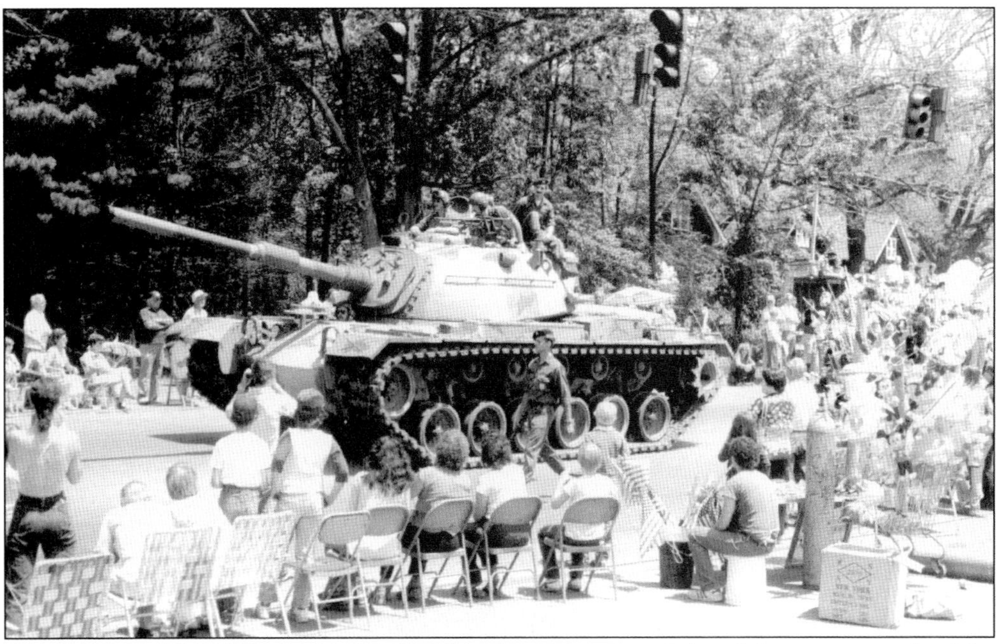

A huge army tank rolls by to the delight of the spectators. People lined the entire stretch of the parade route to see the biggest parade in North Branford history. The Quarry Road houses can be seen at the far right. The traffic signals (now gone) were located at the driveway to Forte's Market. The old slaughterhouse and market are part of the water authority property today. (Totoket Historical Society.)

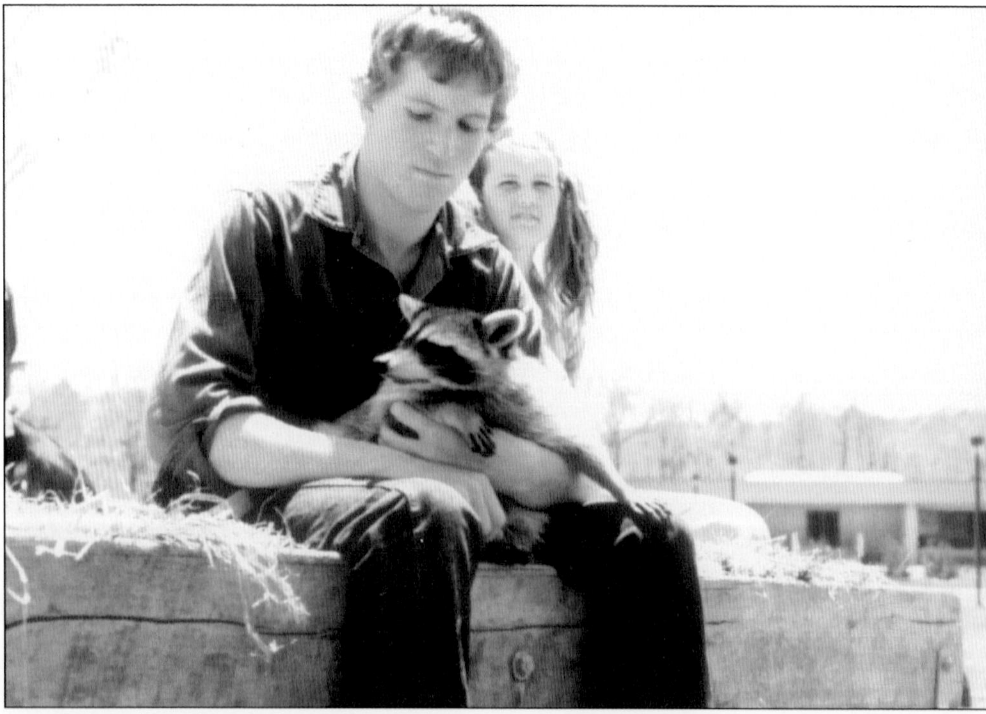

A couple of unidentified youths with a pet raccoon ride on a local farm float in the sesquicentennial parade. (Totoket Historical Society.)

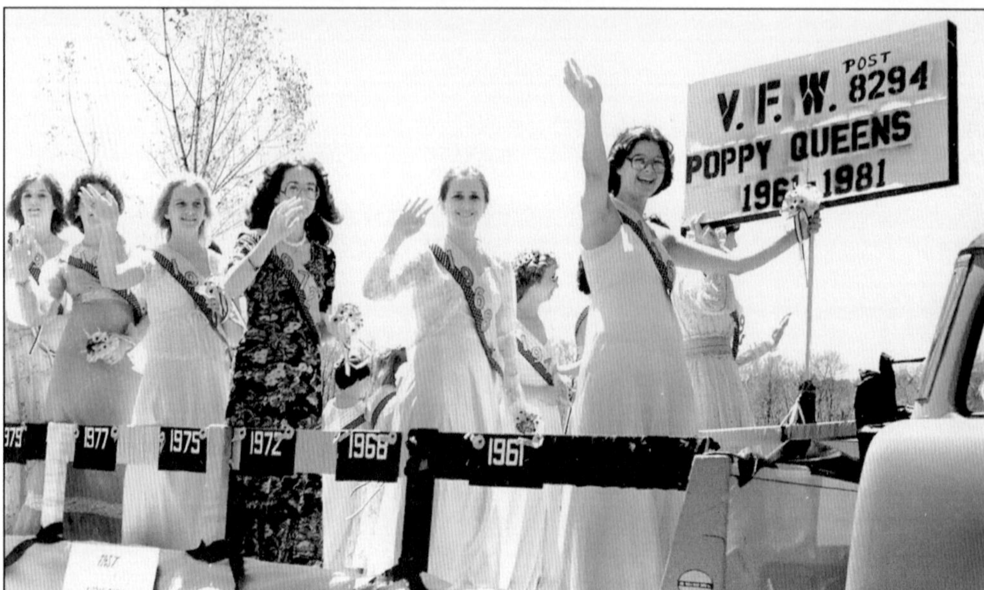

A line of Poppy Queens, selected annually from 1961 to 1981, line up on the V.F.W. Post No. 8294 float to wave to the crowd. They are chosen each year to ride in the Memorial Day parade. From left to right are unidentified (1979), unidentified (1977), Edna Kopylec (1975), unidentified (1972), Mary Doody (1968), and unidentified (1961). Leola Kopylec can be seen in the back between the 1961 and 1968 Poppy Queens. (Totoket Historical Society.)

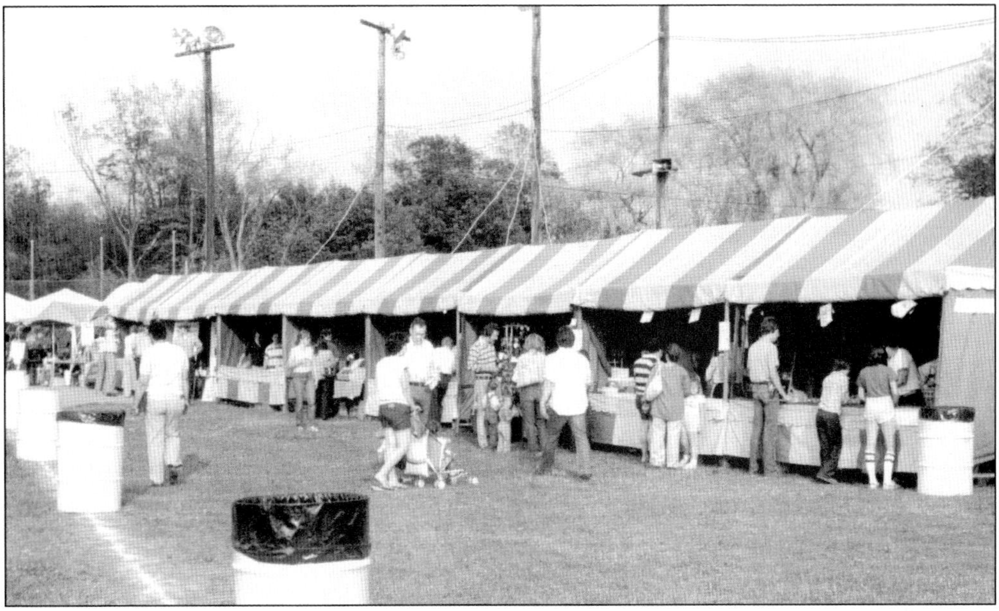

On Wednesday night, a carnival opened on the grounds of the North Branford Intermediate School. It ran for four evenings and all day Saturday. There were rides for the children and adults. Many townspeople, including town officials, "were in evidence everywhere working booths, selling tickets, pizza and popcorn, acting as barkers at games of chance," according to the 1981 annual town report. Shown here is a row of the carnival booths. (Totoket Historical Society.)

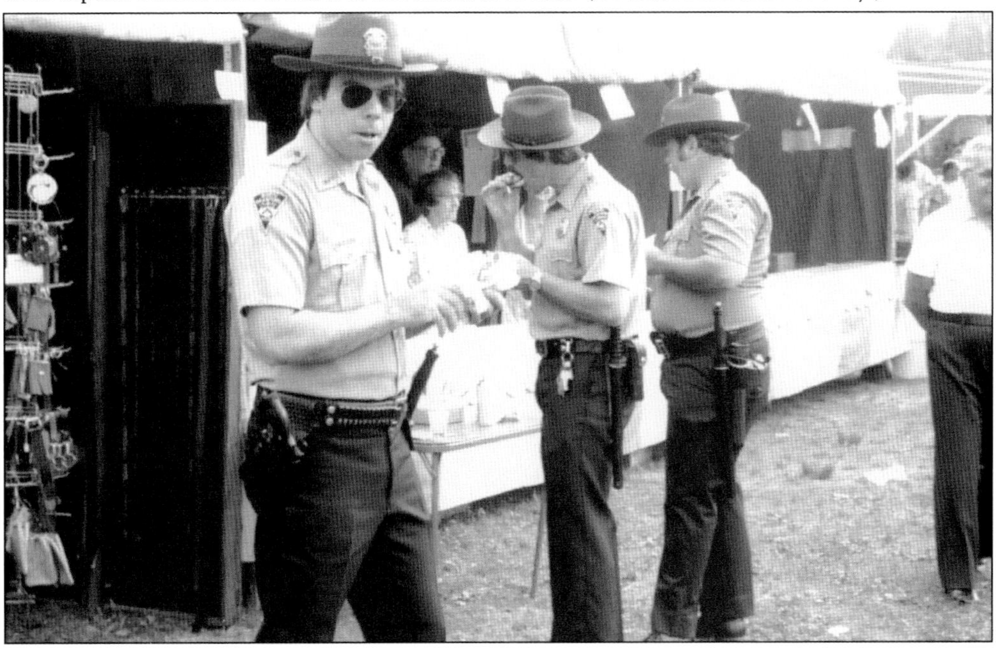

Three town policemen take a break to indulge in some hotdogs at the carnival. They are Mike Doody, Art Hausman, and Norman Andrews, a part-time supernumerary. Ann Nesi can be seen working in the booth as Charles Kulinski (far right) wanders by. According to the 1981 annual report, "The crowds were so large that it seemed everyone in Town was there on one particular night." (Totoket Historical Society.)

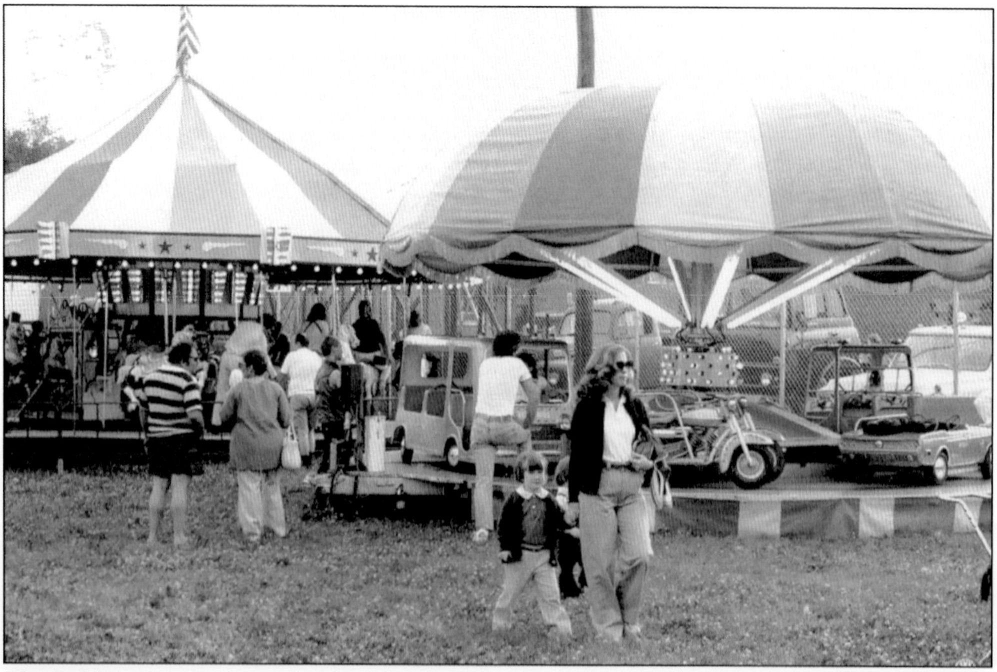

The kiddie rides, as shown in this photograph, were very popular with the younger crowd as they "rode to excitement." In spite of being rained out one night, the carnival was enjoyed by thousands, according to the 1981 annual town report. (Totoket Historical Society.)

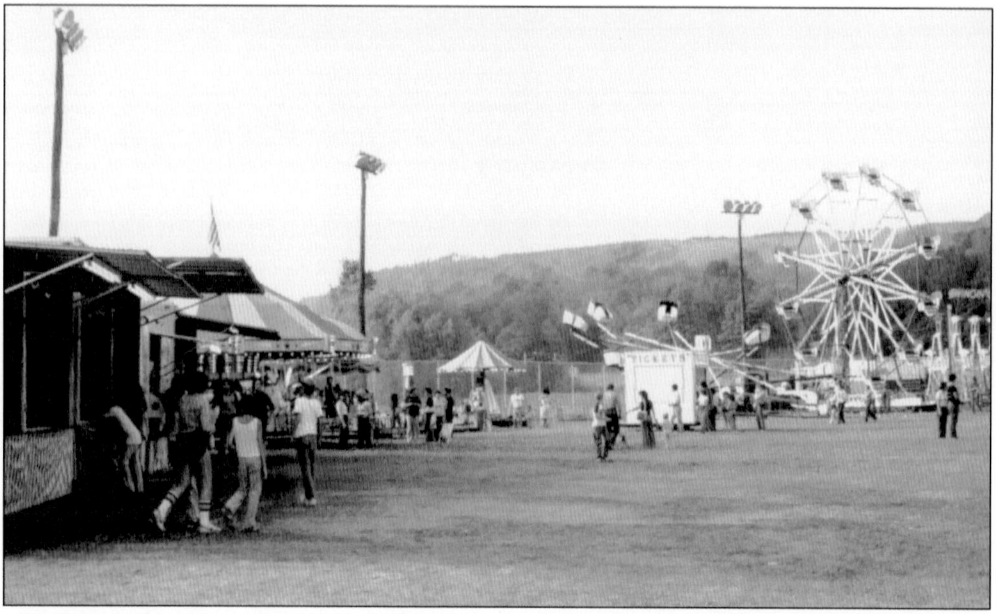

The high point of the sesquicentennial celebration was a fireworks display on Friday night, said to be the largest one in Connecticut that year. The display drew 30,000 people, who flocked to the school grounds, sitting on coats and blankets, "like an old-fashioned 4th of July," according to the 1981 annual town report. When the fireworks began, a hush fell over the crowd as they viewed the display vivid against the summer sky, the noise booming off Totoket Mountain. (Totoket Historical Society.)